D1517131

YES, ITALIAN!

150 delicious, authentic recipes that bring together food, family, and fun

Weight Watchers Publishing Group

Editorial

VP Content/Editor in Chief Theresa DiMasi

Managing Editor Valeria Bloom

Food Editor Eileen Runyan

Project Editor Alice K. Thompson

Contributing Editors Lisa Chernick; Leslie Fink, MS, RD

Copy Editors Diane Pavia, Elzy Kolb

Nutrition Consultants Ariella Sieger, Laureen Jean Leyden

Recipe Developers Terry Grieco Kenny, Frank Melodia, Carol Prager, Julia Rutland

Art

Creative Director, Content Denis Darch

Creative Director Ed Melnitsky

Design Director Daniela A. Hritcu

Production Manager Alan Biederman

Designer Rebecca Kollmer

Illustration Giancarlo Spagnoli

Photo

Photo/On-set Art Director Marybeth Dulany

Photographers Andrea Wyner (food/lifestyle Italy); Johnny Miller (food)

Additional Photographers Lisa Chernick, Theresa DiMasi, Abbey Dulany, Bobby Kollmer, Rebecca Kollmer, Alessandro Mallamaci, Giancarlo Spagnoli

Food Stylist Ugo Adinolfi (Italy); Susan Spungen

Prop Stylist Carla Gonzalez-Hart

Copyright © 2017 by Weight Watchers International, Inc.

Nothing may be reprinted in whole or in part without permission from the publisher. Editorial and art produced by W/W Twentyfirst Corp., 675 Avenue of the Americas, New York, NY 10010.

WEIGHT WATCHERS is a registered trademark of Weight Watchers International, Inc.

SKU #11543

Printed in the USA

Front cover:
Johnny Miller (Roast Shrimp Scampi, page 217)

Back cover:
Andrea Wyner

Back cover (and pages: xii, 180): shot on location at Barone G.R. Macrì.

Only 6 SmartPoints per slice!

Pepperoni Cauliflower-Crust Pizza, page 85

About Weight Watchers International, Inc.

Weight Watchers International, Inc. is the world's leading commercial provider of weight-management services, operating globally through a network of company-owned and franchise operations. Weight Watchers holds more than 36,000 meetings each week, at which members receive group support and learn about healthy eating patterns, behavior modification, and physical activity. Weight Watchers provides innovative digital weight-management products through its websites, mobile sites, and apps. Weight Watchers is the leading provider of online subscription weight-management products in the world. In addition, Weight Watchers offers a wide range of products, publications, and programs for those interested in weight loss and weight control.

eason never ends: Every day an abundance
tables, and fish is plucked from land and
d that same day. Just when you're sad to
to tender, sweet peas, in come bright, juicy
ich eventually give way to dense, orange-
kins, then sunny, refreshing ci us.

Contents

The art of cooking and eating

Italy is delicious.

This is what I'd think as I wandered the streets of my parents' hometowns as a kid. The squares, shops, and markets were filled with food. I'd find baskets of tomatoes, eggplants, zucchini, peppers, and green beans; crates of peaches, plums, blood oranges, and apples; and sacks of dried beans, spices, and chestnuts. The market sold fish of all kinds: tuna, sardines, red mullet, swordfish, squid, and salted cod. Prosciutto, salami, and provolone cheese hung from shop ceilings, and barrels of salted capers, wrinkled olives, and anchovies in oil lined the floors. It was all so colorful and vibrant. In nearby farms (or our small backyard), chickens ran free in the meadows, eating bugs, while cows and pigs grazed on fresh grass. Nuns in the local convent shaped pasta and made sweets for the upcoming festivals of the saints.

At home, I'd ask my Zia (aunt) Santa, "How much basil for the tomato sauce?" And she'd say, "To the eye." We baked loaves of bread at our community oven and I'd pedal down to the local farm for fresh milk, still warm when I tasted it. At 12:30 my family, and other families, gathered in their homes to eat lunch, trade stories, and gossip. And while we were eating, we'd talk about what we were going to have for dinner the next day.

At bars (which are more like what we call cafés or coffee shops in the United States), people walked through beaded curtains and would meet someone who'd say they were related. That distant cousin-in-law would buy them a drink and then another and another. There was always a bite of this, and a bite of that, and some sort of snack for everyone. Waiters bent over small tables packed with guests eating gelato and arguing over politics and who made the best gnocchi. I'd walk back home from the bar and another zia, Maria, would call down from the balcony, inviting me up for a *caffè* and a little something to eat.

When we traveled up north, we'd stop at neon-lit rest stops on *l'autostrada* and see people stand at the counter munching on made-to-order panini, drinking fresh-squeezed juices, and ending the meal with espresso. Life was good.

And it's still good in Italy. Within a day of visiting any part of the country, you can immediately see, feel, and taste the passion and zeal people have for food, family, and life. There's no doubt—Italians love food and everything about it, including shopping for it, cooking it, and eating it. To them, life is meant to be enjoyed, and food is an integral part of that enjoyment. I have never met an Italian who hasn't brought up food at some point in our conversation.

Weight Watchers celebrates food too—its pleasures and its power to nourish us, physically and emotionally. More and more of our Members want to eat food that makes them feel good. They want more vegetables and less meat. They're less excited about desserts and special-occasion dishes, and more excited about making delicious everyday food. They're asking us for advice on cooking chicken or how to make a quick, comforting soup. Their local markets are selling a variety of vegetables and they want to know what to do with them. In this book, we use the principles of Italian cooking and how Italians approach day-to-day living to help you eat and live well.

Why Italian? Because of what and how they eat (and it's the recipes you keep asking us for). Italian food is so much more than spaghetti, meatballs, and eggplant parmesan: Italians enjoy vegetables, legumes, seafood, chicken, a little meat, and fruit for dessert. And they like to keep things simple. They don't interfere too much with food, avoiding complicated cooking methods and complex sauces. Instead they let the natural, fresh flavors of food shine.

My tribe, through the years

1. Zio (uncle) Ilario
2. Cooking with Zia (aunt) Santa, and cousins Maria and Enzo.
3. The kids
4. Lunch
5. Zio Nicolino and Zia Rina

Family album **1.** Mom and Dad walking in Rome. **2.** My kids and niece and nephew canning tomatoes. **3.** Making new friends at the beach. **4.** Preserving summer. **5.** Another family get-together.

I learned how to cook from my mother, and she from her mother before that. I never sensed fear or insecurity when I watched them cook. These days we're being told we're not competent enough to cook—we need the right gadgets and the right ingredients and the right this and that. I'm hoping this book will help you understand that cooking doesn't have to be a grand production. Once you learn a few basic techniques for getting the most flavor out of food and what ingredients you need to stock your pantry and refrigerator with (see page xix), you too can whip up something good to eat. We want you to develop a feel for food. Everything in this book is doable: We highlight changes you can make at your local market (buy seasonal!), in your kitchen (freeze or preserve fresh food!), and at your table (put electronic devices away!). And really, all you need for a quick meal is a ripe tomato, some torn up basil, and some fresh bread and you have something delicious to eat. Or crack open an egg and make a frittata with whatever vegetables you have in the refrigerator.

Simple food relies on just a few ingredients, so do what the Italians do and buy fresh food that's in season. Most Italians wouldn't dream of eating figs in January. Try it: Let what you find at the market or pick from a garden dictate what you eat today. Italians also opt for local ingredients. To them, there's no such thing as Italian food—each of the 20 regions has its own specialties, based on its unique history, geography, and climate. The northern regions, with close proximity to France, Switzerland, and Austria, feature fertile valleys and lush mountainsides, perfect for producing milk, butter, pork, beef, and rice. Central and Southern Italy also have mountains, but climates there are drier and the volcanic soil is rich, so they produce pasta and grains, vegetables, olive oil, beef, and pork. Fish and seafood are caught along the coasts and near rivers, and mushrooms, boar, and wild game are found in and near forests.

Respect for the flavors and ingredients connected to a specific place and people means you're eating traditionally and authentically, and most likely the food will taste more delicious. Great Italian cooking is less about duplicating a particular dish you ate in Venice and more about cooking with local ingredients, especially produce from local farms. Having said that, I don't ever want to sacrifice flavor, so I'll buy balsamic vinegar from Modena or prosciutto from Parma when I can. It's difficult to ignore the thousands of hours people have spent perfecting such delicacies.

I often get asked how I can get dinner on the table so quickly, mostly made from scratch, and make it taste like I've been cooking for hours. Here, too, I do what my very resourceful and inventive relatives have taught me and have basics on hand, such as broth, salsa verde, anchovy sauce, and jars of tomatoes I have canned. I also have a well-stocked pantry and vegetables in the freezer— ones I've frozen when they were in season and at peak flavor. It takes me a little extra work on a weekend, every few weeks or so, but it's worth it when I come home from a long day at work and want to make something quick and homemade for the family.

Preserving food is inspired by *la cucina povera* ("the cooking of the poor"). Its philosophy is simple: Do what you can with what you have, and extract the most flavor possible out of an ingredient. And don't waste anything. My aunt would leave stale bread on top of the wood-burning stove and throw it into *ribollita* (bread soup) the following day or save leftover chicken for stews later in the week. I use wilted greens for soups, leftover vegetables for frittata. Sometimes I even cook extra so I have leftovers. Simplicity and economy go hand in hand, and it feels good to create a meal that's greater than the sum of its parts.

In Michigan where I grew up, our pantry was stocked with jars of canned tomatoes, vegetables, and fruits that came from my father's garden. We'd also go to a farm and pick our own peppers, eggplants, summer squash, strawberries, and peaches. A few things were pickled, a few others roasted and marinated; but canning tomatoes was the big project for the end of summer. The whole family would get in on the fun, setting ourselves up assembly-line fashion for the undertaking.

Not only did my family cook together, we—and every other family I knew—ate together. No matter how modest the meal, Italians make time to sit down and eat with their family and friends. They bring out the real cutlery and the real napkins and they never seem to run out of conversation. Anyone who sits at the table is instantly part of the family. You never know what will happen during the course of a meal—singing, dancing, someone shouting out a marriage proposal. My husband also visited Italy as a child, and when I first met his aunts, uncles, cousins, and the friends he grew up with, they all gave me a hug and a kiss on both cheeks before I even had a chance to talk, and invariably invited me to lunch the next day. That's the way it works in Italy.

Of all the lessons I've learned from Italians, the most powerful is the belief that good fresh food is an inherent right. Whether you're rich or poor, everyone should eat delicious, high-quality food. You can see it in the many festivals and *sagre* (food fairs) Italians celebrate weekly, monthly, and yearly. Food is made in the town piazza in giant cooking vessels and enjoyed by all. You can see it when you step into a fine restaurant and "peasant" food like polenta is served to all patrons. Or in a home kitchen where a lasagna is made with slices of soppressata (a spicy salami), baskets of creamy ricotta, and extra-virgin olive oil by a family that owns a few olive trees and a cow. And also in the tradition of a *caffè* or pizza *sospeso* (suspended), where people order espresso or a slice of pizza, drink it or eat it, then pay for two of what they ordered, leaving the receipt for the second for someone in need to use. You see these acts of kindness and generosity all the time in Italy, but it also speaks to an Italian's belief that even in hard times, though one might lack some things, good food shouldn't be one of them.

Food has the power to bring people together. Italians have suffered many hardships, both in Italy and as immigrants coming to America, leaving the safety of their old culture to try life in a different one. They had to learn a new language and leave behind their extended families. But they didn't have to give up their food. They grew fresh vegetables and fruit in their yards, a skill most learned from their parents in the old country, and many opened Italian food specialty shops that brought foods like pasta, pizza, and cannoli to a very appreciative audience.

This is the legacy my parents have given me. They created a bridge that stretched from their home and life in the United States to the one remembered in Calabria, Italy. The connection between the two was great food, good wine, music, family, dance, and a tenacious, generous spirit. Appreciate life. Make something out of nothing. Find beauty where none seems to exist. Make every minute count. When you're living on the edge of a volcano, these things are important.

Right now in Italy, people are visiting bars for espresso and *cornetti* (brioche-like croissants), reading newspapers, and then going to neighborhood *fruttivendoli* (greengrocers) and *macellai* (butchers) to buy food for lunch or dinner. They're lovingly preparing food for their families and sitting with them to eat. Then at night they'll stroll, arm in arm, back and forth along the streets, for their *passeggiata*.

We hope this cookbook gets you started on a path to eating and living well in your own way. The message is simple: Enjoy your life. Live as simply as possible. And eat great food.

Salute (to your health)!

Theresa DiMasi
EDITOR IN CHIEF/VP, CONTENT
theresa@weightwatchers.com

The Italian
table is where
the fun begins.

At the Barone G.R. Macrì, an *agriturismo* (farm-stay) in Calabria, a nap follows a relaxing midday lunch.

Living *la dolce vita* (the sweet life) on the Amalfi Coast

About Our Recipes

While losing weight isn't only about what you eat, Weight Watchers realizes the critical role it plays in your success and overall good health. That's why our philosophy is to offer great-tasting, easy recipes that are nutritious as well as delicious. Our recipes emphasize the kind of foods we love: lots of fresh fruits and vegetables, most of which have 0 SmartPoints® value, and delicious lean proteins, some of which have 0 SmartPoints and others that are low in SmartPoints. We also try to ensure that our recipes fall within the recommendations of the U.S. Dietary Guidelines for Americans—lower in saturated fat and sugar with plenty of fruits and vegetables, lean proteins, and low-fat dairy—so they support a diet that promotes well-being and reduces the risk for disease. If you have special dietary needs, consult with your health-care professional for advice on a diet that is best for you, then adapt these recipes to meet your specific nutritional needs.

get started, keep going, and enjoy good nutrition

At Weight Watchers, we believe that eating well makes life better, no matter where you are in your weight-loss journey. These delicious recipes are ideal, whether you're just getting started or have already reached your goals on the SmartPoints system. Unlike other weight-loss programs, which focus solely on calories, the SmartPoints plan guides you toward healthier foods that are lower in sugar and saturated fat, and higher in protein. But this isn't a diet—all food is "in." Eating well should be fun, energizing, and delicious, so that smart food choices become second nature. To get maximum satisfaction, we suggest you keep the following information in mind while preparing our recipes:

❥ On the WW Freestyle™ Program, eating a mix of foods (rather than all 0 SmartPoints meals) can help you avoid feeling bored or deprived. Remember, there's room for all SmartPoints foods in your plan—variety is key to a healthy and livable eating style.

❥ SmartPoints values are given for each recipe. The SmartPoints value for each ingredient is assigned based on the number of calories and the amount of saturated fat, sugar, and protein per the ingredient quantity. The SmartPoints values for each ingredient are then added together and divided by the number of servings, and the result is rounded.

❥ Recipes include approximate nutritional information: They are analyzed for Calories (Cal), Saturated Fat (Sat Fat), Sodium (Sod), Total Carbohydrates (Total Carb), Sugar, Dietary Fiber (Fib), and Protein (Prot). The nutritional values are obtained from the Weight Watchers database, which is maintained by registered dietitians.

❥ To boost flavor, we often include fresh herbs or a squeeze of citrus instead of increasing the salt. If you don't need to restrict your sodium intake, feel free to add a touch more salt as desired.

❥ Recipes in this book that are designated gluten free do not contain any wheat (in all forms, including kamut, semolina, spelt, and triticale), barley, or rye, or any products that are made from these ingredients, such as breads, couscous, pastas, seitan, soy sauce, beer, malt vinegar, and malt beverages. Other foods such as salad dressings, Asian-style sauces, salsa and tomato sauce, shredded cheese, yogurt, and sour cream may be sources of gluten. Check ingredient labels carefully on packaged foods that we call for, as different brands of the same premade food product may or may not contain gluten. If you are following a gluten-free diet because you have celiac disease, please consult your health-care professional.

❥ For information about the Weight Watchers basic plan, please visit WeightWatchers.com/us/m/cms/plan-basics.

calculations not what you expected?

SmartPoints values for the recipes in this book are calculated without counting the 0 SmartPoints foods—fruits, most vegetables, and some lean proteins that are part of the plan. However, the nutritional information does include the nutrient content of these ingredients. This means you may notice discrepancies with the SmartPoints values you calculate using the nutrition information provided for the recipe versus the SmartPoints values listed for the recipe. That's because the SmartPoints values for the recipes that contain 0 Points ingredients have been adjusted to reflect those ingredients, while the nutrition information provided includes the nutrition for all ingredients. For tracking purposes use the SmartPoints value listed for the recipe. Also, please note, when fruits and veggies are liquefied or pureed (as in a smoothie), their nutrient content *is* incorporated into the recipe calculations. These nutrients can increase the SmartPoints.

Alcohol is included in our SmartPoints calculations. Because alcohol information is generally not included on nutrition labels, it's not an option you can include when using the handheld or online SmartPoints calculator or the Weight Watchers Mobile app. But since we include the alcohol information that we get from our database in our recipes, you might notice discrepancies between the SmartPoints you see here in our recipes and the values you get using the calculator. The SmartPoints listed for our recipes are the most accurate values.

SIMPLY FILLING (THE NO-COUNT OPTION)

If counting SmartPoints isn't your thing, try Simply Filling, a no-count technique. To follow it, eat just until satisfied, primarily from the list of Simply Filling foods found in the Tracker online. For more information, see your meeting room materials or go online if you are a subscriber.

CHOOSING INGREDIENTS

As you learn to eat healthier and add more wholesome foods to your meals, consider the following:

● LEAN MEATS AND POULTRY

Purchase lean meats and poultry, and trim them of all visible fat before cooking. When poultry is cooked with the skin on, we recommend removing the skin before eating. Nutritional information for recipes that include meat, poultry, and fish is based on cooked, skinless boneless portions (unless otherwise stated), with the fat trimmed.

● SEAFOOD

Whenever possible, our recipes call for seafood that is sustainable and deemed the most healthful for human consumption so that your choice of seafood is not only good for the oceans but also good for you. For more information about the best seafood choices and to download a pocket guide, go to the Environmental Defense Fund at seafood.edf.org, the Monterey Bay Aquarium at seafoodwatch.org, or the Safina Center at safinacenter.org.

● PRODUCE

For best flavor, maximum nutrient content, and the lowest prices, buy fresh, local produce such as vegetables, leafy greens, and fruits in season. Rinse them thoroughly before using, and keep a supply of cut-up vegetables and fruits in your refrigerator for convenient healthy snacks.

● WHOLE GRAINS

Explore your market for whole-grain products such as whole wheat and whole-grain breads and pastas, brown rice, bulgur, barley, cornmeal, whole wheat couscous, oats, farro, and quinoa to enjoy with your meals.

Introducing WW Freestyle™

Welcome to WW Freestyle! Our newest program makes deciding what to eat much easier, with much less tracking, so you can focus on what really matters in your weight-loss journey—nourishing your whole self and doing more of the things that you enjoy.

How does it work?

The WW Freestyle program uses our incredibly effective SmartPoints® system to guide you toward go-to foods that are the foundation of healthy eating.

- Every food is assigned a SmartPoints value, based on its nutrition.
- If the value is high, that means it is higher in sugar and saturated fat, and lower in protein than some other foods.
- If the value is low, it is lower in sugar and saturated fat, and higher in protein.

All foods are yours for the eating and enjoying: You choose based on their SmartPoints value, your personalized SmartPoints Budget, and what you're in the mood for.

More freedom and flexibility

With WW Freestyle, you have a wide list of go-to foods that are zero SmartPoints value! These zero SmartPoints foods include: chicken and turkey, seafood, plant-based proteins, eggs, veggies, unsweetened, fat-free, plain yogurt*, and fruits. These foods don't need to be tracked or measured so you can spend less time planning and counting, and more time enjoying food and your life. And you'll still lose weight!

That's where this book comes in

Almost every one of these delicious Italian recipes includes at least one (and sometimes many more!) zero SmartPoints foods, so every dish is full of flavor, and designed to help you achieve success.

At Weight Watchers, we want to help you reach your health goals while enjoying the foods you love. We offer the most up-to-date research on what works for effective weight loss and the tools to support you on your journey. And we think one of the essentials for success is this collection of memorable, crowd-pleasing recipes that are as delicious as they are easy to prepare. *Yes, Italian!* is your newest go-to source!

* When yogurt is used in these recipes we refer to it simply as plain, fat-free yogurt.

MILAN ·   VERONA   VENICE ·

TURIN ·

GENOA ·

BOLOGNA

PISA ·   FLORENCE ·

PERUGIA ·

ORVIETO ·

Adriatic Sea

ROME ·

NAPLES ·

BARI ·

SARDINIA

Tyrrhenian Sea

CAGLIARI ·

CAULONIA MARINA

ROCCELLA IONICA

Ionian S

PALERMO ·

SICILY

CATANIA ·

Mediterranean Sea

The Italian Pantry

Deciding what to cook depends on a number of factors: Are you in the mood for something light and refreshing, rich and toothsome, or smoky and crisp? Do you want chicken, pork, beef, or beans? What equipment do you have—an oven, a grill? How much time do you have? What ingredients do you have on hand?

With a well-stocked pantry you have options. And cooking is always easier when you don't have to search for ingredients every time. The trick to stocking your pantry is to use the best-quality ingredients you can afford: It makes sense to spend a little extra on the staples that you'll turn to again and again. And remember that you can take your time building up your pantry—there's no need to spend a lot of money at the start.

The following items are what we use in our kitchens day in and day out. We also recommend that you have the following in your refrigerator, freezer, or cupboard so you can always throw together quick meals: chicken breast; ground meats (beef, pork, turkey); lemons; onions, carrots, celery, and a variety of vegetables in season; milk; nuts (walnuts, pine nuts); red-wine vinegar; canned or homemade broth; coarse and fine sea salt; canned tuna; homemade bread crumbs; and fresh bread.

Our **NONNA'S TIP** suggestions give you a little extra advice—the kind a seasoned cook or an Italian grandma ("nonna") might have!

Anchovies These savory little fish may be tiny but they pack a ton of flavor. They add deep umami richness to sauces and stews, and are equally happy taking on a starring role in such dishes as *bagna cauda* or Caesar salad. Briny and intensely flavorful, they mellow when cooked or blended with other ingredients. We recommend buying the meatiest you can find. Anchovies sold stateside are typically **oil-packed fillets** and should be drained and patted dry. We prefer **salted anchovies,** common in Italy and in shops specializing in Italian foods; if these are not deboned, lift out the spine and rinse the fillets well under cold running water.

NONNA'S TIP If using anchovies in tins, roll up leftover fillets and keep refrigerated in a small jar covered with olive oil.

Balsamic Vinegar Rich, dark, and sweet, balsamic vinegar is a staple in Italian kitchens and now accounts for nearly half of all vinegar sales in the United States. You can buy a bottle for just a few dollars in most supermarkets, but it won't be true *aceto balsamico tradizionale*—the real thing is produced in Modena or Reggio Emilia and aged at least 12 years. A small bottle of this silky handcrafted vinegar can cost hundreds, though a medium-priced vinegar can do the trick. Look for the D.O.P. seal or the word *condimento* or the abbreviation IGP on the bottle. The good news: Balsamic is usually meant to enhance, not replace, wine vinegar, so often you only need to use a

drizzle in salad dressings and sauces.

NONNA'S TIP Want to improve the quality of cheaper balsamic? Simmer it for a few minutes to concentrate its flavor.

Beans Ubiquitous, earthy, economical, and packed with great nutrition, beans are both a rustic staple and treasured ingredient in Italian cuisine. Some favorite varieties are **chickpeas, cannellini, borlotti (cranberry),** and **fava beans. Canned beans** are convenient for impromptu cooking, so we recommend you have some on hand. Many cooks, however, prefer the texture and taste of dry beans prepared from scratch—they're generally more buttery and chewier. If you'd like to cook your own, a 15-ounce can is about 1⅔ cups. (Bonus: Beans cooked from dried are about half the price of the canned ones, and freeze excellently for 3 to 4 months.) See page 30 for more on cooking dried beans.

NONNA'S TIP Lots of dishes are associated with a specific type of bean, but Italians tend to use whatever beans are on hand or in season. Feel free to substitute varieties with abandon.

Canned Tomatoes Fresh tomatoes are a favorite in the Italian kitchen, but their canned brethren are tops when it comes to getting big, bold, consistent tomato flavor year-round. Italy is known worldwide for the export of its canned **San Marzano tomatoes,** a variety widely considered the king of cooking tomatoes.

You can find these and a host of other high-quality domestic and imported products in supermarkets. We recommend using **whole, peeled plum tomatoes** in minimal juices, and crushing them with the back of your spoon. If whole tomatoes are not possible, opt for **chopped** or **crushed. Tomato paste** (*estratto* in Italian) is ideal for adding a quick punch of flavor to everything from pasta sauce to soups and stews. Note that the chemical Bisphenol A (BPA) is sometimes found in the interior coating of cans. Although the FDA has concluded that the amount that may leach into foods is too small to be a health risk, you can opt for cans and cartons labeled BPA-free.

NONNA'S TIP Canned tomatoes can differ greatly in flavor. Savvy cooks know to taste a tomato-based dish before serving it: If the flavor is a bit tart, add a pinch of sugar; if it's a bit sweet, add a squeeze of lemon or drizzle of red-wine vinegar. If you find the flavor all-around flat, perk it up with a drizzle of balsamic.

Capers Tangy, sharp, briny capers are a staple in puttanesca sauce, caponata, butter sauces, and toppings for seafood. They also add a bit of piquancy to pasta, pizza, salads, and sandwiches. The capers we're most familiar with are small buds picked from the caper bush and pickled, although capers dry-packed in salt are available in Italian markets (rinse the latter thoroughly before using). We prefer the salt-packed ones. **Caperberries** are a separate product. If the buds are allowed to flower, an olive-size berry forms on the bush. These are sold brined with a long, curved stem attached and are a fantastic addition to an antipasti plate. Add capers at the end of cooking.

NONNA'S TIP Some jars of capers sold stateside are marked "nonpareil," meaning that the smallest buds have been selected. These petite capers are typically firmer and denser and may have a deeper flavor. If you use larger capers, you may want to chop them to distribute their flavor better throughout a dish.

Dried Herbs and Spices Many Italian herbs retain excellent flavor when dried and are good alternatives to fresh for long-cooked dishes like sauces and stews, as well as for dry rubs. Jars of **oregano, bay leaves, rosemary, marjoram, sage,** and **thyme** are good to have on hand; not so much for dried basil, parsley, and mint, which lose character and often taste dusty when dried. Common Italian spices include **fennel seeds,**

coriander, black pepper, and **nutmeg** (opt for whole nutmeg to grate freshly rather than ground nutmeg, and whole peppercorns for grinding). In a class by itself is ***peperoncino*** (hot chile pepper), adding sultry flavor to myriad dishes. Ropes of scarlet peperoncini strung up to dry are a bright feature in many an Italian kitchen. The dried peppers can be used whole (often a good strategy to flavor olive oil), crushed, or powdered. **Red pepper flakes** are a generic equivalent and fine if you don't have imported chile on hand; just make sure your flakes are fairly fresh, preferably no more than 6 months old.

NONNA'S TIP Dried herbs can lose their potency within just a few months of purchase. Give herbs the smell test before you rely on them for flavor. A distinct, fresh aroma is what you want; a musty, dull aroma means they're past their prime.

Fresh Herbs The aroma, flavor, and brightness of fresh herbs are can't be beat. They're central to innumerable classic dishes, from pesto to saltimbocca, and enhance the flavor of just about everything that comes to the table. Italy's predominately Mediterranean climate means that herbs grow in most regions with year-round abandon, so it's no surprise that cooks turn to them constantly. **Basil, flat-leaf parsley, rosemary, sage, oregano, marjoram,** and **mint** are the most popular. Choose leaves that are young, bright, and fragrant. Better yet, think like an Italian: Grow herbs in your garden or in an indoor window box as a cost-effective way to keep a superfresh variety on hand.

NONNA'S TIP Embrace the aroma of herbs in your dishes. Think about chopping herbs and garnishing foods just before serving to maximize the release of their essential oils, or gently bruise whole sprigs of rosemary before adding them to a stew pot or roasting pan. Breathe in deeply and enjoy the natural aromatherapy!

Fresh Tomatoes Fragrant, juicy, sweet-tart tomatoes are so integral to Italian food that it's hard to imagine that Italians only warmed to *pomodori* in the 1800s, and then mostly in the southern part of the country. When you think of Italian food today, you probably automatically think red: Tomatoes are abundant in everything from antipasti to salads to pizza and, of course, sauce. Although canned tomatoes are a household staple (see page xix for more on them), fresh, ripe tomatoes in season are an irresistible choice. Italy is famous for popularizing varieties grown especially for cooking and canning. These

Italians live off the bounty of the land: fresh fruit and vegetables, dairy, and fish. When an ingredient is in abundance, it's preserved for later use.

elongated, egg-sized tomatoes are commonly known as **plum, Italian,** or **Roma** tomatoes in the United States. Their flesh is dense and meaty, ideal for sauce and long-cooked dishes, but a bit dry for eating raw. Juicy varieties that are better in salads and other uncooked dishes include large slicing tomatoes like **beefsteak** and numerous **heirloom varieties.** Small **cherry** or **grape tomatoes** typically have a high sugar content, making them consistently good year-round. Whatever variety you're looking for, you'll find the best flavor and aroma from tomatoes that have been fully ripened in the sun. These tomatoes are extremely perishable, so growing your own or buying from farmers' markets in season is always your best choice. If you're faced with a glut of ripe tomatoes, you may want to cook up a big batch of sauce and freeze it. See our Quick-Cook Tomato Sauce (page xxxii) for an easy, delicious recipe that's excellent for freezing. We also freeze whole tomatoes by first blanching them for 1 to 2 minutes, removing stems and seeds, then putting the fruit in storage bags and freezing it.

NONNA'S TIP How to choose the most deeply flavored tomatoes? Aroma rather than color or firmness is often the best indicator. Fresh, sun-ripened tomatoes should have a heady smell that's an appetizing blend of earthy and herbaceous.

Garlic Italian cooking without garlic? Most of us find it unimaginable. Southern Italian and Italian-American dishes tend to use it most generously, with crowd-pleasing results: Garlic contains a number of chemical compounds that work together to excite our senses of taste and smell, one reason it's so popular. Raw garlic is pungent and sharp, but cooking mellows it and brings out sweet and nutty notes. The more you mince, the stronger the garlic flavor. Spaghetti *aglio e olio* (with garlic and oil) is an excellent example of the alchemy of heat on garlic: Sliced cloves are cooked slowly in olive oil to create a pasta sauce of simple perfection. However you use garlic—and however much you use—make sure it's fresh to avoid harsh flavor. The cloves should be firm and plump and tightly packed in the bulb, and there should be no yellowing or sprouting. Store garlic at room temperature.

NONNA'S TIP If you accidently burn garlic when sautéing, it's best to start over; the taste and aroma of charred garlic is particularly unpleasant and is likely to spoil the dish.

Gorgonzola This rich blue-veined cheese is named for the town outside Milan where it was originally produced. Today it's made throughout Northern Italy and celebrated worldwide for its buttery texture and pungent flavor. It's a superb melting cheese, making it popular in pasta and risotto and over pizza and other hot dishes. But its piquant flavor and incredibly creamy texture means it's also ideal on a cheese plate or crumbled over salads.

NONNA'S TIP Need a quick dessert? Place a wedge of Gorgonzola on a plate and serve with fruit in season like apples, pears, peaches, plums, figs, or grapes. Add a few handfuls of nuts if you like.

Lentils Thick, hearty lentils are an Italian favorite and grown in several regions. They form the basis of many simple and delicious meals, including soups, stews, and salads, and they're often paired with greens and flavored with small amounts of pork. Our favorite variety is Castelluccio lentils from Umbria—they're tiny, green, and tender, with a delicate flavor. They hold their form during cooking, so they won't fall apart when used for making soups or stews. If you can't find Castelluccio, we also like Puy lentils, sometimes known as "poor people's caviar." Puy are especially terrific in salads. If neither is available, you can opt for larger brown lentils; they too will hold up to longer cooking times.

NONNA'S TIP The acid in ingredients like tomatoes can slow the cooking of lentils and beans. If you're making a soup or stew that includes a lot of tomato, you may want to wait and add it after the lentils have begun to soften.

Mozzarella Soft, mild, sometimes tangy mozzarella is one of the most popular cheeses worldwide, and with good reason: Not only is it deliciously sweet and creamy as is, it's also one of the all-time great melting cheeses, deepening in flavor and becoming irresistibly gooey in pizza and baked dishes such as eggplant parmigiana. **Fresh mozzarella,** usually sold packed in water, is a revelation in milky flavor and tender texture. If you can, buy it and eat it within hours of its being made. **Packaged mozzarella** has the benefit of a longer shelf life, and also comes in low-fat and fat-free varieties; low-fat is a good compromise for a product with a favorable nutritional profile that still preserves much of its flavor and melting qualities. Most mozzarella is made from cow's milk, but a delicious exception is **buffalo mozzarella.** This rich, super-creamy, grassy-flavored cheese is made from the milk of water buffalo that have traditionally grazed in the Campania region of Italy. Its mouthfeel is other-worldly, both solid and meltingly soft.

NONNA'S TIP Using just a small amount of cheese in a recipe? Sprinkling it on top will often give you more impact than incorporating it into the dish.

Olive Oil

The hills of Italy are dotted with olive trees, making the country one of the biggest producers of olive oil in the world, second only to Spain. Olive oil is an indispensable ingredient in Italian cooking and is used for sautéing, frying, drizzling, preserving, and even baking. Oils vary greatly in flavor, ranging from buttery and mild to herbaceous, sharp, peppery, or fruity. The oils from Northern Italy tend to be lighter, while the ones from central and Southern Italy more peppery or fruity. Tasting a few can give you an idea of the range of flavors and point you toward your personal favorite. We recommend having at least two types of oil in your pantry: one for drizzling and one for cooking. Highest-grade **extra-virgin olive oil** (EVOO) is best for dressings, dipping, and drizzling. EVOO comes from the first pressing of olives and is extracted without using heat or chemicals for superior taste and aroma. Because heat neutralizes much of an oil's character, select a less expensive one for sautéing and other hot tasks: A lower-priced extra-virgin oil is always a good choice, or choose one labeled as just plain olive oil. Italy produces more olive oil than just about any other country, but it is also a major importer of oil from other countries. "Packed in Italy" doesn't necessarily mean that an oil is pressed from Italian olives; look for specifics on the label if you want a true Italian product.

NONNA'S TIP Exposure to light and heat will affect olive oil's quality so be sure to use a bottle within a few months, or keep it in a cool cabinet or refrigerated for longer periods.

Olives

Italy grows many of the world's best-tasting olives, and not all of them end up in oil. Lucky for us—we get to enjoy their salty, pungent taste all on their own. Some popular varieties include big, meaty **Cerignolas**, excellent for snacking; the **Castelvetrano**, Italy's most ubiquitous olive, used for both oil and eating; petite but flavor-packed **Taggiasca** (Ligurian) olives; and tart, tangy **Gaetas**. For the best texture and brightest flavor seek out olives from a well-stocked supermarket olive bar, a cheese shop, or specialty food store, or buy imported olives in jars; give canned olives a pass.

NONNA'S TIP Need to pit olives? Place them on your cutting board and press down on them with the flat side of a chef's knife until they split; you'll be able to slip the pits out easily.

Parmesan

This delicious cheese is hard, grainy and used primarily for grating. It's an essential ingredient in pesto, chicken Parmesan, and Caesar salad. It's also excellent on its own, cut into chunks and drizzled with aged balsamic vinegar. The higher quality the Parmesan, the more impact you'll get from small quantities. The name **Parmigiano-Reggiano** is used for cheeses that meet strict production standards and minimum aging times (up to 2 years or more). It's nutty and lightly tangy, with a crumbly, almost crystallized texture. Look for the words Parmigiano-Reggiano stamped on its rind. A less expensive but good-quality alternative is **Grana Padano**. Its production process is not quite as strict, and it's aged for a minimum of 9 months, making its flavor less assertive. The field of non-Italian Parmesans includes products that vary considerably in quality. Whatever type you buy, grate it yourself: **Pre-grated Parmesan** loses moisture and aroma quickly, becoming flat and chalky. Parmesan will last for weeks (and even months) in the fridge, so buying a big chunk when it's on sale is a great idea.

NONNA'S TIP Don't throw away the tough rind once you've finished a piece of good Parmesan. Save it to drop into soups or stews for an extra layer of flavor.

Pecorino Romano

Briny, sharp pecorino Romano is a terrific grating cheese that's popular throughout Italy. Much of pecorino's flavor and character come from the fact that it's made from sheep's milk, not cow's milk like its cousin Parmesan. This gives it a distinctive tang and an earthier taste than Parmesan. It's also saltier and stronger in flavor, so be careful not to overwhelm your dishes with it. Look for **imported pecorino Romano** to experience this cheese at its best. Domestic cheeses labeled **"Romano"** may not be made from 100 percent sheep's milk or aged the full 5 to 8 months that imported pecorino is aged.

NONNA'S TIP Mixing grated pecorino and Parmesan together delivers a blend of pungent and nutty flavors.

Pasta

Italians categorize pasta into three types: fresh, filled, and dried. **Fresh pasta** is usually egg-based and sold freshly cut or refrigerated. **Filled pastas** include ravioli, tortellini, mezzelune, agnolotti, pansotti, and numerous other regional varieties. Most Italians opt for **dried pasta,** and with more than 300 types available—from long, thin strands of capellini and tube-shaped rigatoni to butterfly-shaped farfalle (sometimes colored

Pasta shapes

Lasagna

Rigatoni

Spaghetti

Ditalini

Orzo

Campanelle

Pappardelle

Ziti

Fusilli

Fettucine

Bucatini

Cavatappi

Gemelli

Manicotti

Linguine Fini

Fregola

Shells

Elbows

Linguine

Farfalle

Tortellini

Orecchiette

Tagliatelle

Penne

Rotelle

Capellini
(Angel Hair)

Rotini

with vegetables or even squid ink)—one could eat a different pasta almost every night of the year. See our chart on the page xxv for some of the most popular shapes. Traditionally the finest pasta was made from durum semolina and water, sometimes with egg as a binding ingredient. But welcome to a whole new world of noodles: Changing tastes and dietary concerns are packing the market with alternative pastas. Whole-grain varieties include nutty, toothsome **farro pasta** and **whole wheat semolina pasta;** gluten-free **quinoa, rice, corn,** and **mixed-grain pastas;** and **grain-free pastas** based on legumes. And you can even leave traditional pasta completely behind and try **spiralized vegetables** or gorgeously stringy **spaghetti squash.**

NONNA'S TIP No matter what you choose, cook pasta like the Italians do: Start with a large pot and plenty of water. Bring it to a rolling boil, add salt, and when it starts boiling again, add the pasta. Cook until al dente, the point at which it's soft on the outside and still offers a bit of bite at the center but isn't chalky white in the middle; this is usually 1 to 2 minutes less than what the package says. And don't rinse the pasta unless you're making pasta salad—the starchy coating helps sauces to adhere. You can even remove pasta from its cooking water with tongs and add it straight to the simmering sauce. If your sauce is too thick, add some of the cooking water to loosen it. Eat pasta hot and fresh.

Polenta Originally a staple in Northern Italian cooking, but now widely eaten across Italy, polenta can be served as a side dish, a main as a substitute for pasta, and even as an alternative to bread. It's simple to make—ground cornmeal is cooked in salted water or broth and sometimes enriched with butter, Parmesan, or mascarpone. We recommend regular polenta, but if dinner needs to be on the table quickly we use quick-cooking or instant—regular polenta cooks in about 40 minutes, while the quick-cooking version is done in around 5 minutes. Polenta can be either yellow or white, and coarsely or finely ground. Our favorite is white and coarsely ground. Once polenta is smooth and thick it can be served immediately as a soft, wonderfully comforting porridge; as a side dish; or topped with thick sauces or stews. When it cools, its texture changes dramatically, becoming firm and bouncy, ideal for slicing. Reheat sliced polenta in a skillet or grill pan.

NONNA'S TIP If you're making polenta to serve fresh under a stew or as a side dish, consider making a double recipe and spreading the leftovers on a greased pan and refrigerating it. You can slice and reheat it for another meal.

Porcini Mushrooms Italians are devoted to porcinis, and with good reason: This prized mushroom is remarkably rich in flavor, with a pungent, woodsy taste and aroma rivaled by few other ingredients. **Fresh porcinis** have a brief season, but since **dried porcinis** are readily available they can be a year-round staple. They're hugely popular in risotto, stews, soups, and pasta sauces; just inhale deeply over a dish containing porcinis to experience their seductiveness. These mushrooms only grow wild, so they're predictably expensive, but their concentrated flavor means a little goes a long way. Keep a small package of dried porcinis on hand to easily add depth and intensity to your cooking. Rehydrate them in warm water for about 20 to 30 minutes. The soaking water is loaded with flavor, so don't throw it out. If grit or sand sinks to the bottom, pour the liquid away, leaving sediment behind, or strain the liquid through cheesecloth.

NONNA'S TIP Look for dried porcinis consisting of large slices without a lot of crumbs or powder. These will rehydrate with less waste and are usually more intense in flavor.

Prosciutto and Pancetta Italians are famous for their love of pork, and these two cured products are an easy way to work its flavor into numerous dishes. **Prosciutto** is cured ham that is salted and air-dried for concentrated flavor. Its intensely funky and sweet flavor means even rosy paper-thin slices bring big impact to your dishes. **Pancetta,** like bacon, is made from pork belly. This fatty but delicious cut is seasoned with pepper and spices for distinctive character. Diced and sautéed, it brings deep, cured-pork flavor to sauces, stews, vegetables, and more. Both prosciutto and pancetta are so savory that you'll find a little goes a long way.

NONNA'S TIP Thinly sliced prosciutto dries out quickly, losing its silky texture and delicious aroma; keep it well wrapped and use sliced-to-order prosciutto within a day or two and packaged prosciutto a few days after opening. Pancetta is sturdier, but should still be used within a week of slicing or unpacking. Pancetta should be sliced thinly or finely diced and not cooked too long or it will turn chewy and hard.

Rice **Arborio** and **Carnaroli** rice are the most famous in Italy and the basis for traditional risotto.

These short-grain varieties have a high starch content that, when cooked and stirred with broth, creates the naturally creamy texture for which risotto is famous. Both are usually imported, although high-quality domestically grown versions are now also available in the United States.

NONNA'S TIP Don't rinse the rice grains before making risotto; rinsing will remove the outer powdery coating of starch that's an important element of the dish.

Ricotta
Soft, scoopable ricotta is the freshest of Italy's staple cheeses. If you find ultrafresh **handmade ricotta** in Italy or at a specialty store, try it: Its rich, sweet, milky flavor and smooth texture are unforgettable. Packaged ricotta can also be delicious, with the benefit that it comes in **low-fat** and **fat-free** varieties; as with mozzarella, low-fat ricotta is a smart compromise, delivering good flavor and texture while keeping your recipes leaner.

NONNA'S TIP Commercial ricottas, particularly low-fat ones, can have a slightly grainy texture. For a smoother, creamier cheese, you can whirl it in a food processor for a minute or two.

Wine
Italy has more than 2,400 recognized styles of wine. These are made in every region of Italy, not only by celebrated winemakers but also in households, trattorias, and osterias across the country. Besides enjoying wine with meals, Italians use wine freely in cooking. It adds moisture, acidity, sweetness, and notes of fruit to dishes. In addition, wine's alcohol actually enhances the flavors around it, much like salt does. Just about any Italian wine that you like to drink is fine for cooking, with inexpensive **Primitivo, Chianti,** or **Pinot Grigio** being excellent choices. Sweet varieties like **Marsala, Moscato,** or **Vin Santo** should be used only where their sweetness will add to a dish's flavor, not clash with it. As for as drinking wine with your meal, see our Wine Pairing suggestions included with selected recipes throughout the book.

NONNA'S TIP Prefer not to cook with wine? Substitute broth mixed with a little red- or white-wine vinegar; a mild fruit juice like grape or pear is a good replacement for sweet wines.

A Note About Our Wine Pairings

We selected two dozen Italian wines that are widely available in the United States, then matched them to our most wine-friendly recipes. For practical reasons we've kept our suggestions relatively broad, highlighting a grape varietal (such as Pinot Grigio or Primitivo) or a general style or regional classification (such as Chianti or Barolo). We think these designations are a practical way to navigate through Italy's 2,400 recognized styles, and an absolutely staggering number of producers—more than any other country in the world.

Our wine focus is on Italy, but feel free to hop countries or continents to suit what you find available. A New Zealand Pinot Noir can go just as wonderfully with pizza or a rich tomato sauce as Dolcetto does. The staff at a good wine store should be able to lead you to many other compatible wines beyond the ones we've covered.

Salute!

7 Easy Skills for Cooking Italian

Onions, garlic, tomatoes, and more! Knowing how to prep these go-to ingredients will speed up your cooking and give your flavors a boost. Here are some of the most common techniques to master for the recipes in this book.

Peeling Garlic

1. Place the unpeeled clove on a cutting board and press down with the flat side of a chef's knife until the clove cracks.

2. Remove the papery skin with your fingers. Repeat with the number of cloves needed for your recipe. Now you can slice, chop, or mince the cloves.

Dicing an Onion

1. With a sharp chef's knife, cut the onion in half vertically, from top to root end. Peel off the papery skin and place the onion halves flat side down on a cutting board. Make two or three horizontal cuts toward the root end, stopping before you cut all the way through.

2. Make vertical cuts about ¼ inch apart, keeping the root end intact. Then make perpendicular cuts, chopping the onion into uniform cubes.

Chopping Herbs

1. Pull the leaves off the stems of the herbs. Gather the leaves in a pile on a cutting board. With a sharp chef's knife, cut across the herbs to chop the leaves coarsely.

2. Carefully steadying the top of the blade with the palm of your hand, rock the knife up and down without lifting the tip from the cutting board, moving back and forth over the herbs until minced.

Exception: Basil. Tear with hands or snip with scissors.

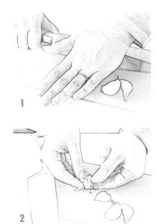

Peeling Tomatoes

1. Bring a pot of water to a boil. With a paring knife, cut a shallow X on the bottom of each tomato. One or two at a time, lower the tomatoes into the boiling water; boil until the edges of the X begin to curl back, 20 to 30 seconds. Remove them with a slotted spoon and place in a bowl of cold water.

2. When cooled, use the edge of a paring knife or your fingers to peel off the skin. To seed tomatoes, slice them in half crosswise and use your fingers to scoop out the seeds.

Peeling and Deveining Shrimp

1. Starting at the head end, use your fingers to loosen the shell sections on the underside of the shrimp and peel them off. Peel off the tail section if desired.

2. To devein the shrimp, use a paring knife to make a shallow cut down the back of the shrimp to expose the dark vein. Use the tip of the knife or your fingers to pull and lift out the vein.

Toasting Nuts

1. To toast nuts in the oven, preheat the oven to 350°F. Spread the nuts across a shallow baking pan. Bake, shaking the pan every few minutes, until the nuts are golden and fragrant, about 8 minutes. Cool on a plate.

2. To toast them on the stovetop, put the nuts in a heavy skillet just large enough to hold them in a single layer. Place it over medium heat and cook, shaking the pan every 30 seconds or so, until the nuts become golden and fragrant, 3 to 5 minutes depending on their size. Cool on a plate.

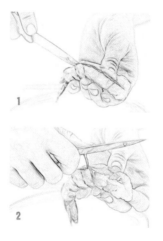

Removing Eggplant's Bitterness

Eggplants can become bitter with age, so always try to get nice, firm, shiny ones, free of bruises. If you're particularly sensitive to this veggie's bitterness you can use this technique many cooks swear by: Slice or cube the flesh and put it in a colander. Sprinkle generously with salt (preferably coarse or kosher) and place the colander in a bowl to catch the liquid the eggplant will release. Drain up to an hour, then rinse and pat dry and the eggplant is ready to cook. To avoid bitterness altogether, buy Japanese eggplant—the long, skinny, purple kind.

Building-Block Recipes

We're constantly inspired by the way Italians are able to quickly create extraordinarily delectable meals *daily*, always with ease, style, and grace. Much of it is due to the quality of the ingredients they use, and the fact that they start with well-stocked pantries (see page xix for tips on how to build yours). Italian home cooks also rely on a few foundational building-block recipes. These recipes provide depth of flavor and background support to the main ingredients of a dish, and they encourage cooks to improvise—the possibilities are endless! I spend a few hours on a weekend afternoon every other month or so making these recipes. I keep jars of them in my fridge, or I pour them into metal muffin tins, silicone molds, or ice-cube trays and freeze them so they'll last longer. This is how my parents cooked—you "save for a rainy day," and when you don't have much, you treasure what you do have and make the most of it.

Soffritto

makes 2 cups • gluten free • vegetarian

This mix of finely diced vegetables and a fat (usually olive oil) is the base for practically any soup, sauce, ragu, and braise in Italian cooking. This is where the flavor of a dish starts. A classic mix includes carrots, celery, and onions, and depending on the region, garlic, parsley, and even pancetta or anchovies are added. The key is to cook gently until vegetables are soft, melting and lightly browned.

¼ cup olive oil

1 large onion, diced

3 cloves garlic, finely chopped

2 celery stalks, diced

2 carrots, diced

1 sprig rosemary (optional)

Salt, to taste

Freshly ground black pepper, to taste

1 Heat skillet or large saucepan over medium heat. When hot, add oil. Add onion and cook, stirring frequently, until onion is translucent, about 6 minutes. Add garlic and continue to cook until onion is pale gold, 5–7 minutes longer.

2 Stir in celery, carrots, rosemary (if using), and salt and pepper. Cook, stirring occasionally, until vegetables are very tender and caramelized, 10–15 minutes, stirring bottom of pan frequently to release any browned bits. Remove and discard rosemary. Use immediately as base for sauces, soups, or stews, or transfer to jar and refrigerate up to 1 week.

Per serving (2½ tablespoons): 52 Cal, 4 g Total Fat, 1 g Sat Fat, 66 mg Sod, 3 g Total Carb, 1 g Sugar, 1 g Fib, 0 g Prot. **SmartPoints:** 1

Quick-Cook Tomato Sauce

serves 8 • gluten free • vegetarian • under 20 minutes

Nothing compares to sauce made with fresh, ripe plum tomatoes that have been basking in the sun all summer long. To prepare tomatoes, peel and seed them (see page xxix), chop them, then pour them into a saucepan that already has onions and garlic sizzling. This fresh sauce is excellent over pasta, or as a topping for spaghetti squash, grilled eggplant, and meatballs. Want to freeze it? Just leave out the basil.

3 tablespoons olive oil

1 small onion, chopped

4 large garlic cloves, minced

2 pounds ripe tomatoes, cored and diced

1 tablespoon tomato paste

2 teaspoons kosher salt

½ cup chopped fresh basil

1 Heat oil in large saucepan over medium heat. Add onion and cook, stirring, until softened, about 5 minutes. Add garlic and cook, stirring frequently, until fragrant, about 30 seconds.

2 Add tomatoes with their juice, tomato paste, and salt; cook, stirring, until tomatoes break down and begin to soften, 4–5 minutes. Stir in basil.

Per serving (½ cup): 73 Cal, 5 g Total Fat, 1 g Sat Fat, 490 mg Sod, 6 g Total Carb, 4 g Sugar, 2 g Fib, 1 g Prot. **SmartPoints:** 2

Classic Tomato Sauce

serves 12 • gluten free • vegetarian

We like canned San Marzano plum tomatoes imported from Italy for this sauce. Garlic, finely minced, is an essential ingredient too. When you add garlic to the pan, sauté it slowly until the color is close to a pale gold, no longer! Throw in fresh basil at the very last minute, just before serving, for a hit of herbaceous flavor.

1 tablespoon olive oil

2 onions, chopped

4 garlic cloves, minced

2 (28-ounce) cans whole peeled tomatoes, drained and broken up

¼ cup tomato paste

1 teaspoon salt

½ teaspoon black pepper

1 Heat oil in Dutch oven over medium heat. Add onions and garlic; cook, stirring, until onions are softened, about 5 minutes.

2 Add all remaining ingredients to Dutch oven and bring to boil. Reduce heat and simmer, partially covered, until flavors are blended and sauce is slightly thickened, about 25 minutes.

Per serving (½ cup): 34 Cal, 1 g Total Fat, 0 g Sat Fat, 195 mg Sod, 6 g Total Carb, 3 g Sugar, 1 g Fib, 1 g Prot. **SmartPoints:** 1

Basil Pesto

serves 6 • gluten free • vegetarian • under 20 minutes • no cook

This is a lively, fragrant sauce made of fresh basil crushed with Parmesan, garlic, and pine nuts. Pesto is a classic sauce for pasta, and is delicious spread on crostini, pizza, and panini. A dollop in soup is wonderful too.

2 cups lightly packed fresh basil leaves (from about 1 bunch)

3 tablespoons pine nuts

2 tablespoons water

1 tablespoon extra-virgin olive oil

2 garlic cloves, minced

¼ teaspoon salt

½ cup plus 2 tablespoons grated Parmesan

1 Combine all ingredients except Parmesan in food processor or blender and puree. Add cheese and pulse until mixed.

2 Transfer pesto to jar with tight-fitting lid; spray top of pesto with olive oil nonstick spray to prevent browning. Can be refrigerated in airtight container up to 3 weeks or frozen up to 3 months.

Per serving (generous 3 tablespoons): 144 Cal, 12 g Total Fat, 3 g Sat Fat, 324 mg Sod, 4 g Total Carb, 0 g Sugar, 1 g Fib, 6 g Prot. **SmartPoints:** 5

Artichoke Pesto

serves 8 • gluten free
• vegetarian • under 20 minutes
• no cook

Use this tasty alternative to classic pesto as a topping for crostini, a sauce for gnocchi, or for dipping vegetables.

1¼ cups canned artichoke hearts (not oil-packed), drained and rinsed

1¼ cups lightly packed fresh basil leaves

¼ cup pine nuts, toasted

3 tablespoons grated Parmesan

3 tablespoons water

1 garlic clove, quartered

½ teaspoon salt

Combine all ingredients in food processor and pulse a few times, then process until finely chopped but not smooth. Transfer pesto to jar with tight-fitting lid; spray top with olive oil nonstick spray to prevent browning. Can be refrigerated in airtight container up to 2 days.

Per serving (3 tablespoons): 46 Cal, 3 g Total Fat, 1 g Sat Fat, 305 mg Sod, 4 g Total Carb, 1 g Sugar, 2 g Fib, 2 g Prot. **SmartPoints:** 1

Salsa Verde

serves 8 • gluten free
• vegetarian • under 20 minutes
• no cook

Want to brighten up grilled fish, chicken, boiled vegetables, or a steak? This zesty, lemony sauce does the trick. You can add a pinch or two of red pepper flakes for heat or a few teaspoons of chopped capers for a bit of punch. Sometimes finely chopped anchovies are added too.

½ cup finely chopped fresh parsley

2 tablespoons finely chopped fresh marjoram or oregano

1 garlic clove, minced

1 tablespoon finely grated lemon zest

2 tablespoons lemon juice

2 tablespoons extra-virgin olive oil

¼ teaspoon salt

Combine all ingredients in bowl and stir well. Allow flavors to blend at least 10 minutes before serving. Will keep refrigerated up to 2 days.

Per serving (1 tablespoon): 49 Cal, 5 g Total Fat, 1 g Sat Fat, 75 mg Sod, 1 g Total Carb, 0 g Sugar, 0 g Fib, 0 g Prot. **SmartPoints:** 2

Light Aïoli

serves 6 • gluten free
• vegetarian • under 20 minutes
• no cook

Serve this deeply garlicky mayonnaise over roasted vegetables, grilled chicken, or seafood. It's also terrific as a dressing for sliced tomatoes.

5 tablespoons low-fat buttermilk

3 tablespoons light mayonnaise

1 garlic clove, minced

½ teaspoon finely grated lemon zest

1 teaspoon lemon juice

¼ teaspoon salt

⅛ teaspoon black pepper

Whisk together all ingredients in small bowl. Refrigerate for at least 10 minutes to let flavors blend. Will keep refrigerated for 2 days.

Per serving (1½ tablespoons): 31 Cal, 3 g Total Fat, 0 g Sat Fat, 175 mg Sod, 1 g Total Carb, 1 g Sugar, 0 g Fib, 1 g Prot. **SmartPoints:** 1

Italian Béchamel

makes 2¼ cups • vegetarian • under 20 minutes

This easy, lightened-up version of white sauce is flavorful and rich-tasting, excellent for tomato-free pasta like our Winter Squash Lasagna on page 118. Also use it in vegetable gratins and potatoes, and to add thickness and creaminess to soups.

¼ cup all-purpose flour

2½ cups evaporated fat-free milk

2 garlic cloves, finely chopped

⅓ cup grated Parmesan

½ teaspoon salt, or to taste

¼ teaspoon black pepper, or to taste

⅛ teaspoon freshly grated nutmeg

Place flour in small saucepan and very gradually whisk in milk. Whisk in garlic. Warm over low heat, stirring constantly, until sauce simmers and is thickened, about 3 minutes. Remove from heat and stir in Parmesan, salt, pepper, and nutmeg.

Per serving (generous ¼ cup): 76 Cal, 1 g Total Fat, 1 g Sat Fat, 250 mg Sod, 10 g Total Carb, 7 g Sugar, 0 g Fib, 6 g Prot. **SmartPoints:** 3

Beef Broth

makes 12 cups • gluten free

Homemade beef broth is rich and flavorful, and once you get used to cooking with it you may not want to go back to canned broth. It adds deep flavor to soups and stews, and can be used to make risotto. Beef broth has also become a popular hot beverage stateside, sometimes known as bone broth—try it spiked with a little cider vinegar and chopped fresh herbs.

4 pounds meaty beef soup bones

14 cups water

1 large onion, quartered

2 carrots

1 celery stalk

1 large leek, sliced and rinsed

2 garlic cloves

6 fresh parsley sprigs

1 bay leaf

½ teaspoon peppercorns

1½ teaspoons salt

1 Preheat oven to 400°F. Place bones in roasting pan and roast until lightly browned, about 30 minutes.

2 Transfer bones to large pot and add all remaining ingredients. Bring to simmer over medium heat, skimming off foam that rises to surface. Reduce heat and simmer, partially covered, 4 hours, skimming off foam that rises to surface.

3 Line colander with double thickness of cheesecloth; set over large bowl. Strain broth, pressing hard on solids to extract all liquid; discard solids.

4 Let broth cool; refrigerate until fat rises to surface and solidifies, at least 4 hours or up to overnight. Scrape off fat and discard. Use broth at once or refrigerate up to 2 days. Or transfer to 1-cup freezer containers and freeze up to 6 months.

Per serving (1 cup): 31 Cal, 0 g Total Fat, 0 g Sat Fat, 475 mg Sod, 3 g Total Carb, 1 g Sugar, 0 g Fib, 5 g Prot. **SmartPoints:** 1

Chicken Broth

makes 8 cups • gluten free

A few chicken wings (or bones from yesterday's roast chicken), some vegetables, a handful of herbs and peppercorns. That's all it takes to make this classic rich *brodo*. Broths do need a little tending, but the actual hands-on time is minimal. We simmer gently (not boil) and from time to time skim off any foam that forms on top. Chicken broth is also excellent for sipping: try it with a squeeze of lemon juice.

4 pounds chicken wings, backs, or legs

12 cups water

1 large onion, quartered

2 carrots, coarsely chopped

2 large celery stalks with leaves, thickly sliced

1 large leek, sliced and rinsed

8 fresh parsley sprigs

2 fresh thyme sprigs

12 black peppercorns

1½ teaspoons salt

1 Combine chicken and water in stockpot; bring to simmer over medium heat, skimming off foam that rises to surface. Add all remaining ingredients; reduce heat and simmer, partially covered, 2 hours, skimming off foam that rises to surface.

2 Line colander with double thickness of cheesecloth; set over large bowl. Strain broth, pressing hard on solids to extract all liquid; discard solids.

3 Let broth cool; refrigerate until fat rises to surface and solidifies, at least 4 hours or up to overnight. Scrape off fat and discard. Use broth at once or refrigerate up to 2 days. Or transfer to 1-cup freezer containers and freeze up to 6 months.

Per serving (1 cup): 14 Cal, 0 g Total Fat, 0 g Sat Fat, 580 mg Sod, 1 g Total Carb, 0 g Sugar, 0 g Fib, 2 g Prot. **SmartPoints:** 0

Vegetable Broth

makes 8 cups • gluten free
• vegetarian

This deep, restorative broth proves you don't need meat to enjoy a bowl of rich sustenance. If you're in the mood, add a handful of sliced mushrooms, spinach, or leeks to the broth, or even *pastina* (tiny pasta). Try broth instead of water when cooking grains or beans for more intense flavor.

1 tablespoon olive oil

4 onions, quartered

3 leeks, sliced and rinsed

2 celery stalks with leaves, coarsely chopped

2 parsnips, coarsely chopped

1 carrot, coarsely chopped

12 cups water

6 large dried mushrooms or 12 fresh mushrooms

3 fresh parsley sprigs

6 fresh dill sprigs

12 black peppercorns

1½ teaspoons salt

1 Heat oil in stockpot over medium heat. Add onions, leeks, celery, parsnips, and carrot; cook, stirring occasionally, until vegetables begin to soften, about 10 minutes. Add all remaining ingredients; bring to simmer, skimming off any foam that rises to surface. Cook at bare simmer, partially covered, 2 hours.

2 Line colander with double thickness of cheesecloth; set over large bowl. Strain broth, pressing hard on solids to extract all liquid; discard solids.

3 Use broth at once or let cool and refrigerate up to 2 days. Or transfer to 1-cup freezer containers and freeze up to 6 months.

Per serving (1 cup): 28 Cal, 2 g Total Fat, 0 g Sat Fat, 667 mg Sod, 2 g Total Carb, 1 g Sugar, 0 g Fib, 1 g Prot. **SmartPoints:** 1

Italian Vinaigrette

serves 8 • gluten free
• vegetarian • under 20 minutes
• no cook

This vinaigrette is perfect over greens, pasta, or grain salads. It also doubles as a marinade for chicken, seafood, or vegetables.

¼ cup minced shallots

¼ cup red-wine vinegar

¼ cup vegetable broth or water

2 tablespoons extra-virgin olive oil

1 teaspoon Italian seasoning blend

½ teaspoon sugar

½ teaspoon salt

¼ teaspoon black pepper

Combine all ingredients in small jar with tightly fitting lid. Seal jar and shake until mixed well. Can be refrigerated up to 4 days; shake well before using.

Per serving (1½ tablespoons): 37 Cal, 3 g Total Fat, 0 g Sat Fat, 167 mg Sod, 1 g Total Carb, 1 g Sugar, 0 g Fib, 0 g Prot. **SmartPoints:** 1

Love & Marriage:

1. San Vittorio's church in Roccella Ionica where my parents got married.
2. Frank and Filomena were married for more than 50 years: he with a tough-guy look and warm smile, and she with the confidence that comes from keeping a family together. Though they were accustomed to working from the moment they woke to the moment they went to sleep, at day's end they'd come together and look out at the same sunset, and know they had each other.

Chapter 1

Starters (antipasti)

Prosciutto-Arugula Focaccia
FOCACCIA CON PROSCIUTTO E RUCOLA

serves 6 • under 20 minutes

This recipe couldn't be easier to make. *Antipasto* means "before the pasta" in Italian, and serving a few tasty bites is a fun way to invite your family and friends to the table and to set the stage for the coming meal. I like to keep it simple and let the quality of the ingredients do the work: cherry tomatoes, a chunk of Parmesan, a bowl of olives, salted anchovies, or marinated artichokes. Crispy, chewy focaccia is also a guest favorite. I top mine with rosy, paper-thin prosciutto and peppery arugula for a touch of spiciness.

1 (4-ounce) piece plain focaccia or flatbread, split horizontally if thick

2 teaspoons extra-virgin olive oil

2 garlic cloves, finely chopped

1½ cups lightly packed baby arugula

2 teaspoons red-wine vinegar

¼ teaspoon black pepper

Pinch salt

3 ounces very thinly sliced prosciutto (about 6 slices), cut into strips

1 Preheat broiler.

2 Cut focaccia or flatbread into 6 equal pieces. Place pieces on baking sheet. Brush tops of each with oil and sprinkle with garlic. Broil 6 inches from heat until browned in spots, about 1 minute.

3 Toss, arugula, vinegar, pepper, and salt in medium bowl. Divide mixture evenly among focaccia pieces and top each evenly with proscuitto.

Wine pairing:

Pinot Grigio, if you'd like to pour white; a light Dolcetto, if you'd prefer red.

Per serving (1 piece focaccia and ¼ cup arugula mixture): 110 Cal, 6 g Total Fat, 2 g Sat Fat, 569 mg Sod, 6 g Total Carb, 0 g Sugar, 0 g Fib, 6 g Prot.

Choose a simple focaccia or other flatbread for this appetizer, and split the bread horizontally with a serrated knife if it's thicker than about ¾ inch.

Prosciutto-Arugula
Focaccia

Pea-and-Ricotta Crostini
CROSTINI CON PISELLI E RICOTTA

serves 24 • vegetarian

Italians adore crostini. Slices of baguette or ciabatta are grilled or toasted, rubbed with garlic and olive oil, and topped with all kinds of goodies, depending on what is available at the greenmarket. We like ours with whipped peas, mint, creamy ricotta, a wedge of cherry tomato, and a sprinkling of freshly cracked black pepper for a pop of flavor. A plate of these two-bite morsels is a perfect start to a meal.

10 ounces frozen green peas or fresh spring peas

½ cup part-skim ricotta

¼ cup firmly packed fresh mint leaves, plus 24 small mint leaves for garnish

2 tablespoons grated Parmesan

1 tablespoon extra-virgin olive oil

1 garlic clove, chopped

½ teaspoon salt, or to taste

¼ teaspoon black pepper, or to taste

6 ounces Italian bread or ciabatta, cut into 24 even slices

6 cherry tomatoes, cut into 4 wedges each

Freshly cracked black pepper

1 Bring medium saucepan half full of water to boil; add peas. Return to boil; boil 1 minute to soften skins. Drain and rinse under cold water; drain again.

2 Put drained peas into bowl of food processor; add ricotta, ¼ cup mint leaves, Parmesan, oil, garlic, salt, and pepper. Process until mixture is smooth but still has a little bit of texture. Scrape mixture into small bowl; let stand at least 15 minutes for flavors to blend, or cover and refrigerate up to 2 days.

3 Preheat oven to 375°F. Coat large baking sheet with nonstick spray. Place bread slices on prepared baking sheet and spray lightly with nonstick spray; bake until lightly browned, flipping once, 8–10 minutes. Place bread slices on wire rack to cool.

4 To assemble crostini, mound 1 tablespoon pea mixture on each bread slice. Top each with cherry tomato wedge and small mint leaf. Sprinkle with cracked pepper.

 Per serving (1 crostino): 43 Cal, 1 g Total Fat, 0 g Sat Fat, 117 mg Sod, 6 g Total Carb, 1 g Sugar, 1 g Fib, 2 g Prot.

You can make and refrigerate the spread up to 2 days in advance, and store the cooled toasts in an airtight container up to 1 day.

Tomato Bruschetta
BRUSCHETTA AL POMODORO

serves 24 ● *vegetarian*

I admit it: I like just about anything on toast. This bright, colorful tomato dish is bursting with summery goodness. And the fact that it takes just a few minutes of prep time is an added bonus.

2 garlic cloves

1 (10-ounce) loaf French baguette, cut on diagonal into 24 slices

3 tomatoes (about 1¼ pounds), diced

1 cup loosely packed fresh basil leaves, chopped

¼ cup finely chopped red onion

1 tablespoon extra-virgin olive oil

2 teaspoons red-wine vinegar

¾ teaspoon salt

¼ teaspoon black pepper

1 Preheat oven to 375°F. Coat large baking sheet with nonstick spray.

2 Slice 1 garlic clove in half. Rub cut sides of garlic over one side of each bread slice; place bread on baking sheet and spray lightly with nonstick spray. Bake until lightly browned, flipping once, 8–10 minutes. Place bread on wire rack to cool.

3 Meanwhile, mince remaining garlic clove. Combine tomatoes, basil, onion, oil, vinegar, salt, pepper, and minced garlic in large bowl and toss. Let sit 10 minutes for flavors to blend. Spoon tomato mixture evenly onto bread slices.

Per serving (1 bruschetta): 41 Cal, 1 g Total Fat, 0 g Sat Fat, 145 mg Sod, 7 g Total Carb, 1 g Sugar, 1 g Fib, 1 g Prot.

**Pea and Cherry
Tomato Frittata**

Pea and Cherry Tomato Frittata
FRITTATA DI PISELLI E POMODORINI

serves 6 • gluten free • vegetarian

In Italy, eggs are rarely eaten for breakfast. Instead, they're often made into frittatas, a terrific starter or a quick meal that works for dinner, lunch, or brunch. This egg dish is essentially a blank canvas—whatever vegetables, meats, and cheese are in your refrigerator can go into a frittata. And then leftovers can be eaten for lunch the next day. When reserves are low but I still want something substantial, this is what I make. Nothing fancy here.

½ ounce dried porcini mushrooms

2 teaspoons olive oil

1 onion, diced

3 garlic cloves, finely chopped

1 teaspoon dried basil

1 cup cherry tomatoes

1 cup frozen peas

4 large eggs, lightly beaten

2 egg whites, lightly beaten

3 tablespoons grated Parmesan

½ teaspoon salt

¼ teaspoon black pepper

1 Place mushrooms in small bowl and cover with warm water by 1 inch. Let stand until softened, about 20 minutes. Lift mushrooms out with slotted spoon (grit may have sunk to bottom of bowl); chop mushrooms.

2 Heat oil in 10-inch cast-iron or other ovenproof skillet over medium-high heat. Add mushrooms and onion; cook, stirring occasionally, until onion begins to brown, about 5 minutes. Stir in garlic and basil. Add cherry tomatoes and peas; cook until tomatoes and peas soften, 2–3 minutes.

3 Preheat broiler. Whisk together eggs, egg whites, Parmesan, salt, and pepper in medium bowl. Pour over mushroom mixture, stirring gently to combine. Reduce heat to medium and cook until eggs are almost set, 7–8 minutes. Place frittata under broiler and broil 5 inches from heat until top is lightly browned, about 2 minutes. Let stand at least 5 minutes before slicing and serving. Serve warm or room temperature.

Wine pairing:

Prosecco or Pinot Grigio.

Per serving (⅙ of frittata): 120 Cal, 6 g Total Fat, 2 g Sat Fat, 345 mg Sod, 9 g Total Carb, 3 g Sugar, 2 g Fib, 9 g Prot.

If the handle of your skillet is not ovenproof, wrap it with foil to protect it from the heat of the broiler.

Make It Your Own: Frittata

Frittatas are exceptionally flexible and easy to make. Simply mix eggs and your favorite ingredients together in a skillet and pop it in the oven, no fiddling necessary. Eggs have a starring role in this dish, so start with the freshest possible.

I like to eat my frittata with a salad. I choose seasonal leaves and dress them lightly: in summer, escarole, sorrel, or tender young Swiss chard; in winter I go for bitter leaves, such as *cicoria*, radicchio, endive, or hot mustard greens. Spinach and peppery arugula work well any time of year. I like to add fresh herbs to my salads, whether it's mint, flat-leaf parsley, basil, or marjoram.

CHOOSE A MAIN VEGETABLE (STEAMED, SAUTÉED, OR OTHERWISE PRECOOKED)	ADD A BACKUP VEGETABLE TO BOOST THE MAIN VEG	CHOOSE AN HERB OR SPICE FOR AN ACCENT FLAVOR	ADD SOME RICHNESS
Asparagus	A few artichokes, pickled or *sott'olio* (in oil)	Chopped flat-leaf parsley	Chicken or turkey sausage, browned and crumbled
Broccoli		Fresh thyme	
Broccoli rabe, cut into segments	Roasted red peppers (water-packed) from a jar	Fresh dill	Ham (*prosciutto cotto*)
Boiled or roasted potatoes		Tarragon	
	Spinach leaves	Red pepper flakes	Freshly grated pecorino Romano
Cauliflower	Cherry tomatoes	Torn basil leaves	Freshly grated Parmesan

 + +  +

	Thinly sliced zucchini	Paprika	Pancetta
Diced red onion			Provolone
Diced red or yellow bell peppers			Ricotta
Leeks			
Porcini mushrooms			
Zucchini blossoms			

Clams Oreganata with Pancetta

VONGOLE CON ORIGANO E PANCETTA

serves 8

I think of this recipe as a marriage of earth and sea: briny, succulent clams and sweet, mountain-cured pork. It's a cross between two Italian-American dishes: clams oreganata (bread crumbs and oregano) and clams casino (bread crumbs and bacon). It uses littleneck clams, native to the North Atlantic coast and larger than most clam varieties found in Italy.

2 dozen littleneck clams, shucked by your fish seller, shells and liquor reserved

¼ cup (1½ ounces) diced pancetta

1 garlic clove, minced

⅓ cup panko (Japanese bread crumbs)

2 tablespoons olive oil

2 tablespoons chopped fresh oregano leaves

2 tablespoons grated Parmesan

½ teaspoon grated lemon zest

¼ teaspoon black pepper

Lemon wedges

1 Place 24 clam shell halves in colander and scrub under cold water to remove any grit; pat dry and arrange on baking sheet. Place 1 clam meat in each shell. Carefully spoon some reserved clam liquor over each clam, avoiding any grit that settles to the bottom.

2 Put pancetta in small nonstick skillet and place over medium-low heat. Cook, stirring occasionally, until lightly browned, about 4 minutes. Add garlic; continue to cook, stirring, until garlic is fragrant, about 30 seconds longer. Remove from heat; push pancetta to one side of skillet and pour off and discard rendered fat.

3 Stir panko and 1 tablespoon oil into pancetta until crumbs are evenly moistened; cool slightly. Add oregano, Parmesan, lemon zest, pepper, and any remaining clam liquor and stir until combined.

4 Preheat oven to 475°F.

5 Spoon heaping teaspoon of panko mixture loosely over each clam (do not pack crumbs down). Place on baking sheet and drizzle tops with remaining 1 tablespoon oil. Broil clams until crumbs are golden brown and crisp and clams are just cooked through, about 10 minutes. Serve hot with lemon wedges.

Wine pairing:

Light red, like Primitivo, or rich white, like Pinot Bianco.

Per serving (3 clams): 101 Cal, 6 g Total Fat, 1 g Sat Fat, 254 mg Sod, 4 g Total Carb, 0 g Sugar, 0 g Fib, 6 g Prot.

Clams Oreganata
with Pancetta

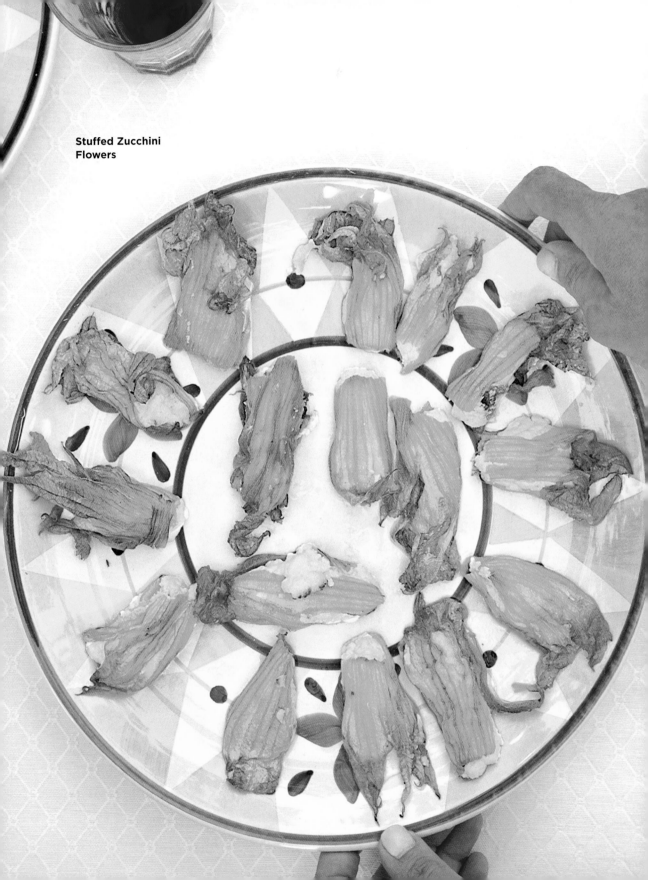

**Stuffed Zucchini
Flowers**

Stuffed Zucchini Flowers
FIORI DI ZUCCA RIPIENI

serves 4 • gluten free • vegetarian

Zucchini flowers, also called zucchini blossoms or squash blossoms, are popular in Italy, especially in the Campania and Calabria regions, but when I was growing up in Michigan, none of my friends knew what they were. Other kids got PB&J sandwiches in their lunchboxes; my brother and I would get zucchini fritters in ours—that is, if there were any left over: We'd pop them in our mouths minutes after my mom lifted them out of the pan, still warm and luscious. Blossoms taste like zucchini, but with a light, ephemeral quality. They're delicious stuffed with ricotta and Parmesan, and if you make these beauties, I guarantee you'll impress your friends.

8 zucchini flowers
⅔ cup part-skim ricotta
3 tablespoons grated Parmesan
1 tablespoon lightly beaten egg white
¼ teaspoon salt
⅛ teaspoon black pepper

1 Preheat oven to 400°F. Spray baking sheet with nonstick spray.

2 Carefully spread petals of each zucchini flower; pinch off stamen and discard. Holding flowers by stem, quickly dip one at a time in cold water. Pat flowers dry; place stem ends up on paper towels to drain.

3 In small bowl, stir together ricotta, Parmesan, egg white, salt, and pepper.

4 Carefully spoon about 1 heaping tablespoon filling into each flower, twisting petals loosely at ends to close.

5 Place stuffed flowers on baking sheet; spray with nonstick spray. Bake until filling is hot, about 15 minutes. Serve warm.

Wine pairing:
Crisp white like Vernaccia or Vermentino.

Per serving (2 stuffed flowers): 83 Cal, 5 g Total Fat, 3 g Sat Fat, 249 mg Sod, 4 g Total Carb, 1 g Sugar, 0 g Fib, 7 g Prot.

Wild Mushrooms on Baked Polenta

FUNGHI SELVATICI SU POLENTA AL FORNO

serves 8 • gluten free • vegetarian

Crisp, earthy, delicious. I like to spoon on the mushroom mixture and eat them immediately, though you can make these savory little rounds ahead of time. Just reheat in a 350°F oven for about 10 minutes before serving. It's a perfect gluten-free option!

1 (18-ounce) log prepared polenta, sliced into 16 rounds

8 teaspoons grated Parmesan

2 teaspoons olive oil

1¼ pounds mixed mushrooms, tough stems trimmed, sliced

2 garlic cloves, finely chopped

1½ teaspoons chopped fresh rosemary leaves

¼ teaspoon salt, or to taste

¼ teaspoon black pepper

3 tablespoons light cream cheese (Neufchâtel)

¼ cup vegetable broth

2 tablespoons chopped fresh parsley leaves

1 Preheat oven to 450°F. Spray baking sheet with nonstick spray.

2 Arrange polenta on baking sheet in single layer. Lightly coat polenta with nonstick spray and sprinkle each round with ¼ teaspoon Parmesan; bake until Parmesan is lightly browned, 15–18 minutes.

3 While polenta rounds bake, prepare mushroom topping. Heat oil in large skillet over medium-high heat. Add mushrooms and cook, stirring frequently, until they release most of their liquid, about 12 minutes. Stir in garlic, rosemary, salt, and pepper; cook until fragrant, about 1 minute.

4 Stir cream cheese and broth into skillet; cook over medium-low heat until cream cheese melts and mixture looks creamy, 2–3 minutes.

5 To assemble, place about 2 tablespoons mushroom mixture onto each polenta round. Sprinkle each round with ¼ teaspoon Parmesan and garnish with parsley.

3 SmartPoints value™

Per serving (2 polenta rounds): 94 Cal, 3 g Total Fat, 1 g Sat Fat, 340 mg Sod, 13 g Total Carb, 2 g Sugar, 2 g Fib, 4 g Prot.

Gorgonzola-Fig Stuffed Endive

INDIVIA CON GORGONZOLA E FICHI

serves 8 • gluten free • vegetarian • under 20 minutes • no cook

Creamy Gorgonzola, seedy figs, and crisp endive: This antipasto is as much about texture as flavor. Texture is one of those things I think we forget about when we're making ourselves something to eat, until one day we realize it makes all the difference in the world. And Gorgonzola—named after a town in Lombardy, just outside Milan—delivers strong, pungent flavor, even in small amounts.

3 tablespoons light cream cheese (Neufchâtel), softened

1 ounce (about ¼ cup) Gorgonzola cheese or other blue cheese

24 small Belgian endive leaves

3 dried figs, stems trimmed, figs cut into 8 pieces each

1 In small bowl, mash together cream cheese and Gorgonzola.

2 Top base of each endive leaf with about 1 teaspoon cheese mixture and 1 piece fig.

Wine pairing:

Festive sparkling white, like Prosecco.

Per serving (3 stuffed leaves): 43 Cal, 2 g Total Fat, 1 g Sat Fat, 77 mg Sod, 5 g Total Carb, 2 g Sugar, 2 g Fib, 2 g Prot.

Bagna Cauda with Vegetables

BAGNA CAUDA CON VERDURE

serves 8 • gluten free

Bagna cauda translates as "hot bath," a poetic name for this rich garlic-and-anchovy sauce from the Piedmont region. Farmers would come home weary from working the fields and gather with family around the *bagna cauda* to dip vegetables or crusty bread into this warm, savory sauce. It's similar to fondue or crudités and dip. Enjoy the condiment with seasonal artichokes, radicchio, fennel, cauliflower, carrots, radishes, asparagus, celery, Broccolini, and summer squash, or use it to dress vegetable dishes and meats.

2 garlic bulbs, cloves separated but not peeled

1¼ cups chicken broth

1 (2-ounce) can flat anchovies in olive oil, drained and rinsed

2 tablespoons extra-virgin olive oil

1 tablespoon unsalted butter

¼ teaspoon kosher salt

¼ teaspoon black pepper

6 cups assorted cut-up raw vegetables, such as bell peppers, baby radishes, carrots, summer squash, snap peas, cauliflower, broccoli, Romanesco, and celery

1 Preheat oven to 350°F. Combine garlic and ½ cup broth in 8- or 9-inch square baking dish. Cover with foil; roast until cloves are soft and most broth has been absorbed, about 1 hour.

2 When cloves are cool enough to handle, squeeze pulp out of papery skins back into baking dish. Pour remaining ¾ cup broth into dish; scrape bottom with rubber spatula. Pour mixture into blender, add anchovies, and puree.

3 Combine mixture with oil, butter, salt, and pepper in small saucepan. Bring to simmer over medium-low heat, whisking, until butter is melted and dip is emulsified and smooth, about 5 minutes.

4 Pour mixture into small fondue pot or chafing dish set over warming candle or canned-heat cooking fuel. Serve immediately with vegetables for dipping.

Wine pairing:

Fruity red, such as a young Barbera from Piedmont.

Per serving (2 tablespoons dip and ¾ cup vegetables): 113 Cal, 6 g Total Fat, 2 g Sat Fat, 428 mg Sod, 12 g Total Carb, 2 g Sugar, 2 g Fib, 5 g Prot.

Bagna Cauda
with Vegetables

Marinated Peppers, page 19

Roasted Eggplant Caponata, page 20

Tomato Bruschetta, page 5

Marinated Peppers

PEPERONI MARINATI

serves 4 • gluten free • vegetarian

This dish is one of my favorites. It's colorful, simple, and luscious. Be sure to roast the peppers until they collapse and blister. As they cook, they'll release a syrupy sweet and smoky liquid. Green peppers are quite watery, so I use only red and yellow. I sometimes tear up extra parsley and scatter it on top.

1 tablespoon extra-virgin olive oil

2 small garlic cloves, very finely sliced or minced

⅛ teaspoon red pepper flakes

4 red, yellow, or orange bell peppers (or a mix), halved and seeded

2 tablespoons regular or white balsamic vinegar

2 tablespoons capers, rinsed and drained

½ teaspoon kosher salt

2 teaspoons chopped fresh parsley leaves

1 Combine oil, garlic, and pepper flakes in small glass bowl. Let garlic mixture stand until ready to serve.

2 Preheat broiler. Place bell pepper halves, cut side down, on foil-lined baking sheet. Broil 6 inches from heat source until skins are blistered and charred all over, about 10 minutes. Rotate peppers occasionally, if necessary. Place peppers in large bowl and cover with plastic wrap. Let steam 10 minutes.

3 Peel peppers and cut or tear into 1-inch-wide strips. To serve immediately, place on serving platter and drizzle garlic oil over peppers, then drizzle with vinegar and sprinkle with capers, salt, and parsley. Or combine peppers with remaining ingredients in airtight jar and refrigerate up to 3 days; let come to room temperature before serving.

Per serving (½ cup): 64 Cal, 4 g Total Fat, 0 g Sat Fat, 396 mg Sod, 8 g Total Carb, 4 g Sugar, 2 g Fib, 1 g Prot.

Roasted Eggplant Caponata
CAPONATA CON MELANZANE AL FORNO

serves 10 ● gluten free ● vegetarian

When I was growing up, my family would go on a lot of "visits." These visits with friends always included talking about politics and the old country, card games, and a table filled with food made from scratch. Because my parents had lots of Sicilian friends, caponata was always on the menu. Each cook had her own version, but all used eggplant and tomatoes as a base. The salty, sweet, and sour quality came from the addition of capers, olives, raisins, and vinegar. Our version includes hints of cinnamon and cocoa for deep flavor and a nod to Sicily's North African and Spanish influences.

The trick to a good caponata, I was told, is to cook the vegetables separately and mix them together afterward. This is a bit finicky, I know, but I'm willing to take the extra step because caponata can be made a day ahead. In fact, I prefer to make it in advance because it gives the flavors an opportunity to meld. I serve this dish on its own or as a relish to complement grilled fish, roast chicken, or polenta.

1 large (2-pound) eggplant, trimmed

2 tablespoons olive oil

½ teaspoon kosher salt

6 plum tomatoes, halved lengthwise

1 onion, diced

3 celery stalks with leaves, stalks diced, leaves chopped

½ cup tomato sauce

¼ cup golden raisins

12 pitted green olives, coarsely chopped

3 tablespoons balsamic vinegar

2 tablespoons capers, rinsed and drained

⅛ teaspoon red pepper flakes

1 teaspoon unsweetened cocoa (optional)

¼ teaspoon cinnamon (optional)

1 Adjust oven racks to middle and bottom positions. Preheat oven to 425°F. Spray 1 large and 1 medium baking sheet with nonstick spray.

2 Cut eggplant into ¾-inch cubes and toss with 1 tablespoon oil and salt on large baking sheet; spread in even layer. Arrange tomatoes, cut-side down, on medium baking sheet.

3 Roast eggplant on middle rack and tomatoes on bottom rack. Roast eggplant, stirring once or twice, until lightly browned and tender; roast tomatoes until skins are wrinkled and flesh is soft, about 20 minutes. Cool; pull off tomato skins and discard.

4 Heat remaining 1 tablespoon oil in large nonstick skillet over medium heat. Add onion and diced celery; cook, stirring often, until vegetables are just tender, about 8 minutes. Add roasted tomatoes and tomato sauce, breaking up tomatoes with wooden spoon.

5 Stir in raisins, olives, vinegar, capers, and pepper flakes until combined. Stir in cocoa and cinnamon, if using. Stir in eggplant; cook over low heat, stirring a few times, until flavors blend, about 8 minutes. Stir in celery leaves. If caponata is too thick, stir in water a tablespoon at a time until sauce coats vegetables. Serve warm, or cool and refrigerate. Bring to room temperature before serving.

Per serving (about ½ cup): 74 Cal, 4 g Total Fat, 0 g Sat Fat, 260 mg Sod, 11 g Total Carb, 6 g Sugar, 3 g Fib, 1 g Prot.

Marinated Olives
OLIVE MARINATE

serves 12 • gluten free • vegetarian • no cook

We varied the classic garlic-fennel-orange flavor combo by adding lemon zest and swapping in thyme for fennel (though stick with fennel if you want a licoricelike flavor). I use bright-green Castelvetrano olives from Sicily because they're meaty and buttery. Press on the olives with the side of a large knife and the pits will pop right out.

½ pound (about 24) brine-cured green and/or black olives

2 (3-inch) strips orange zest

2 (3-inch) strips lemon zest

2 garlic cloves, lightly crushed with side of large knife

¾ teaspoon dried thyme

½ teaspoon extra-virgin olive oil

Generous pinch cayenne

1 Stir together all ingredients in medium bowl. Refrigerate, covered, at least 1 day or up to 1 week.

2 To serve, transfer olive mixture to serving bowl. Let come to room temperature.

Per serving (2 olives): 25 Cal, 2 g Total Fat, 0 g Sat Fat, 139 mg Sod, 2 g Total Carb, 0 g Sugar, 1 g Fib, 0 g Prot.

Chapter 2

Soups (zuppe)

Chicken-and-Escarole Soup

ZUPPA DI POLLO E SCAROLA

serves 6 • gluten free

As the season for fresh produce wanes and the frost arrives, soups become more substantial. In this recipe we use escarole, a lettuce that's hardy enough for long simmers and has a good bitter flavor that Italians love. The two proteins–beans and chicken–are staple ingredients, and the red pepper flakes provide a nice back note of heat and spice. Don't forget to sprinkle the bowls of soup with Parmesan cheese before serving. Italians add grated cheese to almost all their soups, except fish-based ones.

1 ounce pancetta or thick-cut bacon, chopped

1 large onion, chopped

4 garlic cloves, minced

3 cups chicken broth

1 (14½-ounce) can whole tomatoes, chopped, juice reserved

4 (5-ounce) skinless boneless chicken thighs

2 cups tightly packed rinsed and chopped escarole

1 (15-ounce) can cannellini (white kidney) beans, rinsed and drained

2 tablespoons chopped fresh basil leaves or 2 teaspoons dried basil

¼ teaspoon red pepper flakes

2 tablespoons grated Parmesan

1 Spray Dutch oven or large saucepan with nonstick spray and set over medium heat. Add pancetta and cook until crisp, 4–5 minutes; transfer to plate with slotted spoon.

2 Pour off all but about ½ teaspoon pancetta fat from Dutch oven. Add onion; cook, stirring frequently, until golden, 7–10 minutes. Stir in garlic and cook 1 minute. Add broth, tomatoes and juice, and chicken; bring to boil. Reduce heat and simmer, covered, until chicken is cooked through and tender, about 30 minutes. Remove chicken and set aside until cool enough to handle. Shred and return to soup.

3 Stir escarole, beans, basil, and pepper flakes into soup; return to boil. Reduce heat and simmer until escarole is wilted and softened, about 5 minutes. Sprinkle with crisped pancetta and Parmesan just before serving.

Per serving (1½ cups soup, 1 teaspoon pancetta, and 1 teaspoon Parmesan): 250 Cal, 7 g Total Fat, 2 g Sat Fat, 929 mg Sod, 18 g Total Carb, 4 g Sugar, 4 g Fib, 27 g Prot.

Chicken-and-
Escarole Soup

Wedding
Soup

Wedding Soup
MINESTRA MARITATA

serves 4

There are some evenings when I feel like I've absorbed the day, the frenzy of it staying with me. That's when I turn to this recipe for calming. I love the repetition of rolling ground turkey into little meatballs; when the kids were younger I'd get them in on the act, just as I helped my mom when I was a kid.

½ **pound ground skinless turkey breast**

1 **large egg white, lightly beaten**

2 **tablespoons plain dried bread crumbs**

1½ **tablespoons grated Parmesan**

1½ **teaspoons dried oregano**

½ **teaspoon granulated garlic**

8 **cups low-sodium chicken broth**

2 **cups thinly sliced escarole**

½ **cup thinly sliced sweet onion**

⅓ **cup shredded carrot**

1 Combine turkey, egg white, bread crumbs, Parmesan, oregano, and garlic powder in medium bowl and mix gently. Shape into balls about ¾ inch in diameter.

2 Bring broth to boil in large saucepan. Stir in escarole, onion, carrot, and meatballs. Return soup to boil, then adjust heat so soup just simmers. Cook, uncovered, until meatballs are cooked through and float, and escarole is tender, about 15 minutes.

Per serving (about 2 ¼ cups soup and about 8 meatballs): 193 Cal, 6 g Total Fat, 2 g Sat Fat, 269 mg Sod, 13 g Total Carb, 2 g Sugar, 2 g Fib, 24 g Prot.

Pasta, Bean, and Sausage Soup
PASTA E FAGIOLI CON SALSICCIA

serves 6

This "pasta fazool" is more a stew than a soup, so I serve it as a main course with a mess of seasonal greens on the side that I've dressed simply with a squeeze of lemon juice. My husband prefers his *minestre* (soups) thinner and brothier, so if the soup is too thick when it's finished cooking, I'll add a bit more water or stock to thin it out.

1 teaspoon olive oil

3 (3½-ounce) links fresh hot Italian turkey sausage, casings removed

2 large carrots, diced

2 celery stalks, diced

1 small onion, chopped

4 garlic cloves, finely chopped

4 cups reduced-sodium chicken broth

1 (14½-ounce) can whole tomatoes, chopped, juice reserved

½ teaspoon fennel seeds

¼ teaspoon salt

1 (15½-ounce) can cannellini (white kidney) beans, rinsed and drained

1 cup ditalini or other small pasta shape

½ cup coarsely chopped fresh parsley leaves

2 tablespoons grated Parmesan

1 Heat oil in large saucepan over medium-high heat. Add sausage and cook, breaking sausage into chunks with side of spoon, until lightly browned, about 3 minutes.

2 Add carrots, celery, and onion; cover and cook over medium-high heat, stirring occasionally, until vegetables are tender, about 7 minutes. Stir in garlic and cook 1 minute.

3 Stir in broth, tomatoes and juice, fennel seeds, and salt. Mash half of beans with fork; stir in mashed and whole beans and bring to boil. Reduce heat and simmer, uncovered, for flavors to blend, about 5 minutes.

4 Stir in pasta and cook, stirring occasionally, until pasta is tender, about 8 minutes.

5 Remove from heat and stir in parsley. Ladle soup into 6 bowls and sprinkle evenly with Parmesan.

Per serving (2 cups soup and 1 teaspoon Parmesan): 244 Cal, 6 g Total Fat, 1 g Sat Fat, 1,174 mg Sod, 29 g Total Carb, 4 g Sugar, 5 g Fib, 19 g Prot.

Pasta, Bean, and
Sausage Soup

Bean Cuisine

Beans and lentils are grown throughout Italy and are the stars in many popular dishes. In fact, a reliance on beans is one of the reasons traditional Italian cooking is so healthful. They're packed with fiber and lean protein, and on the WW Freestyle program beans, lentils, and peas are all 0 SmartPoints foods. Enjoy them without tracking!

Borlotti, cannellini, and fava beans, along with chickpeas and lentils, are Italian favorites that turn up in soups, stews, pastas, and salads. They're often the main protein source in a meal—simply seasoned and drizzled with a little extra-virgin olive oil—or a perfect complement to meats (especially sausage and pork), and poultry.

Keep a few types of canned beans on hand for pulling together quick meals. We do recommend you cook with dried beans—they need to be soaked before cooking and take more time on the stovetop, but their wonderful flavor and meaty, chewier texture are well worth it. Plus they're less expensive than canned beans, and you can make a big batch and freeze them for later use. Fresh beans are also wonderful. Usually available in late summer, they take less time to cook then dried and taste like pure sunlight.

A few pointers:

- One pound of dried beans will yield about 6 cups cooked. One pound of dried lentils will yield about 5 cups cooked.

- A 15-ounce can of beans is equivalent to 1⅔ cup cooked beans; keep this in mind if you're substituting home-cooked beans for canned in a recipe

- Lentils don't need soaking.

- Nutritional qualities differ by variety: ½ cup cooked, drained beans or lentils contain 6–9 grams protein, 6–10 grams fiber, and 105–125 calories. And all are 0 SmartPoints.

Cooking Dried Beans

makes about 6 cups

1 Spread 1 pound of dried beans out on a tray; sort through them, picking out any small stones or debris. Pour beans into strainer and rinse well. Put them in a large bowl, cover with plenty of cold water, and soak for 4–8 hours or overnight on the counter.

2 Rinse beans in fresh cold water. Transfer them to large pot and cover by 4 inches with cold water.

3 Add 1 teaspoon salt, a few garlic cloves, and 1–2 bay leaves. Place beans on stovetop and bring to boil. Lower heat and simmer, partially covered, until beans are just tender, 30 minutes–1 hour 30 minutes depending on the variety (see chart below).

4 Drain and cool beans. Discard bay leaves; discard garlic cloves or leave them in. Refrigerate beans in their liquid up to 3 days or freeze up to 4 months.

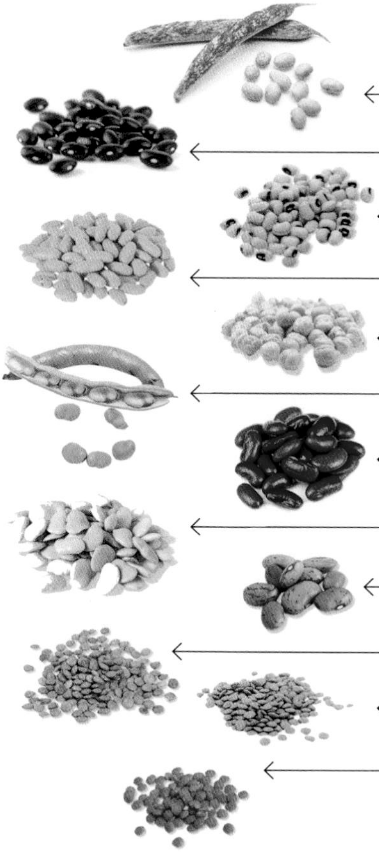

Type of bean or lentil	Simmer partially covered for about
Borlotti (cranberry) beans	1½ hours
Black beans	1½ hours
Black-eyed peas	45 minutes
Cannellini beans	1 hour
Chickpeas	1½ hours
Fava beans	40 minutes (dried)
Kidney beans	1½ hours
Lima beans	1 hour
Pinto beans	1½ hours
Brown lentils	30 minutes
Green lentils	25 minutes
Red lentils	20 minutes

Seafood
Brodetto

Seafood Brodetto
BRODETTO DI PESCE

serves 6

Living in a country with more than 4,500 miles of coastline means Italians eat a lot of fish. Seafood soups called *brodetto, cioppino,* or *cacciucco* were created by fishermen who made them on board their boats, in a big pot, with the catch that hadn't been sold at market that day. The belief in wasting nothing is at the heart of the *cucina povera* (cuisine of the poor) tradition. Our version of *brodetto* is sweet, spicy, and garlicky. Use bread to mop up the savory bits.

6 small (½-ounce) slices Italian bread or ciabatta

5 garlic cloves, 1 clove cut in half, 4 cloves minced

2 teaspoons olive oil

1 onion, chopped

1 cup dry white wine

1 (28-ounce) can crushed tomatoes

2 cups water

½ teaspoon dried oregano

Pinch red pepper flakes

2 dozen mussels, scrubbed and debearded

2 dozen littleneck clams, scrubbed

½ pound cleaned squid, cut into rings and tentacles

½ pound large shrimp, peeled and deveined

¼ teaspoon salt, or to taste

½ cup chopped fresh basil leaves

1 Preheat oven to 375°F. Arrange bread on baking sheet and bake until toasted, about 10 minutes. Rub garlic clove halves over bread and set aside.

2 Heat oil in Dutch oven over medium-high heat. Add onion and cook, stirring occasionally, until softened, about 5 minutes. Stir in minced garlic and cook, stirring, until fragrant, about 30 seconds.

3 Stir in wine and cook 1 minute. Stir in tomatoes, water, oregano, and pepper flakes; bring to boil, reduce heat, and simmer 10 minutes.

4 Stir in mussels and clams and cook, covered, stirring occasionally, until mussels and clams open, about 6 minutes. Discard any that do not open. Spoon mussels and clams into bowl. Stir squid and shrimp into pot and cook, stirring occasionally, until cooked through, about 2 minutes. Remove from heat and stir in salt and basil.

5 Place 1 slice toast in bottom of each of 6 bowls. Top evenly with clams and mussels. Spoon 1 cup soup with shrimp and squid over top of each.

Per serving (1 slice toast, 4 clams, 4 mussels, and generous 1 cup soup): 266 Cal, 5 g Total Fat, 1 g Sat Fat, 1,000 mg Sod, 21 g Total Carb, 5 g Sugar, 2 g Fib, 27 g Prot.

The broth can be made the day before and the toast can be made several hours in advance and stored in an airtight container. Just cook the seafood in the broth shortly before serving.

Clam-and-Fregola Soup

MINESTRA DI VONGOLE E FREGOLA

serves 4

What I love most about this soup is what I love most about Italian food: Its flavors are clear and direct. Fregola is a type of pasta from Sardinia. It's made from semolina dough that has been rolled into balls and toasted in the oven, which gives it a subtle, nutty flavor that's terrific in soups, stews, and salads. If you can't find fregola, Israeli couscous is a good substitute.

I like to cook clams within 24 hours of buying them. Look for shells that are tightly closed. If you're unsure, gently tap them—if the shells don't close, throw the clam out. After cooking, toss any clams with shells that don't open.

⅔ cup (about 4 ounces) fregola

3 teaspoons extra-virgin olive oil

1 large shallot, chopped

2 large garlic cloves, minced

2 large plum tomatoes, chopped

1 cup water

1 cup chicken broth

½ cup dry white wine

Pinch red pepper flakes

2 dozen littleneck clams, scrubbed

¼ cup chopped fresh parsley leaves

1 Bring medium saucepan two-thirds full of salted water to boil. Stir in fregola and cook until al dente, about 6 minutes; drain.

2 Meanwhile, heat 2 teaspoons oil in Dutch oven or large saucepan over medium-high heat. Add shallot and garlic and cook, stirring frequently, until softened, about 2 minutes. Stir in tomatoes and cook, stirring frequently, until softened, about 2 minutes.

3 Add water, broth, wine, and pepper flakes and bring to boil. Add clams; cover and cook until clams open, 6–8 minutes. Discard any clams that don't open.

4 Stir in fregola and cook until heated through. Stir in remaining 1 teaspoon oil and parsley and ladle soup into bowls.

Wine pairing:

Medium-dry white, like Gavi or Soave.

Per serving (6 clams and 1 cup soup): 237 Cal, 4 g Total Fat, 1 g Sat Fat, 521 mg Sod, 28 g Total Carb, 3 g Sugar, 2 g Fib, 14 g Prot.

Clam-and-Fregola Soup

Minestrone with Kale
MINESTRONE CON CAVOLO RICCIO

serves 8 • gluten free • vegetarian

This may be the dish that best reflects what's regional and what's in season. The basic structure of the soup comes from an abundance of fresh vegetables bolstered with a hearty bean or grain—in this case, knobby chickpeas. Think of this recipe as a blueprint for making soup year-round: You can swap in seasonal vegetables like diced zucchini, green beans, or peppers in the summer months; butternut squash, parsnip, or celery root in the fall or winter; and snap peas, asparagus, and leeks in the spring.

2 teaspoons olive oil

1 onion, diced

1 garlic clove, finely chopped

2 zucchini, quartered lengthwise and cut into ¼-inch-thick slices

1 celery stalk, diced

10 baby-cut carrots, halved

3 cups lightly packed coarsely chopped kale leaves

1 (28-ounce) can whole tomatoes, juice reserved, tomatoes chopped

4 cups reduced-sodium vegetable broth

1 (15-ounce) can chickpeas, rinsed and drained

⅓ cup orzo or other very small pasta shape

¼ teaspoon salt, or to taste

¼ teaspoon black pepper

¾ cup grated Parmesan

1 Heat oil in large saucepan over medium heat. Add onion; cook, stirring, until onion is softened, about 3 minutes. Stir in garlic. Add zucchini, celery, carrots, and kale and cook, stirring, until kale wilts, about 5 minutes.

2 Add tomatoes and juice, broth, chickpeas, and orzo. Simmer until carrots and orzo are tender, about 15 minutes. Stir in salt and pepper. Ladle soup evenly into 8 bowls and sprinkle with Parmesan.

Per serving (1 cup soup with 1½ tablespoons Parmesan): 180 Cal, 4 g Total Fat, 2 g Sat Fat, 698 mg Sod, 27 g Total Carb, 7 g Sugar, 5 g Fib, 9 g Prot.

Tomato-Basil Lentil Soup

ZUPPA DI POMODORO E LENTICCHIE AL BASILICO

serves 4 • gluten free • vegetarian

Umbria is famous for its lentils. My favorite kind comes from the town of Castelluccio. They're small and delicate and cook quickly, which means you can get a meal on the table in under 30 minutes. If you can't find Castelluccio lentils, other varieties will do—just know you'll need to cook them a bit longer. I like to make this soup at the end of summer, when basil is at its freshest and I've just canned a few jars of tomatoes.

4 teaspoons olive oil

1 small onion, finely chopped

1 garlic clove, minced

1 cup lentils, picked over and rinsed

4 cups vegetable broth

3 fresh basil sprigs, stems and leaves reserved separately

½ teaspoon salt

¼ teaspoon black pepper

1 (28-ounce) can crushed tomatoes

1 Heat 2 teaspoons oil in large saucepan over medium heat. Add onion and garlic; cook, stirring, until softened, about 3 minutes.

2 Add lentils, broth, basil stems, salt, and pepper to saucepan; bring to boil. Reduce heat and simmer, stirring occasionally, until lentils are just tender, about 20 minutes. Add tomatoes and simmer until lentils are very soft, about 10 minutes longer.

3 Remove and discard basil stems. Tear basil leaves into pieces and sprinkle over soup. Serve drizzled with remaining 2 teaspoons oil.

Per serving (2 cups): 264 Cal, 5 g Total Fat, 1 g Sat Fat, 1,242 mg Sod, 42 g Total Carb, 8 g Sugar, 7 g Fib, 14 g Prot.

Escarole, Bean,
and Pasta Soup

Escarole, Bean, and Pasta Soup
MINESTRA DI SCAROLA, FAGIOLI E PASTA

serves 4 • vegetarian • under 20 minutes

Italians are smitten with beans. This soup is a riff on the classic bean-and-escarole soup popular all over Campania. I find the smack of juicy, bitter escarole in relation to the gentleness of cannellini beans appealing. It's the contrast that counts here. Finishing the soup with lemon juice adds vigor and brightness.

½ cup ditalini or other small pasta shape

2 teaspoons olive oil

2 garlic cloves, minced

4 cups tightly packed rinsed and chopped escarole

6 cups reduced-sodium vegetable broth

½ teaspoon dried oregano

¼ teaspoon salt

¼ teaspoon red pepper flakes

1 (15½-ounce) can cannellini (white kidney) beans, rinsed and drained

2 teaspoons lemon juice

4 tablespoons grated pecorino Romano cheese

1 Cook ditalini according to package directions.

2 Meanwhile, heat oil in large saucepan over medium-high heat. Add garlic and cook, stirring constantly, until fragrant, about 30 seconds. Add escarole and cook, stirring often, until wilted, about 1 minute. Add broth, oregano, salt, and pepper flakes. Cover and bring to boil. Cook until escarole is tender, about 3 minutes.

3 Add beans to saucepan; cook until heated through, about 2 minutes. Stir in ditalini. Remove soup from heat; stir in lemon juice. Ladle soup evenly into 4 bowls and sprinkle with pecorino.

Per serving (about 2 cups soup and 1 tablespoon cheese): 212 Cal, 4 g Total Fat, 1 g Sat Fat, 941 mg Sod, 33 g Total Carb, 4 g Sugar, 5 g Fib, 10 g Prot.

Instead of escarole, you can use chopped kale or collard greens.

Tortellini and Spinach Soup
MINESTRA DI TORTELLINI E SPINACI

serves 4 • under 20 minutes

This soup was created to give pleasure, and I'm happy to report it succeeds.
What's more, it comes together in less than 20 minutes. My family enjoys it hot, ladled
into bowls and eaten immediately.

½ onion, diced

2 garlic cloves, finely chopped

4 cups chicken or vegetable broth

4 ounces frozen cheese tortellini

4 ounces frozen chopped spinach, thawed and squeezed dry

1 (14½-ounce) can diced tomatoes, with juice

¼ teaspoon salt

¼ teaspoon black pepper

2 tablespoons grated Parmesan

1 Coat large saucepan with nonstick spray and set over medium-high heat; add onion and garlic and cook, stirring frequently, until fragrant, about 1 minute.

2 Add broth and tortellini; bring to boil. Reduce heat and simmer, uncovered, 5 minutes.

3 Add spinach, tomatoes, salt, and pepper; simmer, uncovered, 5 minutes. Ladle soup into bowls and sprinkle evenly with Parmesan.

Per serving (1½ cups soup and 1½ teaspoons Parmesan): 169 Cal, 4 g Total Fat, 2 g Sat Fat, 1,208 mg Sod, 21 g Total Carb, 4 g Sugar, 3 g Fib, 12 g Prot.

Broccoli-Cauliflower Soup
VELLUTATA DI BROCCOLI E CAVOLFIORE

serves 6 • vegetarian

It's fair to say I'm pretty much obsessed with this remarkable soup. Steering clear of anything heavy or made with cream, it uses vegetable broth instead of chicken broth for gentle flavor and swaps in milk for cream. The vegetables work well together. I find the cauliflower most interesting, though: Pureeing it brings out its almost mustard-like flavor, and when it's combined with the beans and broccoli, the resulting texture is silky, refined, and light.

2 teaspoons olive oil

1 leek, thinly sliced and rinsed

1 garlic clove, minced

2 tablespoons all-purpose flour

2 cups low-fat (1%) milk

1½ cups vegetable broth

1 large bunch broccoli, stems peeled and chopped and crowns chopped

¼ head cauliflower, cored and chopped (about 5 ounces florets)

½ cup canned white beans, rinsed and drained

1 teaspoon Dijon mustard

¾ teaspoon salt

¼ teaspoon black pepper

½ cup (about 2 ounces) shredded fontina cheese

Lemon wedges for serving

1 Heat oil in large saucepan over medium heat. Add leek and garlic; cook, stirring, until softened, about 5 minutes. Add flour and cook, stirring, 1 minute. Slowly stir in milk and broth and bring to boil, stirring frequently.

2 Add broccoli, cauliflower, beans, mustard, salt, and pepper to milk mixture. Reduce heat and simmer, partially covered, stirring occasionally, until vegetables are very tender, about 10 minutes.

3 Remove soup from heat and let cool 5 minutes. Working in batches, puree soup in blender. (Don't fill the container more than half full. Hold the lid down gently with a folded kitchen towel, and start the blender on low speed.) Stir ¼ cup fontina into soup; reheat if needed. Divide soup among 6 bowls and serve sprinkled with remaining ¼ cup cheese and with lemon wedges.

Wine pairing:

Crisp white, like Vernaccia or Vermentino.

Per serving (1 cup soup and 2 teaspoons cheese): 180 Cal, 6 g Total Fat, 3 g Sat Fat, 691 mg Sod, 22 g Total Carb, 8 g Sugar, 5 g Fib, 11g Prot.

Use caution when blending hot liquids. Their heat can cause the air in the blender to expand and possibly blow the lid off.

The streets of Italy are filled with food—porchetta, chickpea fritters, arancini (rice balls), chestnuts, cannoli, and zeppole. Rain or shine, street vendors are out, making tasty bites. But they're selling more than food: They're selling goodwill and a belief that food must nurture the soul as well as the body.

A cow raised on fresh grass is a happy cow, and a happy cow produces delicious milk.

Why does Italy have an incredible food culture?

Mainly because of its weather and resources—lush mountains, rich volcanic soil, fertile countrysides, winds that create a range of microclimates, and miles of coastline. Italy's port cities also attracted traders and conquerors, bringing with them not just languages and culture, but new culinary traditions and ingredients.

When traveling through Italy there's usually a hill, a mountain, or a body of water that separates villages and towns, and so customs, dialects, and dishes vary from place to place. Food is built into a region's very culture and is a source of local pride and identity. There's no single Italian cuisine—there's only Tuscan, Sicilian, Florentine, and myriad other regional food traditions.

Nothing is wasted in Italy. When fish swimming in shoals bring an abundance of food, what's not sold at the market is salt-cured on the beach.

Eat local

1. People used to love traveling the world and finding a cup of coffee that tasted the same as the one they enjoyed at home. These days, people want something locally produced and special, with a story behind it, like how they bought melons from the back of a truck, sold by a local man whose pants were held up by a piece of string.

2. A fish market.

There's something elemental about cooking with a wood-burning oven.

Food says a lot about a society...

When in Italy, you notice that farmers, merchants, and cooks are enthusiastic. They work with a sense of purpose: to feed and delight you. And they show up with open hearts and generous spirits. Rarely do they act rude or bored. Instead, they move with the dignity of people who are at ease with life.

Unlike haute cuisine, the food of Italy is rooted in home cooking, taught by mothers, grandmothers, and aunts. Italian food was not created for restaurants or luxury hotels, by professional chefs hoping to impress the aristocracy centuries ago. Some eating establishments go back generations with moms and daughters, and fathers and sons working side by side.

Chapter 3

Salads (insalate)

Fig, Prosciutto, and Chicken Salad

INSALATA DI FICHI, PROSCIUTTO E POLLO

serves 4 • gluten free • under 20 minutes

Figs are among the oldest cultivated fruits in the world. Numerous varieties grow across Italy, but they are especially popular in the south, where they flourish along hills and in valleys. We had a fig tree when I was growing up and I couldn't wait for the fruit to ripen. You'll typically see fresh figs in markets from late summer to early fall. If you can't find them, you can substitute a thinly sliced pear or a cup of halved seedless grapes in this recipe.

¾ pound skinless boneless thin-cut chicken cutlets

½ teaspoon salt

2 tablespoons balsamic vinegar

1 tablespoon extra-virgin olive oil

1 teaspoon honey

1 teaspoon Dijon mustard

¼ teaspoon black pepper

6 cups lightly packed mixed salad greens

6 fresh figs, cut lengthwise into quarters

2 ounces thinly sliced prosciutto, cut into strips

1 tablespoon toasted pine nuts

1 Spray ridged grill pan with nonstick spray and set over medium-high heat. Spray chicken lightly with nonstick spray and sprinkle with ¼ teaspoon salt. Add chicken to pan and grill until browned and cooked through, about 4 minutes per side. Transfer chicken to cutting board; let rest 5 minutes. Cut chicken on diagonal into ¼-inch-thick slices.

2 Meanwhile, to make dressing, whisk together vinegar, oil, honey, mustard, pepper, and remaining ¼ teaspoon salt in medium bowl until blended.

3 Place greens on large serving platter. Arrange figs around greens. Top greens with chicken and prosciutto, then sprinkle with pine nuts. Drizzle salad with dressing.

Wine pairing:

Prosecco or medium-dry rosé (*rosato* in Italian).

Per serving (1½ cups): 281 Cal, 11 g Total Fat, 2 g Sat Fat, 847 mg Sod, 20 g Total Carb, 17 g Sugar, 3 g Fib, 27 g Prot.

Prosciutto, Pear, and Goat Cheese

PROSCIUTTO, PERE E CAPRINO

serves 4 • gluten free • under 20 minutes • no cook

When I'm hungry and impatient and want some big flavor, I turn to this recipe.
The prosciutto is salty and earthy, the goat cheese is tangy and creamy, and the pear
delivers juiciness and floral hints. The flavors and textures are bold, but they
somehow meet in the middle and keep things balanced.

6 cups lightly packed baby arugula

2 pears, cored and thinly sliced

½ small fennel bulb, very thinly sliced

2 tablespoons balsamic glaze

1½ teaspoons extra-virgin olive oil

Pinch salt

4 thin (½-ounce) slices prosciutto, cut into strips

1 (3-ounce) log soft goat cheese, cut into 4 disks

Freshly ground black pepper

Toss together arugula, pears, fennel, oil, 1 tablespoon glaze, and salt in large bowl. Divide salad evenly among 4 plates; top evenly with prosciutto and crumble 1 disk goat cheese over each salad. Drizzle salads with remaining 1 tablespoon glaze and sprinkle liberally with black pepper.

Per serving (1 salad): 209 Cal, 10 g Total Fat, 5 g Sat Fat, 686 mg Sod, 21 g Total Carb, 11 g Sugar, 5 g Fib, 11 g Prot.

Drizzle balsamic glaze on grilled fish or poultry, salads, fruit, yogurt, and even ice cream. You can find it in most supermarkets.

Lemony Orzo and Seafood Salad

INSALATA DI ORZO E FRUTTI DI MARE AL LIMONE

serves 4

What's not to love? Beautiful, delicious, ridiculously quick, and evocative. You can almost smell the lemony saltwater in the air.

½ cup whole wheat orzo

3 teaspoons extra-virgin olive oil

1 (1-pound) bag frozen seafood medley (any combination shrimp, calamari, scallops, mussels, clams, or crab meat)

2 cups cherry tomatoes, halved

½ cup diced red onion

1 tablespoon drained capers

Grated zest and juice of ½ lemon

¼ teaspoon black pepper

4 cups lightly packed baby lettuces

1 Cook orzo according to package directions. Drain and rinse under cold running water until cool. Drain again and toss with 1 teaspoon oil.

2 Meanwhile, bring large pot of water to boil. Add seafood and cook just until opaque in center, about 2 minutes. Drain and rinse under cold running water until cool. Drain again and transfer to large bowl. Add tomatoes, onion, capers, lemon zest and juice, pepper, orzo, and remaining 2 teaspoons oil; toss to coat. Serve over lettuces.

Wine pairing:

Soave or Pinot Grigio.

Per serving (1¾ cups seafood salad and 1 cup lettuce): 197 Cal, 5 g Total Fat, 0 g Sat Fat, 335 mg Sod, 20 g Total Carb, 4 g Sugar, 4 g Fib, 18 g Prot.

Lemony Orzo and Seafood Salad

Seafood Salad with Potatoes

INSALATA DI MARE CON PATATE

serves 6 • gluten free

Seafood salads are made all over Italy, and ingredients vary region to region. Ours borrows from more than one and is quite simple to put together: Combine tender shrimp, scallops, and squid—all 0 SmartPoints foods—with diced vegetables and sliced baby potatoes, then spoon onto lettuce leaves. *Molto delicioso!*

½ pound baby potatoes, scrubbed

¾ pound large shrimp, peeled and deveined

¾ pound bay scallops

¾ pound cleaned squid, cut into rings and tentacles

2 celery stalks, diced

1 carrot, diced

1 red onion, diced

½ fennel bulb, cored and diced

3 tablespoons chopped fresh parsley leaves

1 teaspoon grated lemon zest

3 tablespoons lemon juice

2 tablespoons extra-virgin olive oil

¾ teaspoon salt

¼ teaspoon black pepper

6 romaine lettuce leaves

1 Bring large pot filled two-thirds with salted water to boil. Add potatoes and simmer until just tender, 12–15 minutes. With slotted spoon, transfer potatoes to cutting board and let stand until cool enough to handle. Cut potatoes into thin slices and set aside.

2 Meanwhile, return water in pot to gentle simmer. Add shrimp and cook until just opaque in center, 2–3 minutes. With slotted spoon, transfer shrimp to bowl of ice water. Add scallops to pot and simmer until just opaque in center, 2–3 minutes. With slotted spoon, transfer scallops to bowl with shrimp. Add squid to pot and simmer until just tender, about 2 minutes. Drain squid and transfer to bowl with shrimp and scallops.

3 Combine celery, carrot, onion, fennel, parsley, lemon zest and juice, oil, salt, and pepper in large bowl. Add potatoes and seafood; toss to coat.

4 Place a lettuce leaf on each of 6 plates and spoon seafood salad evenly over each.

Wine pairing:

Minerally white, like Verdicchio or Sicilian Vernaccia.

Per serving (1½ cups salad): 221 Cal, 6 g Total Fat, 1 g Sat Fat, 892 mg Sod, 16 g Total Carb, 2 g Sugar, 3 g Fib, 25 g Prot.

Lentil, Orange, and Radicchio Salad
INSALATA DI LENTICCHIE, ARANCE E RADICCHIO

serves 4 • gluten free • vegetarian

Oranges are a popular ingredient in both sweet and savory Italian dishes. In Sicily they are a favorite in salads like this one and are often the red-fleshed blood oranges. If you find blood oranges do try them; otherwise navel oranges will work too. This salad plays the fresh flavors of citrus against the earthy graininess of the lentils. It's bright and sunny, but also substantial.

1 cup green (Puy) lentils, picked over and rinsed

1 teaspoon grated orange zest

¼ cup orange juice

1 tablespoon extra-virgin olive oil

1 teaspoon honey

1 teaspoon chopped fresh rosemary

¼ teaspoon salt

¼ teaspoon black pepper

1 (3-ounce) package baby spinach

2 seedless oranges, peeled, halved, and diced

1 cup thinly sliced radicchio

1 small red onion, halved and thinly sliced

10 pitted black olives, sliced

1 Combine lentils and enough water to cover by 2 inches in medium saucepan. Bring to boil over high heat. Reduce heat and simmer, covered, until lentils are tender but still hold their shape, about 20 minutes. Drain. Transfer to large serving bowl and let cool to room temperature.

2 To make dressing, whisk together orange zest and juice, oil, honey, rosemary, salt, and pepper in small bowl. Pour over lentils and toss to coat. Add spinach, oranges, radicchio, onion, and olives; toss to combine.

Per serving (1¾ cups): 267 Cal, 5 g Total Fat, 1 g Sat Fat, 241 mg Sod, 45 g Total Carb, 11 g Sugar, 8 g Fib, 14 g Prot.

Calamari
over Greens

Calamari over Greens
CALAMARI CON INSALATA

serves 6 • gluten free

Chef Ugo Adinolfi made this dish for us while we were visiting Italy. This salad is what I call a "nowhere-to-hide" recipe because it uses only a few ingredients. That's why quality is important. Fresh squid should smell clean, like the ocean, and look almost translucent. Smaller squid are more tender than large ones, so buy little ones if you can.

2 tablespoons extra-virgin olive oil

1 teaspoon grated lemon zest

2 tablespoons lemon juice

1 garlic clove, minced

½ teaspoon salt

⅛ teaspoon black pepper

1 pound cleaned squid, tubes cut into ½-inch-wide rings

1 cup cherry tomatoes, quartered

6 cups assorted baby lettuce or sliced romaine lettuce

1 Whisk together oil, lemon zest and juice, garlic, salt, and pepper in medium bowl.

2 Bring large saucepan filled two-thirds full with water to boil. Add squid; cover and cook just until opaque, about 1 minute. Drain in colander; rinse under cold running water until cool. Drain again.

3 Add squid to dressing; toss to coat. Cover and refrigerate until flavors are blended, at least 1 hour or up to 4 hours.

4 Toss squid with tomatoes. Place lettuce on platter or in large serving bowl and top with squid mixture.

Per serving (1 generous cup): 125 Cal, 6 g Total Fat, 1 g Sat Fat, 232 mg Sod, 6 g Total Carb, 1 g Sugar, 1 g Fib, 13 g Prot.

Make It Your Own: Bowl Food, Italian-Style

If it were up to me, I'd eat everything out of a bowl. It feels instantly soothing and comes together in a snap. Use a grain or legume as a base, then pile on seasonal vegetables. When putting together your bowl, look for a balance of sweet, sour, salty, bitter, and umami (intensely savory) flavors, with a bit of texture and spice. These flavor elements are the building blocks of any dish you create and the more balanced a dish, the tastier it is. For example, add olives, capers, or anchovies if your bowl needs a touch of saltiness to round out the flavors.

START WITH A HEARTY BASE	CHOOSE ONE OR TWO VEGETABLES	ADD SOME LEAVES	LAYER IN CRUNCH	CHOOSE AN ACCENT FLAVOR	FINISH WITH A DRESSING
Cannellini beans	**Artichoke hearts**	**Arugula**	**Parmesan crisps**	**Anchovies**	**Balsamic vinaigrette**
Chickpeas	Asparagus	Basil	Pine nuts	Bocconcini (mozzarella balls)	
Farro	**Bell peppers (raw or roasted)**	**Endive**	**Toasted almonds**	**Capers**	**Lemon and olive oil**
Fregola (a type of large couscous from Sardinia)	**Grilled or roasted portobello mushrooms**	**Kale**	**Walnuts**	**Goat cheese**	**Pesto**
Lentils	**Fennel (raw or roasted)**	**Radicchio**		**Gorgonzola**	**Red-wine vinegar and olive oil**
Millet	**Peas**	**Romaine lettuce**		**Olives**	
Orzo	**Roasted beets**	**Spinach**		**Parmesan shavings**	
Spelt	**Roasted broccoli**			**Ricotta salata**	
	Roasted cauliflower			**Sun-dried cherries**	
	Roasted pumpkin or butternut squash			**Sun-dried tomatoes**	
	Tomatoes			**Truffle zest**	
	Zucchini				

White Beans and Bitter Greens
FAGIOLI BIANCHI E ERBE AMARE

serves 4 • gluten free • vegetarian • under 20 minutes • no cook

Radicchio is part of the chicory family. It has vibrant, wine-colored leaves and tastes slightly bitter. My favorite variety is Treviso; its leaves are longer and slimmer, and its flavor more intense. Only lettuce grown in Treviso, a town in northern Italy, can be called Treviso. Tear, rather than chop, your lettuce to avoid bruising the leaves.

2 tablespoons water

1½ tablespoons extra-virgin olive oil

1 tablespoon balsamic vinegar

½ teaspoon salt

¼ teaspoon black pepper

1 (15½-ounce) can cannellini (white kidney) beans, rinsed and drained

1 cup grape tomatoes, halved

1 (7-ounce) jar roasted red peppers (not oil-packed), drained and thinly sliced

1 (4-ounce) container baby arugula

1 cup thinly sliced radicchio

1 ounce Parmesan shavings

1 Whisk together water, oil, vinegar, salt, and black pepper in large bowl. Add beans, tomatoes, and roasted peppers and toss until combined.

2 Divide arugula and radicchio evenly among 4 plates; top with bean mixture and Parmesan.

Per serving (2 cups): 192 Cal, 7 g Total Fat, 2 g Sat Fat, 881 mg Sod, 24 g Total Carb, 4 g Sugar, 4 g Fib, 10 g Prot.

Citrus Salad with Fennel
INSALATA DI AGRUMI CON FINOCCHIO

serves 4 • gluten free • vegetarian • under 20 minutes • no cook

In winter, I'm eager to keep the chill dreariness at bay, so I want to eat something bright, colorful, and cheery. That's when I turn to the amazing variety of fragrant citrus fruits that show up at the market. I vary my choices based on what's available: tangerines, blood oranges, clementines, or grapefruit. Crisp fennel adds textural interest to this salad.

2 oranges

1 small grapefruit

5 cups lightly packed mixed baby greens

1 small fennel bulb, halved and thinly sliced

⅓ cup thinly sliced red onion

¼ cup hazelnuts, toasted

¼ cup thinly sliced fresh basil leaves or chopped fennel fronds

1 garlic clove, minced

1 tablespoon white wine vinegar or champagne vinegar

1½ teaspoons extra-virgin olive oil

¼ teaspoon salt

⅛ teaspoon black pepper

1 Cut thin slice off top and bottom of 1 orange. Stand fruit on cutting board and cut down along curve of fruit, removing all peel and white pith. Hold skinless whole fruit over medium bowl and cut along membranes to release each segment, letting segments and juice drop into bowl. Pick out and discard any seeds. Repeat with remaining orange and with grapefruit. Measure out and reserve ⅓ cup juice.

2 Combine citrus fruit, baby greens, fennel, onion, and hazelnuts in large salad bowl.

3 To make dressing, whisk together basil, garlic, vinegar, oil, salt, pepper, and reserved citrus juice in small bowl; pour over salad and toss to coat.

Per serving (about 2 cups): 116 Cal, 5 g Total Fat, 0 g Sat Fat, 167 mg Sod, 16 g Total Carb, 7 g Sugar, 6 g Fib, 5 g Prot.

Shaved Kale Salad with Pecorino

INSALATA DI CAVOLO NERO CON PECORINO

serves 4 • gluten free • vegetarian • under 20 minutes • no cook

This salad is intensely flavorful, relying on crispy kale, spicy radishes, and a rich, creamy dressing. Kale can be tough and fibrous, so we use the Tuscan variety (also known as lacinato, cavolo nero, or dinosaur) because it's the most tender. The acid from the lemon juice helps break down the leaves even more, so be sure to fully coat each with the dressing. Let it sit for 10 minutes, then add pecorino Romano and pine nuts for the same robust creaminess you'd find in a Caesar salad.

2 tablespoons lemon juice

2 teaspoons extra-virgin olive oil

¼ teaspoon salt

⅛ teaspoon black pepper

2 (¾-pound) bunches Tuscan (lacinato) kale, ribs removed and leaves very thinly sliced

3 radishes, thinly sliced

6 tablespoons shredded pecorino Romano cheese

2 tablespoons toasted pine nuts

1 To make dressing, whisk together lemon juice, oil, salt, and pepper in large bowl. Add kale and toss until coated evenly. Let stand at room temperature, tossing occasionally, 10 minutes.

2 Add radishes and toss. Divide kale mixture evenly among 4 plates. Sprinkle each salad with 1½ tablespoons pecorino and ½ tablespoon pine nuts.

 Per serving (2 cups): 161 Cal, 8 g Total Fat, 2 g Sat Fat, 360 mg Sod, 16 g Total Carb, 4 g Sugar, 7 g Fib, 9 g Prot.

Shaved Kale Salad
with Pecorino

Peach, Basil, and Tomato Salad

INSALATA DI PESCHE, BASILICO E POMODORI

serves 4 • gluten free • vegetarian • under 20 minutes • no cook

The essence of summer on a plate. The combo of peach and tomato is exquisite
(tomatoes are fruit, after all). Ricotta salata cheese adds texture and brininess.
Eat it and weep.

*2 tablespoons extra-virgin
olive oil*

*1½ tablespoons balsamic
vinegar*

2 teaspoons minced shallot

½ teaspoon salt

¼ teaspoon black pepper

*1 large beefsteak tomato,
cut into wedges*

*6 cups lightly packed
baby arugula*

*2 large ripe but firm
peaches, sliced*

*¼ cup crumbled ricotta
salata cheese*

*¼ cup lightly packed torn
fresh basil leaves*

1 In medium bowl, combine oil, vinegar, shallot, salt, and
pepper; add tomato and toss to combine. Let stand
5 minutes for flavors to blend.

2 Place arugula in serving bowl; spoon on tomatoes and
dressing. Top with peaches, ricotta salata, and basil; toss
gently to coat.

Wine pairing:

Light red, like Primitivo, or rich white, like Pinot Bianco.

Per serving (about 2 cups): 153 Cal, 10 g Total Fat, 3 g Sat Fat,
436 mg Sod, 13 g Total Carb, 11 g Sugar, 3 g Fib, 5 g Prot.

Ricotta salata is sheep's-milk ricotta
that has been pressed, salted, and
aged. It can be grated, shaved,
or crumbled. If you can't find it,
try substituting ⅓ cup mild feta.

Grilled Caesar Salad

INSALATA DI CAESAR GRIGLIATA

serves 4

Although not strictly Italian, Caesar salad is packed with classic Italian flavors like anchovies, garlic, olive oil, and Parmesan. This grilled version adds a touch of sweetness from balsamic vinegar and agave nectar. All in all, a medley of flavors that dazzle.

1 garlic clove

3 tablespoons grated Parmesan

2 tablespoons reduced-fat mayonnaise

2 anchovy fillets, patted dry

1 tablespoon lemon juice

1 tablespoon white balsamic vinegar

1 teaspoon Worcestershire sauce

½ teaspoon Dijon mustard

½ teaspoon agave nectar or honey

⅛ teaspoon black pepper

4 romaine lettuce hearts

4 (1-ounce) slices whole wheat baguette

¼ teaspoon salt

2 cups cherry tomatoes, halved

1 Spray grill rack with nonstick spray. Prepare grill for medium-high heat cooking.

2 Place garlic in mini–food processor and pulse until minced. Add 1 tablespoon Parmesan, the mayonnaise, anchovies, lemon juice, vinegar, Worcestershire, mustard, agave nectar, and pepper; puree.

3 Cut each romaine heart lengthwise into quarters, leaving cores intact. Pat dry with paper towels. Lightly spray romaine and bread with nonstick spray. Sprinkle romaine with salt.

4 Place lettuce on grill rack and grill, turning once, until lightly charred, but not limp, about 5 minutes. Place bread on grill rack and grill, turning once, until lightly charred, about 4 minutes. Remove cores from romaine. Cut bread into ½-inch cubes.

5 Arrange romaine evenly on 4 plates. Top with bread cubes and tomatoes. Drizzle evenly with dressing and sprinkle with remaining 2 tablespoons Parmesan. Serve at once.

Per serving (1 salad): 210 Cal, 5 g Total Fat, 1 g Sat Fat, 706 mg Sod, 34 g Total Carb, 7 g Sugar, 3 g Fib, 8 g Prot.

Beet
Carpaccio

Beet Carpaccio
CARPACCIO DI BARBABIETOLE

serves 8 • gluten free • vegetarian • no cook

My dad would always say: Do more of what you love and less of what you don't.
One thing that gives me joy is making this gorgeous jewel-toned salad. I adore the taste
of rich and earthy raw beets, the crunch and spiciness of the radishes, the peppery arugula,
and the umami flavor of the Parmesan shavings. When shopping, look for smaller
beets with firm yet yielding texture for the best flavor.

3 tablespoons minced shallot

3 tablespoons red-wine vinegar

½ teaspoon coarse sea salt

¼ teaspoon black pepper

3 tablespoons extra-virgin olive oil

4 radishes

4 beets, peeled

1 (5-ounce) package baby arugula

1½ ounces (about ⅓ cup) thinly shaved Parmesan

1 large lemon, cut into 8 wedges

1 Whisk together shallot, vinegar, ¼ teaspoon salt, and ⅛ teaspoon pepper in small bowl; slowly whisk in oil and set aside.

2 Slice radishes and beets as thinly as possible (use mandoline if you have one), making sure to slice radishes first. Set radishes aside. Combine beets with ¼ cup dressing in medium bowl; toss to coat and marinate at least 10 minutes.

3 Toss arugula with remaining dressing, remaining ¼ teaspoon salt, and remaining ⅛ teaspoon pepper in large bowl. Spread beets out on large platter; arrange arugula mixture over top. Top with radishes and Parmesan; serve with lemon wedges.

 Per serving (1½ cups): 95 Cal, 7 g Total Fat, 2 g Sat Fat, 229 mg Sod, 6 g Total Carb, 4 g Sugar, 2 g Fib, 3 g Prot.

When cooking beets, I like to slow-roast them. I put whole beets in a pan with garlic cloves, a few sprigs of thyme, salt, and a little olive oil, cover with foil and roast at 325°F for about an hour. They're done when the outsides are shriveled and the insides are tender. Slip off their skins and dress them with a bit of balsamic and freshly cracked black pepper.

Everyone's Favorite
Tomato Salad

Everyone's Favorite Tomato Salad

INSALATA DI POMODORI

serves 4 • gluten free • vegetarian • under 20 minutes • no cook

As a kid, I'd spend summers in Italy visiting my family, and this is the one dish my aunt consistently served at our midday meal. It's hardly a recipe, really. We'd dip chewy, crusty homemade sourdough bread in the salad's sweet juices. Whenever friends would visit I'd introduce them to tomato salad. They still talk about it.

The key is to use the best tomatoes you can find. Late summer is when they're at their peak flavor. And use a good-quality olive oil; I like mine full-bodied and fruity. I finish with a tiny sprinkle of flaky Maldon salt for crunch. The whole recipe explodes with flavor.

4 teaspoons extra-virgin olive oil

¼ teaspoon kosher salt

¼ teaspoon black pepper

2 pints cherry tomatoes, halved

½ small red onion, thinly sliced

¼ cup lightly packed fresh basil leaves, thinly sliced

Peperocino (optional)

Whisk together oil, salt, and pepper in large bowl. Stir in tomatoes, onion, basil, and peperocino (if using).

Per serving (1¼ cups): 71 Cal, 5 g Total Fat, 1 g Sat Fat, 128 mg Sod, 7 g Total Carb, 4 g Sugar, 2 g Fib, 1 g Prot.

If you'd like to mellow the flavor of the raw onion, rinse the slices in a sieve under cold running water then drain and pat dry with paper towels before adding them to the salad.

Chapter 4

Pizza, Stromboli, and Calzones (pizza, stromboli e calzoni)

Pizza Dough
PASTA PER LA PIZZA

12 servings, enough for 2 pies • vegetarian

This dough makes enough for two pizzas, so you can freeze half for another day. Thaw it overnight in the refrigerator or on the counter for 1½ hours. If you like, you can let it rise in the refrigerator overnight. You'll find the dough easiest to work with when it's at room temperature.

1½ cups warm water
(105–115°F)

1 teaspoon sugar

1 package (2¼ teaspoons)
active dry yeast

1 tablespoon olive oil

4¼ cups all-purpose flour

1½ teaspoons salt

1 Combine water and sugar in 2-cup measuring cup. Stir in yeast and let stand until foamy, about 5 minutes. Stir in oil.

2 Combine flour and salt in food processor fitted with dough blade. With machine running, scrape yeast mixture through feed tube; process until dough forms a ball, about 1 minute. If necessary, turn dough onto lightly floured surface and knead briefly until smooth and elastic. Form into ball. Spray large bowl with nonstick spray; put dough in bowl and spray top. Cover bowl lightly with plastic wrap and let dough rise in warm spot until double in size, about 1 hour.

3 Gather dough into ball and knead once or twice. Cut in half. Let rest 15 minutes, then stretch or roll to desired shape, or refrigerate for up to 1 day or freeze up to 6 months in floured zip-close freezer bags. Each piece should weigh about 1 pound.

Per serving (2⅔ ounce): 173 Cal, 2 g Total Fat, 0 g Sat Fat, 293 mg Sod, 34 g Total Carb, 0 g Sugar, 1 g Fib, 5 g Prot.

For whole wheat pizza crust, replace up to half the all-purpose flour with whole wheat flour.

How to Shape Pizza Dough

Pizza at home is easy and rewarding. You can mix your own dough or buy dough refrigerated or frozen in most supermarkets. You can also ask your favorite pizzeria to sell you a ball—many will, and they'll probably be flattered that you asked!

These instructions are for forming a single round, Neapolitan-style pizza with a fairly thin crust, but that's not your only option. You can also make your pizzas long or oblong, or you can press the dough into a rectangular sheet pan for Sicilian-style pizza. And if you like, you can even divide dough into balls and let everyone pitch in to form their own individual pizza—a party favorite.

1.Shape the dough into a smooth ball. If the dough is cold, allow it to sit at room temperature, covered with a kitchen towel or plastic wrap, for 30 minutes.

2.Sprinkle flour on a work surface. With lightly floured hands, flatten the dough into a disk. Starting from the center, push the dough outward while spreading your fingers, rotating the dough between pushes to form a circle.

3.Pick the dough up. Move your hands along the edge, rotating the dough and letting gravity pull the dough into a thin circle.

4.If the dough thins too much in one section or rips, return it to the work surface and press it back into even thickness or patch it with a small piece of dough cut from a thicker section. Continue to stretch it with your hands, or you can switch to a floured rolling pin.

5.If the dough resists stretching or pulls back as you work, cover it with a kitchen towel or plastic wrap and let it rest for 10 minutes before continuing.

6.When the dough reaches the desired diameter or thickness, transfer it to a pan or pizza stone and reshape it as needed. Top and bake.

Four Seasons Pizza

PIZZA QUATTRO STAGIONI

serves 6

The name *quattro stagioni*, or "four seasons," is given to a pizza divided into four sections with four different toppings, one for each season. Ours uses artichokes for spring, olives for summer, mushrooms for fall, and prosciutto for winter, though we encourage you to play with different toppings! I sometimes combine the ingredients so I get a taste of all the flavors in one bite. Serve it piping hot with a light green salad on the side.

10 ounces pizza dough, at room temperature

¾ cup prepared pizza sauce

1 cup (about 4 ounces) shredded part-skim mozzarella

½ (10-ounce) package frozen artichoke hearts, thawed, squeezed dry, and quartered

1 cup sliced cremini mushrooms

8 large black olives, pitted and sliced

2 ounces thinly sliced prosciutto, cut into strips

¼ teaspoon black pepper

1 Place oven rack in lower third of oven. Preheat oven to 500°F.

2 Stretch or roll dough out to 12-inch round; if dough begins to pull back, cover it with kitchen towel, let it rest 10 minutes, and then continue rolling. Transfer dough to baking sheet, pressing dough back into shape as needed. Leaving 1-inch border around edges, spread sauce evenly over crust. Sprinkle with mozzarella. Top evenly with artichokes, mushrooms, olives, and prosciutto. Spray pizza lightly with nonstick spray and sprinkle with pepper.

3 Bake until crust is golden and cheese is bubbling, about 20 minutes. Cut pizza into 6 wedges.

Wine pairing:

Young Chianti or Dolcetto.

Per serving (1 wedge): 216 Cal, 8 g Total Fat, 3 g Sat Fat, 775 mg Sod, 25 g Total Carb, 2 g Sugar, 4 g Fib, 13 g Prot.

Four Seasons
Pizza

Ham-and-Gorgonzola Pizza

Ham-and-Gorgonzola Pizza

PIZZA CON PROSCIUTTO COTTO E GORGONZOLA

serves 6

My husband's family is from Borgo Val di Taro, near Parma in Northern Italy, and when we first started dating his parents invited me to dinner quite often. They introduced me to ingredients and dishes I had never tasted before. This recipe is inspired by some of their favorite flavors: *prosciutto cotto* (ham that's been cooked, not cured) and Gorgonzola, a lovely, creamy, blue-veined cheese with a strong, piquant flavor.

1 (10-ounce) prebaked thin whole wheat pizza crust

2½ teaspoons olive oil

1 cup (about 4 ounces) crumbled Gorgonzola cheese

½ cup very thinly sliced red onion

8 thin slices lean low-sodium ham, cut into strips

⅓ cup lightly packed fresh basil leaves, sliced

⅛ teaspoon red pepper flakes

1 Preheat oven to 450°F.

2 Place pizza crust on baking sheet and brush with 1 teaspoon oil. Sprinkle with cheese and onion. Bake until crust is very crisp on bottom, about 12 minutes. Top with ham; bake 1 more minute.

3 Remove pizza from oven and top evenly with basil. Drizzle with remaining 1½ teaspoons oil and sprinkle with pepper flakes. Cut into 6 wedges.

Wine pairing:

Medium-dry rosé (*rosato*).

Per serving (1 wedge): 225 Cal, 10 g Total Fat, 5 g Sat Fat, 581 mg Sod, 22 g Total Carb, 2 g Sugar, 4 g Fib, 12 g Prot.

Clam–Sun-Dried Tomato Pizza

PIZZA ALLE VONGOLE CON POMODORI SECCHI

serves 6

Although thin-crust pies topped with clams (often razor clams, cooked right in their shells) are found in Italy, this recipe takes its inspiration from the pizza popularized in New Haven, Connecticut. Neapolitan immigrants to the area used clams from local waters, just a sprinkling of cheese, and no tomato sauce for this iconic pie. We use ingredients most of us have stashed in the cupboard—cans of briny clams, sweet sun-dried tomatoes—for a quick, midweek dinner.

¼ cup sun-dried tomatoes (not packed in oil)

1 (6½-ounce) can chopped clams, drained

2 garlic cloves, finely chopped

1 tablespoon olive oil

1 (8-ounce) prebaked thin whole wheat pizza crust

1½ cups (about 6 ounces) shredded part-skim mozzarella

2 tablespoons grated Parmesan

1 teaspoon dried oregano

¼ cup chopped fresh basil leaves

1 Preheat oven to 450°F; spray baking sheet with nonstick spray.

2 Place sun-dried tomatoes in cup and add enough boiling water to cover by 1 inch. Let stand until softened, about 10 minutes; drain and chop. Combine clams, garlic, and oil in small bowl; toss well.

3 Place pizza crust on baking sheet. Sprinkle with mozzarella, leaving ½-inch border around edge. Top with Parmesan, oregano, sun-dried tomatoes, and clams. Bake until cheese is bubbly and melted, 8–10 minutes. Sprinkle with basil and cut into 6 wedges.

Per serving (1 wedge): 241 Cal, 9 g Total Fat, 4 g Sat Fat, 397 mg Sod, 21 g Total Carb, 2 g Sugar, 4 g Fib, 19 g Prot.

Clam–Sun-Dried
Tomato Pizza

5-Ingredient
Cheese Pizza

5-Ingredient Cheese Pizza
PIZZA CON 5 INGREDIENTI

serves 8 • vegetarian

Behold the simplicity of a tomato-cheese pizza. The only addition is red pepper flakes, for a bit of heat. Because there are just a few ingredients, I focus on the crust, aiming for a perfectly charred, blistered, and bubbly one. Utterly delicious.

¾ pound pizza dough, at room temperature

Cornmeal for dusting pan

½ cup tomato sauce or pizza sauce

¼ teaspoon red pepper flakes

1 cup (about 4 ounces) shredded part-skim mozzarella

2 tablespoons grated Parmesan

1 Place oven rack in lower third of oven; preheat oven to 500°F.

2 Turn dough onto lightly floured work surface. With lightly floured rolling pin, roll dough into 12-inch round. Sprinkle pizza pan or large baking sheet with cornmeal. Transfer dough to prepared pan, gently pulling dough back into 12-inch round. (If dough begins to pull back, cover it with a clean kitchen towel, let it rest about 10 minutes, and continue rolling.)

3 Spread tomato sauce over dough; sprinkle with pepper flakes. Top evenly with mozzarella and Parmesan. Bake until crust is golden and cheese melts, 12–15 minutes. Cut into 8 wedges.

Per serving (1 wedge): 168 Cal, 6 g Total Fat, 3 g Sat Fat, 417 mg Sod, 20 g Total Carb, 2 g Sugar, 0 g Fib, 9 g Prot.

Robiola and Arugula Pesto Pizza
PIZZA CON ROBIOLA E PESTO DI RUCOLA

serves 8 • vegetarian

This is a pizza for cheese lovers, of whom I am one. We use Robiola, a soft cheese made from a combination of sheep's and cow's milks, popular in the Piedmont and Lombardy regions of Italy. If you can't find Robiola, you can use Taleggio. We balance the richness of the cheese with a fresh and fragrant pesto. The word "pesto" comes from the Italian verb *pestare*, which means "to crush or beat." We let a food processor do the work here, but using a mortar and pestle can be therapeutic at times.

3 cups lightly packed baby arugula

⅓ cup freshly grated Parmesan

3 tablespoons pine nuts, toasted

1 garlic clove, crushed through press

⅛ teaspoon salt

3 tablespoons vegetable broth

2 tablespoons extra-virgin olive oil

1 cup lightly packed fresh basil leaves

1 pound pizza dough, thawed if frozen, at room temperature

½ cup (about 2 ounces) shredded part-skim mozzarella

2 ounces Robiola cheese, finely diced and chilled

1 Place oven rack in lower third of oven. Place large baking sheet or pizza pan on rack and preheat oven to 500°F.

2 Meanwhile, to make pesto, combine 2 cups arugula, the Parmesan, pine nuts, garlic, and salt in blender and blend until coarsely chopped. With machine running, gradually pour in broth and oil; stop to scrape down sides of blender and blend until pureed. Add basil and remaining 1 cup arugula; pulse until combined.

3 On 18-inch sheet of parchment paper, stretch or roll dough out to 13-inch round. If dough begins to pull back, cover it with a kitchen towel, let it rest 10 minutes, and then continue rolling. Slide parchment onto another large baking sheet. Using baking sheet as a guide, slide pizza on parchment onto hot baking sheet in oven.

4 Bake until crust is very crisp on bottom, about 15 minutes. Spread pesto over dough, leaving ½-inch border. Sprinkle top of pizza evenly with mozzarella and then dot with Robiola. Bake until cheeses are melted, about 5 minutes longer. Cut into 8 wedges.

Wine pairing:

Crisp, medium-bodied white, like Gavi or Verdicchio.

Per serving (1 wedge): 237 Cal, 12 g Total Fat, 3 g Sat Fat, 472 mg Sod, 27 g Total Carb, 2 g Sugar, 4 g Fib, 8 g Prot.

Fontina Butternut-Crust Pizza
PIZZA CON BASE DI ZUCCA CON FONTINA

serves 4 • vegetarian

Fontina cheese comes from the Valle d'Aosta region in the Italian Alps, a region famous for its dairy. Cooks from this area bordered by France and Switzerland tend to use more butter and cream in their dishes than those in other regions of Italy. Here we keep the toppings simple, but our mashed butternut squash crust is rich, adding a sweet base-note flavor. I think it's perfect for a chilly fall day.

CRUST
1½ cups mashed cooked butternut squash

½ cup all-purpose flour

½ cup (about 2 ounces) shredded part-skim mozzarella

1 large egg, well beaten

1 tablespoon grated Parmesan

½ teaspoon minced fresh sage leaves

½ teaspoon baking powder

½ teaspoon kosher salt

¼ teaspoon granulated garlic

1 pinch freshly grated nutmeg

1 pinch cayenne pepper

TOPPING
⅓ cup shredded part-skim mozzarella

⅓ cup shredded fontina cheese

2 teaspoons sliced fresh sage leaves

1 pinch freshly grated nutmeg

1 Preheat oven to 375°F. Line large rimmed baking sheet with parchment paper; spray with nonstick spray.

2 To make crust, combine all crust ingredients in large bowl and mix well. Spoon crust mixture into 2 (8-inch) circles on prepared pan; smooth with spoon to form even layer. Bake until browned on bottom, about 25 minutes; carefully flip with spatula. Bake until evenly browned, about 15 minutes longer.

3 For topping, combine mozzarella and fontina in medium bowl; scatter evenly across cooked crusts and sprinkle with sage. Return pizzas to oven; bake until cheese melts, 5–7 minutes. Sprinkle with nutmeg; slice each pizza into 4 wedges.

Per serving (2 wedges): 219 Cal, 9 g Total Fat, 5 g Sat Fat, 585 mg Sod, 18 g Total Carb, 1 g Sugar, 3 g Fib, 13 g Prot.

For crisper results, bake the pizza crusts in a preheated cast-iron skillet or on a baking stone coated with nonstick spray.

Pepperoni
Cauliflower-
Crust Pizza

Pepperoni Cauliflower-Crust Pizza
PIZZA CON BASE DI CAVOLFIORE CON SALAMI

serves 4

The toppings on this pizza are classic, but the cauliflower crust is unique—and low in SmartPoints!

½ *head cauliflower, cut into florets (about 2 cups)*

1½ *cups (about 6 ounces) shredded part-skim mozzarella*

⅔ *cups all-purpose flour*

2 *large eggs*

1 *teaspoon fresh minced oregano*

½ *teaspoon kosher salt*

½ *teaspoon granulated garlic*

⅛ *teaspoon black pepper*

1 *cup tomato sauce*

1½ *ounces thinly sliced turkey pepperoni*

½ *teaspoon dried oregano*

1 *tablespoon sliced fresh basil or small fresh basil leaves*

1 Preheat oven to 450°F. Line large rimmed baking sheet with parchment paper; coat with nonstick spray.

2 Place cauliflower florets in food processor; process to consistency of rice and scrape into large bowl. Add ½ cup mozzarella, the flour, eggs, oregano, salt, garlic, and pepper; stir to combine. Spoon mixture into 2 (8-inch) circles on prepared pan; smooth with spoon to form even layer (mold into a heart shape with your hands, if desired). Bake until browned on bottom, about 20 minutes; carefully flip over. Bake until evenly browned, about 10 minutes longer.

3 Spoon ½ cup sauce over each crust and sprinkle each with ½ cup remaining cheese; top each with half of pepperoni and sprinkle with oregano. Bake until heated through and cheese is melted, about 5 minutes (broil to brown cheese, if desired). Sprinkle with basil. Cut each pizza into 4 wedges.

Wine pairing:
Young Chianti or Dolcetto.

Per serving (2 wedges): 288 Cal, 11 g Total Fat, 6 g Sat Fat, 1,067 mg Sod, 27 g Total Carb, 5 g Sugar, 4 g Fib, 21 g Prot.

Ham-and-Provolone Stromboli
STROMBOLI CON PROSCIUTTO COTTO E PROVOLONE

serves 6

Often when I'd like to indulge the kids, but don't have the energy to cook, I order in pizza.
Unless, that is, I make this recipe, which uses many of the same ingredients as pizza but
somehow seems more fun to create. It's really an assembly job, and the kids love it. Sometimes
they add their own fillings. This recipe sticks to peppers, ham, and cheese.

*1 (11-ounce) tube
refrigerated French
bread dough*

*6 (¾-ounce) slices lean
smoked ham*

*2 bottled roasted red bell
peppers (not packed in oil),
drained, patted dry,
and diced*

*6 (¾-ounce) slices
provolone cheese*

3 scallions, sliced

*1 large egg white,
lightly beaten*

1 teaspoon sesame seeds

1 Preheat oven to 375°F. Remove dough by popping tube open, then slowly unwinding cardboard toward one metal end cap. Carefully tear off cap, then tear off opposite end cap. Slowly unroll cardboard casing. Place dough seam side up on sheet of parchment paper and unfold. Pat dough into a 12 x 14-inch rectangle.

2 Arrange ham slices over dough, slightly overlapping, leaving 1-inch border around edges of dough. Scatter roasted peppers over ham, then top with provolone. Scatter scallions over cheese.

3 Fold dough edges inward over filling. Starting at long side nearest you, use parchment to help roll up dough into compact log. Pinch seam together to seal. Carefully lift roll and place, seam side down, in middle of parchment; slide parchment onto baking sheet. Brush top of stromboli with egg white and sprinkle with sesame seeds. Make 5 evenly spaced 1-inch diagonal slits on top of stromboli.

4 Bake until dough is golden brown and filling is heated through, about 30 minutes. Slide stromboli, still on parchment, onto wire rack. Cool until just warm, about 30 minutes. Cut into 12 slices with serrated knife.

Per serving (2 slices): 246 Cal, 9 g Total Fat, 5 g Sat Fat, 786 mg Sod, 27 g Total Carb, 3 g Sugar, 1 g Fib, 13 g Prot.

Ham-and-
Provolone
Stromboli

Spinach-Artichoke
Calzones

Spinach-Artichoke Calzones
CALZONI CON SPINACI E CARCIOFI

serves 8 • *vegetarian*

The calzone originated in Naples, where it was considered an on-the-go meal, in contrast to the knife-and-fork pizza. This classic is often served stateside with marinara sauce on the side, requiring utensils, but it still makes an excellent portable meal to reheat at the office. Imagine—pizza crust, artichoke hearts, spinach, and cheese all in one bite.

1 pound pizza dough, thawed if frozen, at room temperature

1¾ cups marinara sauce

1⅓ cups (about 5⅓ ounces) shredded part-skim mozzarella

¼ cup grated Parmesan

½ (10-ounce) package frozen artichoke hearts, thawed, squeezed dry, and sliced

1 cup lightly packed baby spinach

1 Heat oven to 425°F. Line large baking sheet with parchment paper.

2 Divide dough into 4 balls. Roll 1 ball out on lightly floured surface to 7-inch circle; transfer to prepared baking sheet.

3 Cover half of circle with 3 tablespoons marinara, ⅓ cup mozzarella, 1 tablespoon Parmesan, ¼ cup artichokes, and ¼ cup spinach, leaving ½-inch border around edges. Fold dough over ingredients. Fold and pinch edges to securely seal calzone. Repeat with remaining ingredients and dough, making 4 calzones.

4 Spray calzones with nonstick spray. Bake until golden brown, about 20 minutes. Let stand 5 minutes, then cut each calzone in half with serrated knife. Warm remaining 1 cup marinara and serve on side with calzones.

Per serving (½ calzone and 2 tablespoons marinara): 263 Cal, 9 g Total Fat, 4 g Sat Fat, 794 mg Sod, 31 g Total Carb, 6 g Sugar, 2 g Fib, 13 g Prot.

Life on parade.

Whatever you call it—a pageant, display, spectacle, drama, or tableau—Italians put on a good show. Streets are filled with people at all hours shouting, laughing, crying, arguing, whistling, singing, or calling out to each other. Ringing church bells and the buzz of a passing Vespa rise above the general cacophony. Older women walk by in housedresses and young men sit on their scooters and make phone calls. The show is so captivating that people watch from their windows, place chairs outside their doors, or sit at cafés and watch all the wonderful characters go by.

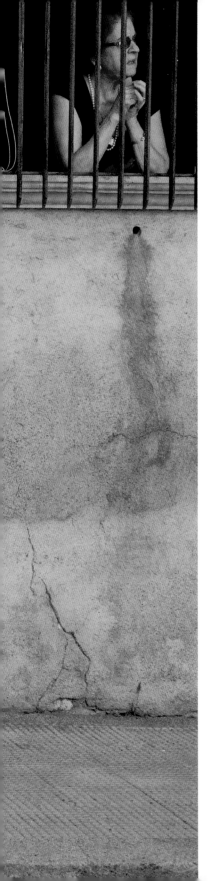

Inside the church.

The street
procession.

Celebrating food and saints

Italians celebrate year-round and the ultimate in spectacle is a festival or street fair. Festivals usually honor a town's patron saint, and street fairs, called *sagre,* honor the bounty of the earth. These food fairs are dedicated to a local dish or ingredient such as chestnuts, grappa, red onions, polenta, steak, truffles, or stuffed eggplant. All festivals and sagre are held in the streets and in the piazza (town square) and usually involve food, music, and a group event like a procession or communal cooking. At the festival of San Fortunato in the Ligurian town of Camogli, people gather and cook fish in the world's largest frying pan!

Here, thousands of visitors flock to Roccella Ionica in Calabria to celebrate the feast of the Madonna delle Grazie, the patron saint of fishermen. Her life-size statue is carried through the streets, accompanied by priests, bands, and people walking barefoot to honor their Madonna. She's then carried to sea and placed on a boat. Fireworks light up the sky that night. The following day the procession continues, ending with the racing of the Madonna up the steps of her church, where she remains until the following year.

The Madonna
brought
to sea.

Cat enjoying
her siesta.

Take your time

In Italy, as in many parts of the world, socializing often takes place over a cup of coffee. Here, men meet at the local bar (our version of a café or coffee shop) and enjoy an espresso, a glass of wine, or a gelato while playing cards and discussing the day's events. This bar is their second home, and multiple visits a day means regular patrons and the barista have all become members of an extended family.

Italians take the time to enjoy life. They *own* their time instead of chasing it.

Homemade
liqueurs.

**Men playing
cards.**

Chapter 5

Pasta and Grains (pasta e cereali)

Manicotti with Sausage
MANICOTTI CON SALSICCIA

serves 10

If you're looking for a dish with lusty, soul-satisfying flavors, look no further. I make this on the chilliest of days and eat it with gusto—and a fine wine.

12 ounces sweet Italian sausage, casings removed

¼ cup dry white wine

½ pound cremini mushrooms, sliced

3 garlic cloves, minced

1 (4-ounce) package fresh spinach

1 (24-ounce) jar pasta sauce

10 manicotti pasta shells (about 6 ounces)

2 cups part-skim ricotta

2 large eggs, lightly beaten

¼ cup chopped fresh parsley leaves

½ teaspoon kosher salt

½ teaspoon coarsely ground black pepper

4 tablespoons shredded Parmesan

¼ cup (about 1 ounce) shredded part-skim mozzarella

1 Cook sausage in large skillet over medium-high heat until browned and crumbly, about 5 minutes, breaking up chunks of sausage with side of wooden spoon. Drain off any fat. Stir in wine, mushrooms, and garlic; cook until mushrooms are tender, about 5 minutes. Add spinach; cook, tossing, until wilted, about 1 minute. Stir in sauce. Set aside.

2 Cook manicotti in boiling water to cover until just tender, about 7 minutes. Drain and rinse under cold water.

3 Meanwhile, stir together ricotta, eggs, parsley, salt, pepper, and 2 tablespoons Parmesan in large bowl.

4 Preheat oven to 425°F. Coat 9 x 13-inch baking dish with nonstick spray. Spread 3 cups meat sauce in bottom of dish. Spoon about ¼ cup ricotta filling into each manicotti shell and place on sauce in baking dish.

5 Spread remaining 2 cups sauce over center of manicotti. Cover with foil and bake until hot and bubbling, about 25 minutes. Uncover and sprinkle with mozzarella and remaining 2 tablespoons Parmesan. Continue to bake, uncovered, until cheese melts, 5–10 minutes longer. Cool 10 minutes before serving.

Wine pairing:
Sangiovese or Barbera.

Per serving (1 filled manicotti shell and ½ cup sauce): 318 Cal, 16 g Total Fat, 7 g Sat Fat, 741 mg Sod, 25 g Total Carb, 8 g Sugar, 3 g Fib, 18 g Prot.

Manicotti with
Sausage

Baked Ziti

ZITI AL FORNO

serves 8

This dish is meant to feed a crowd. My mom comes from a family of nine kids and my dad from a family of five, so when we'd visit relatives in Italy, there would be a lot of meals and a lot of people. The table was always open to a steady stream of guests popping in too. All that had to be said was *"I parenti sono arrivati dall'America"* ("The relatives have arrived from America"), and within minutes 15 Calabresi were gathered around the table, eating cheese, marinated mushrooms, *soppressata* (spicy salami), eggplant fritters, and, yes, *pasta al forno*. Always pasta al forno.

12 ounces ziti

2 teaspoons olive oil

2 garlic cloves, minced

⅓ pound ground lean beef (7% fat or less)

1½ teaspoons dried thyme

1 teaspoon dried rosemary

½ teaspoon salt

½ teaspoon black pepper

1 (28-ounce) can whole tomatoes, tomatoes finely chopped, juice reserved

1 cup (about 4 ounces) shredded part-skim mozzarella

1 Preheat oven to 350°F.

2 Cook pasta according to package directions; drain and set aside.

3 Meanwhile, heat oil in medium saucepan over medium heat; add garlic and cook, stirring, 2 minutes. Add beef and brown, breaking it apart with side of spoon, 3–5 minutes; drain off any fat and set pan back over medium heat.

4 Add thyme, rosemary, salt, and pepper; stir to coat beef. Cook until herbs become fragrant, about 2 minutes. Add tomatoes and juice and bring mixture to boil; reduce heat and simmer 5 minutes.

5 Spoon enough beef-tomato mixture into bottom of 4-quart casserole dish to just cover surface; top with half of cooked ziti. Next, layer with half of remaining beef-tomato sauce and ½ cup mozzarella. Layer with remaining ziti and then top with remaining beef-tomato sauce; sprinkle with remaining ½ cup mozzarella. Bake until heated through and cheese is golden and bubbly, about 30 minutes. Cool at least 5 minutes, then cut into 8 pieces and serve.

Per serving (⅛ of casserole): 258 Cal, 6 g Total Fat, 3 g Sat Fat, 389 mg Sod, 37 g Total Carb, 4 g Sugar, 2 g Fib, 14 g Prot.

Pasta Bolognese
PASTA ALLA BOLOGNESE

serves 6

Ragù (meat sauce) lies at the heart of the cuisine of Emilia-Romagna, a region in Northern Italy. Each city or village has its own version, but the most well-known is *ragù alla Bolognese.* This rich meat sauce contains very little tomato, getting its deep flavor instead from meat slowly braised with aromatic vegetables and wine, then laced with just a bit of tomato paste or canned tomatoes. My mom made ragù every Sunday for the family. I'd wake up to the aroma of *sugo di carne* (that's what she called it) bubbling on the stovetop, wanting to dig in, since I'd been fasting from the night before so I could receive Holy Communion. We'd go to church, and when we returned, my brother John and I would race into the kitchen, ladle a generous portion of *sugo* into a bowl and mop it up with a slice of homemade bread.

My mom used both beef and pork in her sauce because she thought this combo was the most flavorful, but Bolognese is traditionally made with only beef. Whatever meats you choose to use for your sauce, be sure that the beef you select is ground from a braising cut like chuck—and make it the leanest possible. In Southern Italy, ragù is eaten as a full meal and in two courses: first the sauce over pasta as a *primo*, then the meat itself as a *secondo*.

1 teaspoon olive oil

1 onion, diced

1 red bell pepper, diced

3 garlic cloves, finely chopped

½ pound cremini mushrooms, chopped

1 pound ground lean beef (7% fat or less)

½ teaspoon salt

¼ teaspoon black pepper

1 (28-ounce) can whole tomatoes, finely chopped, juice reserved

¼ cup low-fat (1%) milk

8 ounces pappardelle or tagliatelle

3 tablespoons grated pecorino Romano

¼ cup loosely packed fresh basil leaves, thinly sliced

1 Heat oil in large skillet over medium-high heat. Add onion and bell pepper; cook, covered, stirring frequently, until vegetables are tender, about 3 minutes. Add garlic and cook, stirring constantly, until fragrant, about 30 seconds. Add mushrooms and cook, uncovered, stirring occasionally, until tender, about 3 minutes. Add beef, salt, and pepper; cook, breaking apart beef with spoon, until browned, about 5 minutes.

2 Stir in tomatoes and juice; bring to boil. Reduce heat and simmer 10 minutes. Stir in milk and simmer 5 more minutes.

3 Meanwhile, cook pasta according to package directions. Divide pasta evenly among 6 bowls. Top with sauce; sprinkle evenly with pecorino and basil.

Per serving (¾ cup sauce, ⅔ cup pasta, and ½ tablespoon pecorino): 320 Cal, 8 g Total Fat, 3 g Sat Fat, 490 mg Sod, 39 g Total Carb, 7 g Sugar, 3 g Fib, 24 g Prot.

Duck Ragù with
Tagliatelle

Duck Ragù with Tagliatelle
TAGLIATELLE AL RAGÙ D'ANATRA

serves 6

Hearty duck sauces like this one are popular in the Veneto region. They're traditionally served with a local fresh pasta called *bigoli*, a very thick spaghetti that's hollow in the center. Here we use flat, toothsome tagliatelle, but you could also use fettuccine or bucatini.

2 (1-pound) whole duck legs, skin and fat removed

1¼ teaspoons kosher salt

2 large shallots, halved and sliced

2 celery stalks, diced

1 parsnip, peeled and diced

4 garlic cloves, finely chopped

2 (2-inch) strips orange peel, removed with vegetable peeler

½ cup dry red wine

1 (15½-ounce) can whole tomatoes, tomatoes chopped, juice reserved

1¼ cups chicken broth

1 tablespoon chopped fresh sage leaves

1 bay leaf

6 ounces tagliatelle

1 Sprinkle duck all over with ½ teaspoon salt. Spray Dutch oven or large saucepan with nonstick spray and set over medium heat; add duck and brown, about 5 minutes per side. Transfer to plate. Add shallots, celery, parsnip, garlic, and orange peel to pan; cook, stirring frequently, until vegetables soften, about 5 minutes.

2 Add wine and simmer, scraping bottom of pan with spatula to release any browned bits. Stir in tomatoes and juice, broth, sage, bay leaf, and remaining ¾ teaspoon salt; bring to boil. Return duck and accumulated juices to pan. Reduce heat to low and cover. Simmer until duck meat is tender and nearly falling off bones, turning duck once or twice, 1½–2 hours. Remove from heat. Discard bay leaf.

3 Transfer legs to cutting board. When cool enough to handle, pull meat off bones and shred with 2 forks; discard bones. Stir duck back into sauce and cover.

4 To serve, cook pasta in lightly salted water about 1 minute less than package directs. Reheat ragù while pasta cooks. Drain pasta, reserving ½ cup cooking liquid, and add pasta to ragù; add cooking liquid a few tablespoons at a time to loosen sauce. Finish cooking pasta in sauce, gently tossing noodles with large fork or tongs, until pasta is coated and al dente, about 2 minutes longer.

Wine pairing:

Dark, rustic red, like Montepulciano d'Abruzzo.

10 SmartPoints value™

Per serving (about 1 cup): 390 Cal, 10 g Total Fat, 4 g Sat Fat, 775 mg Sod, 36 g Total Carb, 6 g Sugar, 5 g Fib, 24 g Prot.

Linguine with Sardines
LINGUINE CON LE SARDE

serves 4

My uncle (*zio*) Vittorio was a fisherman, and most days he'd leave just before dawn to catch enough fish to sell at the market. Once in a while he'd take my brother and me out with him: "Look for the birds; that's where the fish are," he'd say. My mother, dad, and aunt would meet us at the beach, and we'd walk into the frigid sea with our pants legs rolled up to collect the fish, salt them, and pack them into tins. We'd leave a few unsalted to make for lunch that day.

Pasta con le sarde is one of the classic dishes of Calabria and Sicily. As with any beloved recipe, the ingredients vary from region to region, village to village, even home to home. This version is made with canned sardines (though fresh cooked or frozen can be substituted) and broccoli rabe instead of the usual fennel.

6 ounces whole wheat linguine

1 bunch broccoli rabe, trimmed and cut into 1-inch pieces

1 tablespoon olive oil

1 large onion, chopped

3 garlic cloves, sliced

¼ teaspoon red pepper flakes

¼ teaspoon salt

2 (3¾-ounce) cans sardines in water, drained

1 teaspoon finely grated lemon zest

1 tablespoon lemon juice

4 tablespoons grated Parmesan

1 Cook pasta according to package directions, adding broccoli rabe during last 5 minutes of cooking time. Drain pasta and broccoli rabe, reserving ¾ cup cooking liquid.

2 Meanwhile, heat oil in large deep skillet over medium heat. Add onion and cook, stirring occasionally, until golden brown, about 10 minutes. Add garlic, pepper flakes, and salt; cook, stirring constantly, 1 minute.

3 Remove and discard backbones from sardines and break meat into chunks. Add pasta, broccoli rabe, lemon zest and juice, and sardines to skillet; cook, stirring constantly, just until heated through, 1–2 minutes, adding reserved cooking liquid as needed if mixture seems dry. Divide among 4 plates and sprinkle with Parmesan.

Per serving (1⅔ cups pasta and 1 tablespoon Parmesan): 326 Cal, 11 g Total Fat, 3 g Sat Fat, 422 mg Sod, 40 g Total Carb, 2 g Sugar, 7 g Fib, 22 g Prot.

Lobster Fra Diavolo
SPAGHETTI ALL'ARAGOSTA PICCANTE

serves 4

This bold, audacious "red sauce" pasta is an Italian-American restaurant favorite. The recipe calls for freshly cooked whole lobsters or lobster tails (for ease and expediency), or you can steam your own. It's a very spicy dish, so beware! I believe it's the perfect balance of heat and flavor, but experiment until you find the intensity that works for you.

2 (1¼-pound) lobsters or
2 (8-ounce) lobster tails,
    steamed at market

1 tablespoon olive oil

4 garlic cloves, finely
    chopped

½ cup white wine

1 zucchini or yellow
    squash, diced

½ teaspoon red pepper
    flakes, or to taste

½ teaspoon kosher salt,
    or to taste

1 (28-ounce) can San
    Marzano tomatoes

4 ounces spaghetti

¼ cup chopped fresh
    basil leaves

¼ cup grated Parmesan

¼ teaspoon coarsely
ground black pepper

1 Remove meat from lobster shells; reserve shells. Slice lobster tails into medallions. Coarsely chop any claw meat. Set aside.

2 Heat oil in large skillet over medium heat. Add garlic and lobster shells and cook, stirring, until garlic begins to turn golden and shells are toasted, about 4 minutes. Add wine and cook, scraping bottom of pan, until liquid has evaporated by half, about 3 minutes. Remove and discard shells.

3 Add zucchini, pepper flakes, and salt to skillet; cook, stirring occasionally, until zucchini is tender, about 5 minutes. Stir in tomatoes. Cook over medium-high heat, crushing tomatoes with back of spoon, until sauce is thickened, about 8 minutes. Stir in lobster meat; cook until heated, about 3 minutes. Set aside.

4 Meanwhile, cook pasta according to package directions. Drain and return pasta to pot. Stir in sauce. Stir in basil. Divide pasta among 4 plates or bowls and sprinkle evenly with Parmesan and black pepper.

Wine pairing:

Full-bodied Pinot Bianco or light Sangiovese.

Per serving (1¾ cups pasta and sauce and 1 tablespoon cheese): 277 Cal, 6 g Total Fat, 2 g Sat Fat, 882 mg Sod, 34 g Total Carb, 7 g Sugar, 3 g Fib, 18 g Prot.

Shrimp and Mint Pasta
PASTA CON GAMBERI E MENTA

serves 4

This recipe is straightforward to make, toothsome and comforting to eat. Eggs make the sauce rich and creamy; the trick to having it come out smooth, not like scrambled eggs, is to use very low heat and stir constantly.

6 ounces pappardelle or other wide noodles

2 large eggs

2 tablespoons grated Parmesan

½ teaspoon cornstarch

¼ teaspoon black pepper, or to taste

¼ teaspoon salt, or to taste

1 tablespoon olive oil

1 garlic clove, finely chopped

1¼ pounds medium shrimp, peeled and deveined

¼ cup dry white wine

¾ cup chicken broth

3 tablespoons chopped fresh mint leaves

1 teaspoon finely grated lemon zest

1 Cook pasta according to package directions; drain.

2 Meanwhile, whisk together eggs, 1 tablespoon Parmesan, cornstarch, pepper, and ⅛ teaspoon salt in small bowl.

3 Heat oil in large skillet over medium-high heat. Add garlic and cook, stirring, until fragrant, about 30 seconds. Add shrimp and remaining ⅛ teaspoon salt and cook, stirring frequently, just until pink, about 2 minutes. Add wine and bring to boil; stir in broth and bring to simmer. Slowly whisk ½ cup of hot broth mixture into egg mixture. Remove skillet from heat and slowly add egg-broth mixture to skillet, stirring constantly. Return skillet to low heat and cook, stirring constantly, until sauce is thickened, about 1 minute.

4 Stir in hot pasta. Remove from heat and continue stirring until pasta is coated. Stir in mint and zest. Divide pasta mixture among 4 bowls; sprinkle evenly with remaining 1 tablespoon Parmesan.

Wine pairing:

Full-flavored white, like Soave Classico.

Per serving (about 1¼ cups pasta and ¾ teaspoon Parmesan): 361 Cal, 9 g Total Fat, 2 g Sat Fat, 1,198 mg Sod, 35 g Total Carb, 2 g Sugar, 1 g Fib, 30 g Prot.

**Shrimp and
Mint Pasta**

Pappardelle with Shrimp and Pesto

Pappardelle with Shrimp and Pesto

PAPPARDELLE CON GAMBERI E PESTO

serves 4

In the summer, my dad would pick handfuls of basil from his garden, and my mom would turn it into a fragrant, creamy pesto. She would freeze what she didn't use that day so we could enjoy the taste of summer all winter long. Pesto should always be used raw, at room temperature, and not heated up, which is why Italians allow the heat of just-drained pasta to warm this savory accompaniment.

8 ounces pappardelle

3 cups lightly packed fresh basil leaves

4 teaspoons toasted pine nuts

2 garlic cloves, minced

¾ teaspoon kosher salt

¼ teaspoon plus ⅛ teaspoon black pepper

¼ cup chicken broth

5 teaspoons extra-virgin olive oil

¼ cup grated Parmesan

1¼ teaspoons grated lemon zest

1 pound peeled and deveined small or medium Key West Pink shrimp or regular medium shrimp, thawed if frozen

½ cup quartered cherry tomatoes (optional)

1 Cook pasta according to package directions.

2 Meanwhile, to make pesto, pulse basil, pine nuts, garlic, ½ teaspoon salt, and ¼ teaspoon pepper in blender until coarsely chopped. With machine running, gradually pour in broth and 4 teaspoons oil; blend until thick and paste-like (not too smooth), stopping to scrape down sides once or twice. Stir in Parmesan and lemon zest.

3 Sprinkle shrimp with remaining ¼ teaspoon salt and remaining ⅛ teaspoon pepper. Heat remaining 1 teaspoon oil in large skillet over medium-high heat. Add shrimp and cook, stirring occasionally, just until opaque in center, 3–5 minutes.

4 Drain pasta, reserving ¼ cup cooking liquid. Return pasta to pot; add pesto, shrimp, tomatoes (if using), and reserved cooking liquid and toss to combine.

 Per serving (1¾ cups): 395 Cal, 11 g Total Fat, 2 g Sat Fat, 1,167 mg Sod, 47 g Total Carb, 2 g Sugar, 3 g Fib, 26 g Prot.

We used the smallest shrimp we could find, but you can use medium shrimp if that's more convenient. Gamberetti rosa ("small pink shrimp") are a Mediterranean species with particularly tender, succulent flesh.

Linguine with Peas and Asparagus

LINGUINE CON PISELLI E ASPARAGI

serves 4 • vegetarian • under 20 minutes

Bright green stuff—peas, asparagus, mint—brings spring freshness and vibrancy to a bowl of plain noodles. (I do sometimes substitute fava beans for the asparagus in this recipe.) The ricotta keeps things creamy and light, a welcome change after a winter of heartier, more substantial meals.

6 ounces linguine

1 pound asparagus, trimmed and sliced diagonally into 1-inch pieces

¾ cup frozen green peas

¾ cup part-skim ricotta

2 tablespoons plus 4 teaspoons grated Parmesan

1 teaspoon extra-virgin olive oil

1 teaspoon minced garlic

1 teaspoon finely grated lemon zest, or to taste

½ teaspoon salt

⅛ teaspoon black pepper, or to taste

¼ cup lightly packed chopped fresh mint or basil leaves

1 Cook pasta according to package directions, adding asparagus and peas during last 4 minutes of cooking. Drain pasta and vegetables, reserving 1 cup cooking liquid; set aside.

2 Meanwhile, stir together ricotta, 2 tablespoons Parmesan, oil, garlic, lemon zest, salt, and pepper in serving bowl.

3 Add pasta and vegetables, mint, and ¼ cup reserved cooking liquid to bowl; toss to coat, adding more cooking liquid if desired. Serve sprinkled with remaining 4 teaspoons Parmesan and additional pepper and lemon zest, if desired.

Per serving (about 1¼ cups): 300 Cal, 7 g Total Fat, 3 g Sat Fat, 466 mg Sod, 44 g Total Carb, 5 g Sugar, 5 g Fib, 16 g Prot.

Orecchiette with Broccoli Rabe
ORECCHIETTE CON CIME DI RAPA

serves 4 ● vegetarian

Broccoli rabe is most associated with the cooking of Southern Italy and is known by a number of names: *cime di rapa, broccoli di rapa,* or simply *rapini.* Creamy cannellini beans pair nicely with the greens' bitter, nutty earthiness. Add a little heat from red pepper and you've got a hearty weeknight dinner.

This dish is popular in the Puglia region where their famous orecchiette, a pasta shape that resembles "little ears," is used with this sauce. If you wander down the streets of the villages in this region you might see *nonnas* sitting in their homes, rolling dough into long, skinny tubes, and shaping them into orecchiette.

1 bunch broccoli rabe, tough stems discarded, stalks cut into 2-inch pieces

6 ounces whole wheat orecchiette

2 teaspoons olive oil

3 large garlic cloves, thinly sliced

1 pint grape tomatoes

1 (15½-ounce) can cannellini (white kidney) beans, rinsed and drained

½ teaspoon salt

¼ teaspoon red pepper flakes

⅓ cup grated Parmesan

1 Bring large pot of lightly salted water to boil. Add broccoli rabe and cook 3 minutes; remove with slotted spoon to bowl. When water returns to boil, stir in pasta; cook according to package directions. Drain pasta, reserving 1 cup cooking liquid.

2 Meanwhile, heat oil in large nonstick skillet over medium heat. Add garlic and cook, stirring frequently, until golden, 2–3 minutes.

3 Add broccoli rabe and tomatoes to skillet. Increase heat to medium-high and cook, stirring frequently, until broccoli rabe is tender, about 5 minutes. Add beans, salt, pepper flakes, and ¾ cup reserved cooking liquid. Increase heat to high and cook, stirring frequently, until beans are heated through, 2–3 minutes.

4 Stir in pasta and heat through, about 1 minute; add remaining ¼ cup cooking liquid if mixture seems dry. Remove skillet from heat; stir in Parmesan and serve at once.

Per serving (1½ cups): 328 Cal, 7 g Total Fat, 2 g Sat Fat, 861 mg Sod, 54 g Total Carb, 3 g Sugar, 10 g Fib, 18 g Prot.

Linguine Fini with Eggplant
LINGUINE FINI ALLE MELANZANE

serves 4 ● *vegetarian*

Cooking for family and friends is one of the most personal and generous things you can do. You're providing food that literally sustains them, but also nourishes them with your love and care. I'd say this pasta will drastically improve the quality of their lives and yours.

Both eggplants and tomatoes are grown in Calabria and are staples in Calabrian cuisine. When cooked, an eggplant's spongey texture turns creamy, silky, almost soufflé-like. Both veggies pair well with most anything, but they're especially delicious when they simmer and collapse into a bright, rich, fruity sauce for pasta. You can substitute fusilli or rigatoni for the linguine, but regardless of what pasta you use, the dish works. I like to top the dish with a handful of heady herbs just before serving.

2 pounds plum tomatoes, cored

8 ounces linguine fini or regular linguine

4 teaspoons olive oil

1 small onion, finely chopped

2 large garlic cloves, finely chopped

⅛ teaspoon red pepper flakes

¾ teaspoon kosher salt

1 small (1-pound) eggplant, cut into ¾-inch dice

2 tablespoons grated Parmesan

1 With small, sharp knife, cut shallow "X" on bottom of each tomato. Bring large pot of water to boil. With slotted spoon, add tomatoes and cook until scored skins start to split, about 2 minutes. Drain tomatoes in colander. When cool enough to handle, rub skins off. Halve tomatoes and use your fingers to pull out seeds. Coarsely chop tomatoes.

2 In same pot, cook pasta according to package directions. Drain and keep warm.

3 Meanwhile, heat 2 teaspoons oil in large skillet over medium-high heat. Add onion; cook, stirring occasionally, until golden, about 5 minutes. Add garlic and pepper flakes and cook, stirring constantly, until fragrant, about 30 seconds. Add tomatoes and ½ teaspoon salt; bring to boil. Cook, stirring occasionally, until tomatoes soften and sauce thickens, 5–7 minutes.

4 Heat remaining 2 teaspoons oil in medium nonstick skillet over medium heat. Add eggplant and remaining ¼ teaspoon salt. Cook, covered, stirring occasionally, until eggplant is tender, about 8 minutes.

5 Combine pasta, tomato sauce, and eggplant in large bowl. Serve with Parmesan.

Per serving (1½ cups pasta and sauce and ½ tablespoon Parmesan): 335 Cal, 7 g Total Fat, 1 g Sat Fat, 436 mg Sod, 59 g Total Carb, 10 g Sugar, 6 g Fib, 11 g Prot.

Linguine Fini
with Eggplant

Spaghetti
Puttanesca

Spaghetti Puttanesca
SPAGHETTI ALLA PUTTANESCA

serves 8

The ingredients in this sauce remind me of what I'd find at *il mercato* (the market) in Southern Italy: pasta, olives, briny capers, and tins of salted anchovies. These also happen to be ingredients many people keep in their pantry, so this salty, spicy, and scandalous pasta should come together in a snap.

12 ounces spaghetti

1 tablespoon olive oil

3–4 garlic cloves, minced

1 tablespoon tomato paste

2 teaspoons anchovy paste or 2 finely chopped anchovy fillets

3 pints grape tomatoes, halved

15 pitted Gaeta or Kalamata olives, sliced

3 tablespoons drained capers

½ cup chopped fresh parsley, plus more for garnish

½ teaspoon red pepper flakes

½ teaspoon coarse sea salt, or to taste

¼ cup whole wheat panko (bread crumbs), toasted in dry skillet until browned

1 Bring large pot of salted water to boil and cook pasta according to package directions. Drain, reserving ¾ cup cooking water.

2 Meanwhile, heat oil in large skillet over medium-low heat. Add garlic; cook, stirring, until golden brown, 2–3 minutes. Add tomato paste and anchovy paste; cook, stirring, 2–3 minutes. Add tomatoes, olives, and capers; cook, tossing, until tomatoes are heated through and beginning to soften, about 5 minutes.

3 Add drained pasta to skillet along with reserved cooking water, parsley, pepper flakes, and salt; cook, tossing frequently, until piping hot and sauce thickens enough to coat pasta. Serve sprinkled with parsley and bread crumbs.

Wine pairing:

Sturdy, rustic red, like Valpolicella Ripasso.

Per serving (1 generous cup): 221 Cal, 4 g Total Fat, 1 g Sat Fat, 336 mg Sod, 40 g Total Carb, 4 g Sugar, 3 g Fib, 7 g Prot.

Baked Spinach-Ricotta Shells

CONCHIGLIE AL FORNO CON RICOTTA E SPINACI

serves 6 • vegetarian

Cooking is about throwing some raw materials together and watching them transform into something restorative and nourishing. Here, pasta in a sauce forms an amazing golden crust; the cheese turns oozy and molten; and the spinach, cheese, and basil combine to deliver a lush earthiness. It's comforting and delicious.

18 jumbo pasta shells (about half of 12-ounce box)

1 teaspoon olive oil

1 onion, chopped

2 large garlic cloves, finely chopped

1 (6-ounce) bag baby spinach

1 (15-ounce) container part-skim ricotta

½ cup (about 2 ounces) shredded part-skim mozzarella

2 tablespoons plus 2 teaspoons grated Parmesan

½ cup chopped fresh basil leaves

½ teaspoon salt

¼ teaspoon black pepper

2½ cups fat-free marinara sauce

1 Preheat oven to 375°F.

2 Cook pasta shells according to package directions until just softened. Drain and set aside.

3 Meanwhile, heat oil in large skillet over medium-high heat. Add onion and cook, stirring occasionally, until golden and tender, about 5 minutes. Stir in garlic and cook, stirring frequently, until fragrant, about 30 seconds. Stir in spinach a few handfuls at a time, adding more when wilted. Cook, tossing, just until spinach is tender, about 1 minute. Remove from heat.

4 Transfer spinach mixture to cutting board and chop. Transfer to bowl and stir in ricotta, ¼ cup mozzarella, 2 tablespoons Parmesan, and ¼ cup basil. Stir in salt and pepper.

5 Spread ½ cup marinara sauce on bottom of shallow 3-quart baking dish. Fill shells with cheese mixture and place in baking dish. Spoon remaining 2 cups sauce over and around shells. Sprinkle with remaining ¼ cup mozzarella and remaining 2 teaspoons Parmesan.

6 Cover baking dish with nonstick foil and bake until hot and cheese is melted, about 25 minutes. Sprinkle with remaining ¼ cup basil.

Per serving (3 stuffed shells): 309 Cal, 9 g Total Fat, 5 g Sat Fat, 608 mg Sod, 38 g Total Carb, 6 g Sugar, 3 g Fib, 18 g Prot.

Lasagna with Homemade Sauce
LASAGNE CON SALSA FATTA IN CASA

serves 12 • vegetarian

In Italy, *pranzo*, the midday meal, is usually the most important activity of the day. This is when families come together to connect over a leisurely meal, followed by a nap or time to relax and re-energize. Even people who work far from home make time for a lunch break at a nearby restaurant.

These home meals typically consist of two courses—a *primo* (pasta, risotto, or soup), and a *secondo* (meat or fish) with a few *contorni* (side dishes). Neither course dominates—in Italy a meal is built around a series of small plates that work well together. I like to serve this on the weekend. It's so satisfying that sometimes a second course isn't needed.

1 tablespoon olive oil

2 large onions, diced

6 garlic cloves, finely chopped

2 (28-ounce) cans whole tomatoes, tomatoes diced, juice reserved

1 (6-ounce) can tomato paste

⅓ cup chopped fresh basil leaves or 1 tablespoon dried

¼ teaspoon red pepper flakes

1 teaspoon salt

1½ cups part-skim ricotta

2 large eggs, beaten

¼ cup lightly packed fresh parsley leaves, chopped

4 tablespoons grated Parmesan

12 no-boil lasagna noodles (about 8 ounces)

½ pound fresh whole-milk mozzarella, shredded

1 To make sauce, heat oil in Dutch oven or large heavy saucepan over medium heat. Add onions and cook, stirring occasionally, until onions start to brown, about 10 minutes. Stir in garlic. Add tomatoes and juice, tomato paste, basil, pepper flakes, and salt; stir to combine. Bring sauce to boil; reduce heat to low and simmer, partially covered, stirring and scraping bottom and sides of pot occasionally, until sauce reduces slightly and thickens, about 1 hour.

2 Preheat oven to 350°F. Coat lasagna pan or 9 x 13-inch baking dish with nonstick spray.

3 In medium bowl, combine ricotta, eggs, parsley, and 3 tablespoons Parmesan; stir in about ⅓ cup tomato sauce so ricotta mixture turns pink.

4 Spoon about ½ cup tomato sauce on bottom of prepared pan. Cover sauce with 4 lasagna noodles, breaking some noodles if necessary to form a single layer. Cover noodles with half of ricotta mixture and one-third of mozzarella; spoon one-third of remaining sauce over top. Add another layer of noodles and remainder of ricotta mixture; sprinkle with one-third of mozzarella and another one-third of sauce. Add final layer of noodles and cover with remaining sauce; sprinkle with remaining mozzarella and remaining 1 tablespoon Parmesan.

5 Cover pan with nonstick foil and bake until noodles are tender, cheese melts, and sauce begins to bubble, 45–50 minutes. Remove foil and bake until browned, 15–20 minutes longer. Remove from oven and let lasagna sit 15 minutes before cutting into 12 pieces. The saucy, bubbly lasagna can be assembled a day ahead.

Per serving (1 piece): 258 Cal, 10 g Total Fat, 5 g Sat Fat, 690 mg Sod, 30 g Total Carb, 7 g Sugar, 3 g Fib, 15 g Prot.

Winter Squash Lasagna
LASAGNE ALLA ZUCCA

serves 9 • *vegetarian*

This hearty, fall-inspired meal is a wonderful change of pace from lasagna with red sauce.
The meaty sweetness of the winter squash pairs well with chopped fresh sage, a back note of nutmeg
for warmth, plump golden raisins, and pine nuts for crunch. Béchamel keeps this lasagna moist
as it cools. If you're planning a main course for vegetarians, this is an excellent choice.
The flavors are particularly suited to Thanksgiving.

¼ cup all-purpose flour

2½ cups evaporated
fat-free milk

2 garlic cloves, finely
chopped

⅓ cup grated Parmesan

½ teaspoon salt, or to taste

¼ teaspoon black pepper,
or to taste

⅛ teaspoon freshly
grated nutmeg

10 ounces lasagna noodles,
cooked al dente (about
12 noodles)

2 (10-ounce) packages
winter squash puree,
thawed if frozen

1 cup (about 4 ounces)
shredded part-skim
mozzarella

½ cup golden raisins

2 tablespoons pine
nuts, chopped

1 Preheat oven to 350°F.

2 Place flour in small saucepan and very gradually whisk
in milk and garlic. Warm over low heat, stirring constantly,
until sauce simmers and is thickened, about 3 minutes.
Remove from heat and stir in Parmesan, salt, pepper,
and nutmeg.

3 Spread ¼ cup sauce over bottom of 9 x 13-inch baking
dish and cover with 3 lasagna noodles; top with one-third
of squash and ½ cup sauce. Sprinkle with ½ cup mozzarella
and one-third of raisins. Cover with 3 more lasagna noodles
and spread with half of remaining squash and ½ cup
sauce; sprinkle with one-third of raisins. Cover with 3 more
lasagna noodles and top with remaining squash and raisins;
cover with last 3 lasagna noodles, pressing sheets gently
down. Top with remaining sauce; sprinkle with pine nuts
and remaining mozzarella.

4 Bake until lasagna bubbles around edges and is browned
on top, about 30 minutes. Let cool 10 minutes, then cut
into 9 pieces.

Wine pairing:

Light red, like Barbera d'Asti, or medium-bodied white, like
Pinot Bianco.

9 SmartPoints value™

Per serving (1 piece): 276 Cal, 5 g Total Fat, 2 g Sat Fat, 359 mg Sod,
44 g Total Carb, 15 g Sugar, 2 g Fib, 15 g Prot.

Winter Squash
Lasagna

Gnocchi with
Chickpeas

Gnocchi with Chickpeas

GNOCCHI CON CECI

serves 6 • vegetarian • under 20 minutes

Though I had eaten gnocchi before, my real introduction to this pasta was in Borgo Val di Taro (Borgotaro, for short), on a trip with my husband and in-laws. We foraged for mushrooms—thankfully, my companions were a lot better at it than I—and that evening we feasted on *gnocchi con funghi*.

Gnocchi with mushrooms is a classic dish, but we wanted to try something different. Here, sage is infused into butter and lemon, creating a luxurious and fragrant sauce. Toss with the chickpeas and gnocchi and you're done. The overall taste is earthy, yet fresh.

1 (16-ounce) bag frozen potato gnocchi

2 tablespoons unsalted butter

¼ cup lightly packed fresh sage leaves

1 teaspoon grated lemon zest

1 tablespoon lemon juice

¼ teaspoon salt

⅛ teaspoon black pepper

1 (15-ounce) can chickpeas, rinsed and drained

2 tablespoons grated Parmesan

1 Cook gnocchi according to package directions; drain.

2 Meanwhile, melt butter in large skillet over medium heat. Add sage leaves and cook, stirring occasionally, until butter just begins to brown, 4–5 minutes.

3 Add lemon zest and juice, salt, and pepper; cook 15 seconds. Add chickpeas and cook, tossing, until coated, about 30 seconds. Stir in gnocchi and toss for another 30 seconds. Divide among 6 bowls and sprinkle each with 1 teaspoon cheese.

Wine pairing:

Crisp, fruity white, such as Vernaccia.

Per serving (1 cup gnocchi and 1 teaspoon Parmesan): 251 Cal, 6 g Total Fat, 3 g Sat Fat, 619 mg Sod, 40 g Total Carb, 1 g Sugar, 5 g Fib, 7 g Prot.

Polenta and Vegetable Casserole

CASSERUOLA DI POLENTA E VERDURE

serves 6 • gluten free • vegetarian

This recipe contains two favorite Italian beans: fava beans and cranberry beans (*borlotti* in Italy). Fava beans are green and grassy in flavor; borlotti are cream-colored with red streaks and have a creamy, nutty flavor. Together they form the base of this delicious casserole that's topped with crisp, cheesy polenta rounds.

You can swap in edamame or lima beans in place of favas, and pinto or cannellini beans for borlotti. We use frozen favas and canned cranberry beans in this recipe, but if you find fresh shell beans at the market in summer, I encourage you to try them. Fresh beans are a little more work and take more time because you have to shell them, but less time than cooking beans from dried. The taste is worth it.

1 (15½-ounce) can cranberry beans, rinsed and drained

1 (14½-ounce) can whole tomatoes, tomatoes diced, juice reserved

1 cup frozen fava beans, thawed and skins slipped off, or frozen shelled edamame

1 zucchini, chopped

1 cup marinara sauce

2 garlic cloves, finely chopped

1 teaspoon dried oregano

¼ teaspoon salt, or to taste

1 (16-ounce) log prepared fat-free polenta, cut into 12 (½-inch) slices

1¼ cups (about 5 ounces) shredded reduced-fat Italian cheese blend

1 Preheat oven to 400°F. Spray shallow 2½-quart baking dish with nonstick spray.

2 Combine cranberry beans, tomatoes and juice, fava beans, zucchini, marinara sauce, garlic, oregano, and salt in large saucepan. Place over high heat and bring to boil. Reduce heat and simmer, covered, 10 minutes. Transfer mixture to baking dish. Arrange polenta slices on top, overlapping as needed.

3 Bake until bubbly at edges, about 25 minutes. Sprinkle polenta with cheese and continue to bake until cheese melts, about 5 minutes. Let stand 10 minutes before dividing into 6 servings.

Wine pairing:

Chianti or Primitivo.

Per serving (⅙ of casserole): 267 Cal, 7 g Total Fat, 4 g Sat Fat, 1,040 mg Sod, 37 g Total Carb, 5 g Sugar, 9 g Fib, 15 g Prot.

Polenta and
Vegetable
Casserole

Deep-Dish Polenta Pie
TORTA SALATA DI POLENTA

serves 6 • gluten free • vegetarian

In some towns and villages, polenta is more common than pasta. It used to be thought of as peasant food, but today it's served in fine restaurants around the world. I like to bake it, grill it, or serve it creamy. Here we bake it into a hearty vegetarian pie that can be eaten warm from the oven, packed in a picnic basket, or enjoyed for lunch the next day. We use white cornmeal, commonly found in supermarkets, but you can also use Italian instant polenta; just adjust the cooking time.

1 ounce dried porcini mushrooms or other wild mushrooms

2 cups hot water

1 cup frozen chopped broccoli, thawed

3 tablespoons low-fat (1%) milk

½ teaspoon salt

½ cup white cornmeal

6 tablespoons grated Parmesan

1 tablespoon unsalted butter

1 large egg, lightly beaten

1 small plum tomato, seeded and chopped

Chopped fresh parsley or basil, for garnish

1 Preheat oven to 400°F. Lightly coat bottom and sides of 10-inch deep-dish pie pan with nonstick spray.

2 Combine mushrooms and ½ cup hot water in small bowl; set aside.

3 Place broccoli in colander and squeeze out excess water; set aside.

4 In large heavy-bottomed pot, combine remaining 1½ cups hot water, milk, and salt; bring to boil. Reduce heat to medium-low and slowly drizzle in cornmeal, whisking constantly. Continue to cook, stirring frequently, until polenta is as thick as mashed potatoes, 6–8 minutes.

5 Stir in broccoli, 3 tablespoons Parmesan, and butter. Using slotted spoon, transfer mushrooms to pot. Pour in mushroom soaking liquid, being careful to leave any grit in bottom of bowl. Stir in egg. Spread polenta mixture evenly in prepared pan. Sprinkle with tomato and remaining 3 tablespoons Parmesan. Bake until edges begin to brown, 20–25 minutes. Sprinkle with parsley and cut into 6 wedges. Serve warm or room temperature.

 4 SmartPoints value™

Per serving (1 wedge): 131 Cal, 5 g Total Fat, 3 g Sat Fat, 332 mg Sod, 16 g Total Carb, 1 g Sugar, 2 g Fib, 6 g Prot.

Wild Mushroom Risotto
RISOTTO AI FUNGHI SELVATICI

serves 6 • gluten free • vegetarian

In Italy, risotto is usually served spread out on a large flat plate or in a very shallow bowl. It's then eaten from the outside in, giving the center of the risotto time to cool down.

As with most other food in Italy, versions of risotto reflect regional ingredients: *risotto alla Milanese* with saffron in Milan, risotto with black squid ink in Veneto, and risotto with pumpkin in Lombardy. Ours is inspired by the white truffle and porcini risottos common in Piedmont. Make sure to start out with a good rice and use clear, simmering broth. The risotto is ready when the grains are tender but still have bite and remain separate; the overall consistency should be moist and creamy.

5 cups chicken broth

1 ounce dried porcini mushrooms

1 teaspoon olive oil

¾ pound sliced wild mushrooms or cremini mushrooms

3 large shallots, chopped

1 cup Arborio or Carnaroli rice

¼ cup dry white wine

1 tablespoon unsalted butter

3 tablespoons grated Parmesan

Freshly ground black pepper

2 tablespoons chopped fresh parsley leaves

1 Put broth in medium saucepan and bring to boil over medium-high heat. Remove from heat, add mushrooms, cover, and let stand until mushrooms are softened, about 5 minutes. Strain through fine mesh sieve; remove mushrooms, rinse to remove any grit, and coarsely chop.

2 Return strained broth to saucepan; cover and keep at low simmer.

3 Heat oil in large saucepan over medium heat. Add wild mushrooms and shallots and cook, stirring occasionally, until mushrooms and shallots are tender, about 8 minutes.

4 Stir in rice and cook, stirring, until outer grain is translucent, about 2 minutes. Stir in wine and cook, stirring, until absorbed, about 1 minute. Stir in porcinis. Add broth, ⅔ cup at a time, stirring until absorbed before adding more. Keep stirring and adding broth until rice is just tender but still slightly chewy in center, about 25 minutes from first addition of broth.

5 Remove from heat; stir in butter and Parmesan. Divide among 6 bowls and sprinkle with pepper and parsley.

Wine pairing:

Rich white, like Pinot Bianco, or go earthy with a red, like Brunello.

Per serving (about 1 cup): 242 Cal, 5 g Total Fat, 2 g Sat Fat, 686 mg Sod, 37 g Total Carb, 4 g Sugar, 3 g Fib, 10 g Prot.

Lemon-Chicken
Risotto

Lemon-Chicken Risotto

RISOTTO AL POLLO CON LIMONE

serves 4 • gluten free

Like polenta, risotto used to be known as a peasant dish in Italy. Rice is grown mainly in the Po Valley, stretching across the Piedmont, Lombardy, and Veneto regions. This is where the round- and short-grained Arborio and Carnaroli rice for risotto are farmed.

3 teaspoons olive oil

¾ pound skinless boneless chicken breast

½ teaspoon salt

¼ teaspoon black pepper

1 (9-ounce) package frozen artichoke hearts, thawed, pieces halved if large

5 cups chicken broth

1 small onion, chopped

2 garlic cloves, minced

1 cup Arborio or Carnaroli rice

1 teaspoon grated lemon zest

2 tablespoons lemon juice

¼ cup chopped fresh parsley leaves

3 tablespoons grated Parmesan

1 Heat 1 teaspoon oil in medium skillet over medium-high heat. Sprinkle chicken with ¼ teaspoon salt and ⅛ teaspoon pepper. Add to skillet and cook until browned and cooked through, 5–6 minutes per side. Transfer to cutting board and cool 5 minutes. Cut into ½-inch cubes.

2 Return same skillet to medium-high heat and add artichoke hearts; cook, stirring occasionally, until lightly browned, 4–5 minutes. Transfer artichokes to medium bowl and add chicken.

3 Bring broth to boil in small saucepan; reduce heat so broth just simmers.

4 Heat remaining 2 teaspoons oil in medium saucepan over medium-high heat. Add onion and garlic and cook until softened, about 2 minutes. Add rice and cook, stirring, until outer grain is translucent, about 1 minute. Add 1 cup broth and stir until absorbed. Continue to add broth, ½ cup at a time, stirring until absorbed before adding more. Keep stirring and adding broth until rice is just tender and firm to the bite, and mixture is creamy; cooking time should be about 20 minutes from first addition of broth.

5 Add reserved chicken and artichokes and the lemon zest and juice with last addition of broth. Remove from heat. Stir in parsley, Parmesan, and remaining ¼ teaspoon salt and ⅛ teaspoon pepper and serve at once.

Per serving (1 cup): 378 Cal, 7 g Total Fat, 2 g Sat Fat, 1,140 mg Sod, 47 g Total Carb, 2 g Sugar, 4 g Fib, 29 g Prot.

Rice and Peas

RISI E BISI

serves 6 • gluten free

Risi e bisi is the most Venetian of Venetian dishes. Often described as half risotto and half soup, it is traditionally served on the Feast of St. Mark on April 25, following the ancient tradition of presenting a soup made with the first peas of spring to the *doge* (chief magistrate). Bisi is short for *piselli*, or dried peas. We at WW like to welcome in spring and the arrival of fresh peas. For the sweetest flavor, look for peas that are small, firm, and bright green.

2 teaspoons olive oil

1 onion, finely chopped

1 celery stalk, finely chopped

½ cup Arborio or Carnaroli rice

¼ teaspoon salt

1 (14½-ounce) can chicken broth

2 tablespoons plus ¼ cup water

1 cup small shelled fresh peas or frozen tiny peas

3 tablespoons grated Parmesan

2 teaspoons unsalted butter

¼ teaspoon black pepper

1 Heat oil in medium saucepan over medium-low heat. Add onion and celery; cook, stirring frequently, until onion is translucent, about 4 minutes. Stir in rice and salt and cook, stirring constantly, 1 minute.

2 Add broth and 2 tablespoons water to pan; bring to boil. Reduce heat to low and maintain a gentle simmer, uncovered, for 12 minutes, stirring several times.

3 Stir in peas and remaining ¼ cup water; bring mixture back to boil, reduce heat to low, and continue to gently simmer until rice is just tender, 5–6 minutes. Fold in Parmesan, butter, and pepper until butter is melted and mixture looks creamy.

4 Remove from heat, cover, and let stand 2 minutes. Consistency should be soupier than risotto but thick enough to eat with a fork; if needed, thin with a little more water or broth.

Per serving (½ cup): 135 Cal, 4 g Total Fat, 2 g Sat Fat, 394 mg Sod, 19 g Total Carb, 2 g Sugar, 2 g Fib, 5 g Prot.

Quick Polenta with Cheese
POLENTA AL FORMAGGIO

serves 6 • gluten free • vegetarian • under 20 minutes

Hot, thick and comforting. Served creamy in a bowl, or sliced and grilled. Enough said.

3 cups water

¾ teaspoon salt

¾ cup instant polenta

¼ cup (about 1 ounce) grated Parmesan

2 tablespoons unsalted butter, cut into chunks

Freshly ground pepper for serving

1 Bring water and salt to boil in large saucepan over high heat. Slowly whisk in polenta in slow, steady stream; cook, whisking frequently, until it falls away from the sides of the pan and becomes thick and smooth, about 5 minutes, switching to a spoon if it becomes too thick to whisk.

2 Remove from heat and stir in Parmesan and butter.

3 To serve creamy and soft, spoon hot polenta into bowls or onto plates and grind fresh pepper over top. To serve firm, spread hot polenta into 8-inch square baking pan that has been sprayed with nonstick spray. Cover with plastic wrap and refrigerate at least 1 hour or until firm. When ready to serve, remove from pan and cut into 12 rectangles. Coat both sides with nonstick spray and sprinkle with pepper; cook in ridged grill pan over medium-high heat until browned and heated through, 3–4 minutes per side. Deliciously crisp on the outside and soft on the inside.

Per serving (½ cup soft polenta or 2 pieces firm polenta): 120 Cal, 5 g Total Fat, 3 g Sat Fat, 370 mg Sod, 16 g Total Carb, 0 g Sugar, 2 g Fib, 3 g Prot.

Butternut
Squash–
Farro Bake

Butternut Squash–Farro Bake

ZUCCA E FARRO AL FORNO

serves 12 • *vegetarian*

I could eat winter squash every day. Its bright orange color improves my mood and its mealy-in-a-good-way texture leaves me satisfied. This bake is made with farro, a chewy, nutty grain that's believed to have sustained the Roman legions. (I know it sustains me.) The lightly bitter, mineral-rich flavor of spinach balances the sweetness of the squash, and toasted walnuts add crunch.

3 cups farro

1 tablespoon olive oil

1½ pounds butternut squash, peeled, seeded, and cut into ½-inch dice

2 cups thinly sliced shallot

2 cups diced red bell pepper

2 tablespoons minced garlic, or to taste

5 tablespoons chopped fresh sage

1 teaspoon dried oregano

½ teaspoon cayenne, or to taste

10 ounces baby spinach

½ cup vegetable or chicken broth, warmed

1 tablespoon grated lemon zest

¼ cup lemon juice

1 teaspoon kosher salt

½ teaspoon black pepper

1 cup (about 4 ounces) shredded fontina or Gruyère cheese

1 cup chopped walnuts, toasted

½ cup grated pecorino Romano cheese

1 Cook farro according to package directions until tender; drain any liquid not absorbed (you should have 6–6½ cups farro). Place farro in large bowl and fluff with fork.

2 Preheat oven to 375°F. Coat 9 x 13-inch baking dish with nonstick spray.

3 In large skillet, heat oil over medium heat. Add squash, shallot, bell pepper, and garlic; cook, stirring frequently, until shallot softens, about 5 minutes. Add 3 tablespoons sage and the oregano and cayenne; cook, stirring frequently, until flavors blend, about 3 minutes.

4 Add spinach; cook, stirring, until wilted, about 2 minutes. Add squash mixture to farro; toss to combine. Stir in broth, lemon zest and juice, salt, and black pepper; stir in fontina and spoon mixture into baking dish.

5 In small bowl, combine walnuts, pecorino, and remaining 2 tablespoons sage; sprinkle evenly over farro mixture. Cover with foil and bake 15 minutes. Uncover and cook until casserole is heated through and top is lightly browned, about 5 minutes more.

 9 SmartPoints value™

Per serving (1 generous cup): 337 Cal, 13 g Total Fat, 3 g Sat Fat, 353 mg Sod, 47 g Total Carb, 8 g Sugar, 9 g Fib, 14 g Prot.

Being in a beautiful place makes you feel life is good

Many old buildings in Italy's small towns are simple structures, painted yellow, pink, burnt red, or light blue to match the colors of the earth and sky. If you walk along the narrow streets of these towns, you'll see people talking to each other across the streets through open windows.

Living in art Doors and windows act as transitional elements between public and private life. Though Italians spend most of their day outdoors, shutters are closed at lunchtime and at siesta to keep rooms cool and away from the parching heat.

Chapter 6

Poultry
(pollame)

Rosemary Chicken with Potatoes
POLLO AL ROSMARINO CON PATATE

serves 8 • gluten free

Chicken, garlic, lemon zest, herbs—a simple supper that is simply satisfying. I feel restored just taking in the fragrant aroma wafting through the house.

When I roast chicken, I'm looking to extract every bit of flavor I can. As the meat cooks at a high heat, it leaves crusty gold bits that settle on the bottom of the pan. I pour wine into the pan and scrape away at those bits, encouraging them to dissolve into the wine. The result is a sauce with depth of character and savoriness that I adore with potatoes and chicken. This is what I like most about Italian cooking: Rather than adding flavor to a dish by using stock from other poultry, meat, or vegetables, Italians insist on a sauce that's flavored by a food's own juices, its own heart and soul. This feels natural, intimate, and not contrived.

4 teaspoons chopped fresh rosemary

2 large garlic cloves, minced

1½ teaspoons finely grated lemon zest

¾ teaspoon salt

½ teaspoon black pepper

1 (3½-pound) chicken, skin removed, wings discarded, cut into 8 pieces

6 medium Yukon Gold potatoes (about 2 pounds), sliced

½ cup dry white wine

1 Preheat oven to 400°F. Spray bottom of broiler pan with nonstick spray.

2 Combine rosemary, garlic, lemon zest, ½ teaspoon salt, and ¼ teaspoon pepper in small bowl. Rub herb mixture over chicken pieces. Place chicken in pan. Scatter potatoes around chicken; sprinkle potatoes with remaining ¼ teaspoon salt and remaining ¼ teaspoon pepper.

3 Roast chicken and potatoes 35 minutes. Add wine to pan and turn potatoes. Continue to roast until instant-read thermometer inserted in thighs registers 165°F and potatoes are tender, 10–20 minutes longer.

Wine pairing:
Light red, like Chianti or fruity, spicy rosé (*rosato*).

5 SmartPoints value

Per serving (1 piece chicken with ½ cup potatoes): 292 Cal, 5 g Total Fat, 1 g Sat Fat, 345 mg Sod, 21 g Total Carb, 2 g Sugar, 3 g Fib, 35 g Prot.

Letting your chicken sit at room temperature for 20 minutes before you prepare it helps it cook evenly. Use good wine, but it doesn't have to be expensive.

Rosemary Chicken
with Potatoes

Lemony Chicken Piccata
PICCATA DI POLLO

serves 4

Although sauces with lemon and parsley are common in Italian cooking, particularly with thin slices of veal, chicken piccata is often credited to Italian immigrants in the United States. I first discovered it in high school and had to teach my mom how to make it! It's perfect for weeknight cooking because it comes together in less than 30 minutes with only a handful of pantry ingredients, including the perky caper. I use Meyer lemons when I can find them.

2 tablespoons all-purpose flour

¾ teaspoon salt

¼ teaspoon black pepper

4 (¼-pound) thin-sliced chicken cutlets

2 tablespoons unsalted butter

½ cup chicken broth

¼ cup lemon juice

1 tablespoon drained capers

2 tablespoons finely chopped fresh parsley leaves

1 Combine flour, ½ teaspoon salt, and ⅛ teaspoon pepper in large bowl. Working one at a time, dip both sides of chicken cutlets into flour mixture and shake off excess. Place on large plate.

2 Melt 1 tablespoon butter in large skillet over medium-high heat. Add chicken and cook until lightly browned and cooked through, 3–4 minutes on each side; transfer chicken to plate.

3 Pour broth, lemon juice, and capers into skillet and bring to boil. Reduce heat and simmer until slightly reduced, about 2 minutes. Add chicken and cook, turning to coat, until heated through, about 2 minutes. Remove from heat, move chicken to one side, then swirl in remaining 1 tablespoon butter, remaining ¼ teaspoon salt, remaining ⅛ teaspoon pepper, and parsley.

Per serving (1 piece chicken and 2 tablespoons sauce): 211 Cal, 9 g Total Fat, 4 g Sat Fat, 633 mg Sod, 5 g Total Carb, 0 g Sugar, 0 g Fib, 27 g Prot.

Roast Chicken and Fennel

POLLO E FINOCCHI AL FORNO

serves 4 • gluten free

This recipe brings all its ingredients together in one pan. The minute I get home from work I pull it together, put the pan in the oven, and leave it to cook while I enjoy some time alone before the kids get home from school or hockey practice. The result: meltingly tender chicken with a back note of heat from red pepper.

I adore fennel. I eat it both cooked and raw: Sliced raw it's crunchy and tastes like anise, and when it's cooked it turns soft and sweet. If I have any left over I stir it into pasta for dinner the following day.

1 pound skinless boneless chicken breast

1 teaspoon salt

¼ teaspoon red pepper flakes

1 large red onion, thinly sliced

1 fennel bulb, thinly sliced (reserve greens for garnish)

½ cup white wine

2 teaspoons olive oil

1 Preheat oven to 425°F.

2 Rub chicken on both sides with ½ teaspoon salt and the pepper flakes.

3 Place onion and fennel in roasting pan and toss with remaining ½ teaspoon salt; place chicken on top. Add wine and roast until chicken is cooked through, about 20 minutes. Remove chicken from pan; stir vegetables and place back in oven. Reduce oven to 325°F; roast vegetables, uncovered, until completely caramelized, 35–40 minutes more.

4 Shred chicken with two forks.

5 When vegetables are done, remove pan from oven and add chicken; toss well to coat. Drizzle with oil and toss again. Garnish with fennel greens.

Wine pairing:

Pinot Grigio (good for cooking with too!).

Per serving (about 1¼ cups): 213 Cal, 5 g Total Fat, 1 g Sat Fat, 666 mg Sod, 9 g Total Carb, 2 g Sugar, 2 g Fib, 27 g Prot.

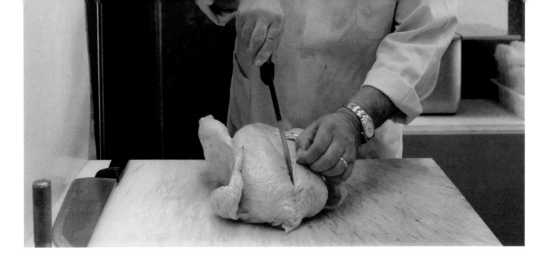

Chicken... with an Italian Accent

Chicken breast is called *petto di pollo* in Italian, and with the new WW Freestyle program, it just got even tastier: This popular protein is a zero SmartPoints food,* which means you don't need to track or measure it—one more reason to make it a dinner staple. Think of chicken as a blank canvas—depending on the cooking method and flavorings you choose, the possibilities are endless. Here we suggest some of our favorite sauces to complement the juicy meat. It's all about what you're in the mood to eat.

Grill

1 Start with breasts about 5 or 6 ounces each. If they're thicker than ¾ inch or very uneven in thickness, place them between two sheets of plastic wrap and pound them lightly with the bottom of a small heavy saucepan or rolling pin. Pat them dry with paper towels and season generously with salt and pepper. Rub each breast with 1 teaspoon olive oil.

2 Prepare an outdoor grill for medium-heat cooking or heat a ridged grill pan over medium-high heat. Place breasts on grill and cook 3 minutes; rotate breasts a quarter turn (this will give you nice grill marks) and continue to grill until the bottom is well browned, about 3 minutes more. Flip breasts with tongs and repeat on the other side. Test for doneness by using the tip of a paring knife to peek into the center of a breast; it will look moist and ivory-colored with no noticeable pink when it's done (it should register 165°F on an instant-read thermometer).

Flavor boost

- Dab with Basil Pesto (page xxxii), and sprinkle with cracked pepper.

- Drizzle with Salsa Verde (page xxxiii) that you've spiked with a few pinches of red pepper flakes.

- Slice and serve over a bed of pasta or Skinny Noodles with Classic Tomato Sauce (page xxxii).

*NOTE *that although chicken breast itself is a zero Points food, cooking it in olive oil, as recommended for grilling and pan-searing, will add 1 SmartPoints per teaspoon of olive oil used; remember to calculate the per-serving SmartPoints accordingly. Our serving and sauce suggestions will also add SmartPoints. See individual sauce recipes and consult your program guide for complete information.*

Pan-Sear

1 Start with breasts about 5 or 6 ounces each. If they're thicker than ¾ inch or very uneven in thickness, place them between two sheets of plastic wrap and pound them lightly with the bottom of a small heavy saucepan or rolling pin. Pat them dry with paper towels and season generously with salt and pepper.

2 Choose a heavy skillet that will hold your chicken in a single layer with enough space to turn the pieces easily; a 9- or 10-inch skillet typically works for two breasts, and a 12-inch skillet is usually good for four. Place the pan over medium-high heat. When hot, add 2 teaspoons oil. When the oil is hot and almost shimmers, add the chicken. Let sit undisturbed for 1 minute, then give the skillet a firm shake by the handle to loosen the breasts (this will help them cook without sticking). Cook until the underside is browned, 3 to 4 minutes.

3 Flip the breasts with tongs and repeat on the other side. Test for doneness by using the tip of a paring knife to peek into the center of a breast; it will look moist and ivory-colored with no noticeable pink when it's done (it should register 165°F on an instant-read thermometer). If it needs a few more minutes, lower the heat, cover the skillet, and test again in 2 minutes.

Flavor boost

- Cover with Quick-Cook Tomato Sauce (page xxxii) and melt mozzarella on top.

- Spoon on Italian Béchamel (page xxxiv) and top with sautéed mushrooms.

- Drizzle with Light Aïoli (page xxxiii) and sprinkle with basil and lemon zest.

Poach

1 Place chicken breasts in a deep skillet that will hold them in a single layer. Pour in enough water to just cover them and season the water generously with salt. You can add aromatics like a few smashed garlic cloves, bay leaves, or sprigs of herbs if you like. Bring to a bare simmer over high heat; lower the heat so the water just simmers and cook until breasts are no longer pink in the center, 10 to 15 minutes depending on their size and thickness.

2 Remove the breasts from the cooking liquid (save the liquid to use as broth if you like). You can enjoy the poached chicken warm, room temperature, or chilled.

Flavor boost

- Fan slices over fresh greens and drizzle with Italian Vinaigrette (page xxxv).

- Drizzle with Light Aïoli (page xxxiii) and top with capers and diced anchovy.

- Dice the chicken and toss with Artichoke Pesto (page xxxiii) and use it as a sandwich or wrap filling.

**Chicken Milanese
with Arugula**

Chicken Milanese with Arugula

POLLO ALLA MILANESE CON RUCOLA

serves 4

My kids love their nonna's chicken *cotoletti* (cutlets) and ask for them over and over again. When I make this dish, which is similar, I sometimes change up the greens: frisée for its delicate flavor, or Oakleaf lettuce for its nuttiness.

3½ tablespoons lemon juice

2½ teaspoons extra-virgin olive oil

¾ teaspoon salt

¾ teaspoon black pepper

6 cups lightly packed baby arugula

½ fennel bulb, very thinly sliced (about 1 cup)

1 cup thinly sliced red onion

1 cup grape tomatoes, quartered

2 tablespoons all-purpose flour

⅓ cup plain dried bread crumbs

1 large egg

3 large egg whites

¼ cup finely chopped fresh parsley leaves

¼ cup grated pecorino Romano cheese

4 (¼-pound) thin-sliced chicken cutlets

1 tablespoon unsalted butter

1 To make dressing, whisk together 1½ tablespoons lemon juice, 2 teaspoons oil, ¼ teaspoon salt, and ¼ teaspoon pepper in large bowl. Place arugula, fennel, onion, and tomatoes on top of dressing (do not mix). Set aside.

2 Spread flour and bread crumbs on separate sheets of wax paper. Whisk together egg, egg whites, parsley, and pecorino in large shallow bowl.

3 Sprinkle cutlets on both sides with remaining ½ teaspoon salt and ½ teaspoon pepper. Coat chicken with flour, one piece at a time, shaking off excess. Dip into egg mixture, then lightly coat with bread crumbs.

4 Heat remaining ½ teaspoon oil in large nonstick skillet over medium-high heat. Add ½ tablespoon butter and heat until melted. Add 2 chicken cutlets and cook until crumb coating is golden and chicken is cooked through, about 3 minutes per side; transfer chicken to plate and keep warm. Repeat with remaining ½ tablespoon butter and 2 chicken cutlets.

5 Toss salad with dressing until coated evenly. Place chicken on 4 plates; sprinkle with remaining 2 tablespoons lemon juice. Top evenly with salad.

Per serving (1 chicken breast with 2 cups salad): 325 Cal, 12 g Total Fat, 4 g Sat Fat, 738 mg Sod, 19 g Total Carb, 4 g Sugar, 3 g Fib, 34 g Prot.

The chicken and salad can be prepared through step 3, then refrigerated up to 2 hours ahead. When you're ready to eat, cook the chicken and toss the salad.

Porchetta-Spiced Chicken

POLLO IN PORCHETTA

serves 4 • gluten free

Porchetta is a revered and celebrated dish throughout Italy, originating from the Lazio region. The pork roast consists of a boned suckling pig fantastically seasoned with herbs and spices. Our version swaps in chicken breast for pork but keeps all the aromatic seasonings: rosemary, fennel, and a generous amount of garlic. Nothing may beat a real-deal porchetta, but this comes pretty darn close. We pair it with a simple side of gorgeous Broccolini.

¾ teaspoon fennel seeds

¼ teaspoon red pepper flakes

2 large garlic cloves, minced

2 teaspoons finely chopped fresh rosemary leaves

1 teaspoon finely chopped fresh sage leaves

½ teaspoon kosher salt

¼ teaspoon black pepper

4 (5-ounce) skinless boneless chicken breasts

2 (¾-ounce) very thin slices prosciutto, each slice halved

1 bunch (about 1 pound) Broccolini, trimmed, large stalks halved lengthwise

2 teaspoons olive oil

1 Preheat oven to 400°F. Coat small baking dish and small rimmed baking sheet with nonstick spray.

2 Toast fennel seeds and ⅛ teaspoon pepper flakes in small skillet over medium heat until fragrant, about 1 minute; transfer to plate to cool. Finely grind spices in spice mill or with mortar and pestle. Transfer spices to small bowl and stir in garlic, rosemary, sage, ¼ teaspoon salt, and the black pepper.

3 Place chicken between 2 sheets of wax paper; using rolling pin, pound each breast to about ⅛-inch thickness.

4 Remove and discard top piece of wax paper. Divide half of garlic mixture among chicken breasts. Fold in bottom and sides of each chicken breast; roll up. (Discard bottom piece of paper.) Place rolled chicken, seam side down, in prepared dish. Cover each roll with 1 piece of prosciutto; spoon remaining garlic mixture on top.

5 On prepared baking sheet, toss together Broccolini, oil, remaining ¼ teaspoon salt, and remaining ⅛ teaspoon pepper flakes. Spread Broccolini in single layer.

6 Bake chicken and Broccolini on middle rack until chicken is cooked through and Broccolini is tender, 16–18 minutes for chicken and 20–22 minutes for Broccolini.

Wine pairing:

Light red, like Chianti or Primitivo.

Per serving (1 rolled chicken breast and 3 to 4 stalks broccolini): 242 Cal, 9 g Total Fat, 2 g Sat Fat, 688 mg Sod, 9 g Total Carb, 2 g Sugar, 3 g Fib, 33 g Prot.

Porchetta-Spiced
Chicken

Chicken Parmigiano
POLLO ALLA PARMIGIANA

serves 4

Who doesn't love a lightened-up riff on an Italian-American classic? Cue the Sinatra, please.

4 (5-ounce) skinless boneless chicken breasts

2 large egg whites, lightly beaten

½ cup plain dried bread crumbs

2 teaspoons dried oregano

½ teaspoon dried crushed rosemary

½ teaspoon dried thyme

⅛ teaspoon salt, or to taste

1 teaspoon olive oil

1½ cups tomato sauce

½ cup (about 2 ounces) shredded part-skim mozzarella

2 tablespoons grated Parmesan

1 Preheat oven to 350°F. Coat large baking dish with nonstick spray.

2 Place chicken between 2 sheets of wax paper; using rolling pin, pound chicken to ¼-inch thickness.

3 Place egg whites in shallow bowl. In another shallow bowl, combine bread crumbs, oregano, rosemary, thyme, and salt. Dip chicken in egg whites, then in bread crumb mixture; turn to coat.

4 Spray large skillet with nonstick spray and add oil; heat over medium-high heat. When hot, add chicken and cook until lightly browned and cooked through, about 4 minutes per side (cook chicken in batches if necessary).

5 Pour ½ cup sauce into prepared baking dish; place chicken in dish in single layer. Pour remaining 1 cup sauce evenly over chicken; sprinkle with mozzarella and Parmesan. Bake until chicken is cooked through and cheese is bubbly, about 25 minutes.

Wine pairing:
Sturdy red, like Chianti Classico.

4 SmartPoints value

Per serving (1 piece chicken): 312 Cal, 9 g Total Fat, 3 g Sat Fat, 842 mg Sod, 16 g Total Carb, 4 g Sugar, 2 g Fib, 41 g Prot.

Slow-Cooker Chicken Cacciatore

POLLO ALLA CACCIATORA

serves 4 • gluten free

Cacciatora means "hunter-style." It's the type of food hunters would eat after getting home from a long morning in the countryside. These dishes typically combine meat and broth with onions, mushrooms, and tomatoes; bell peppers and wine are optional. The sweetness and punch of onion rounds out the dish. Throw it all in a slow cooker and you'll end up with tender, fragrant meat, melting vegetables, and an intense broth. It's low-and-slow cooking at its best.

1 (14½-ounce) can diced fire-roasted or crushed tomatoes

¼ cup red wine

1 tablespoon tomato paste

2 garlic cloves, finely chopped

¾ teaspoon dried oregano

¾ teaspoon salt, or to taste

¼ teaspoon black pepper

4 (5-ounce) skinless bone-in chicken thighs

2 cups sliced mushrooms

1 green bell pepper, thinly sliced

1 small onion, chopped

¼ cup chopped black olives

1 Whisk together tomatoes, wine, tomato paste, garlic, oregano, salt, and pepper in 3- to 5-quart slow cooker. Add chicken, mushrooms, bell pepper, and onion. Cover and cook for 6–7 hours on low or 3–3½ hours on high.

2 Sprinkle with olives and serve.

Wine pairing:

Rich red, like Amarone or Valpolicella Ripasso, both from Veneto.

Per serving (1 thigh and about ¾ cup vegetables): 247 Cal, 7 g Total Fat, 2 g Sat Fat, 862 mg Sod, 11 g Total Carb, 5 g Sugar, 3 g Fib, 32 g Prot.

**Braised Chicken Legs
with Oranges**

Braised Chicken Legs with Oranges

COSCE DI POLLO BRASATE CON ARANCE

serves 4 • gluten free

Cooking is a chance to experience something new, and share it with friends and family. I remember the grilled branzino I made at my son's baptism party, and the steamed mussels we ate at a family picnic on the beach, and the blueberry pancakes I made for the photographers and stylists on a shoot in Costa Rica. I think of all the parties my mom and dad had when I was a kid—30, 40, 50 people at a time. My dad was in charge of the decor and the alcohol, my mom in charge of the food, my brother and I in charge of the music. Friends still talk about those parties down to the details of what we ate.

This recipe can be made for a crowd. It's a braise that features oranges, the pride of Sicily. A sprinkling of meaty, buttery Sicilian Castelvetrano olives or other green olives makes an excellent garnish.

4 (8-ounce) bone-in chicken legs, skin removed

½ teaspoon kosher salt

½ teaspoon black pepper

1 teaspoon olive oil

2 seedless oranges

1½ cups chicken broth

¼ cup balsamic vinegar

⅛ teaspoon red pepper flakes

1 (12-ounce) package frozen quartered artichoke hearts, thawed

1 red bell pepper, sliced

2 teaspoons cornstarch

2 teaspoons water

12 green olives, pitted and halved

1 Sprinkle chicken with salt and black pepper. Heat oil in large nonstick skillet with tightly fitting lid over medium heat. Add chicken and brown on all sides, about 8 minutes.

2 Juice 1 orange. Trim ends of second orange and cut orange into thin round slices. Combine orange juice, broth, vinegar, and pepper flakes in large glass measuring cup; pour over chicken. Add artichokes, bell pepper, and reserved orange slices to pan. Bring to boil over high heat. Cover, lower heat, and simmer until chicken is cooked through and very tender, turning once, about 35 minutes.

3 Transfer chicken and vegetables to large shallow bowl with slotted spoon. Cover and keep warm. Combine cornstarch and water in small bowl. Stir into broth mixture in skillet. Bring to boil; stir until slightly thickened, about 1 minute. Pour over chicken or serve on the side. Garnish with olives.

7 SmartPoints value

Per serving (1 chicken leg, 1 cup vegetables, and ½ cup sauce): 385 Cal, 12 g Total Fat, 3 g Sat Fat, 945 mg Sod, 18 g Total Carb, 10 g Sugar, 6 g Fib, 48 g Prot.

Chicken Sausage Skewers

SPIEDINI DI SALSICCIA DI POLLO

serves 4 • gluten free

These skewers can be made in a flash, especially if you do the prep work ahead of time. You can assemble the dish through step 2 and refrigerate it up to 8 hours before cooking. Let the skewers come to room temperature while you prepare the grill or heat your grill pan. Enjoy!

12 ounces cooked spicy Italian chicken sausage, sliced diagonally into 16 pieces

1 large yellow bell pepper, cut into 16 pieces

1 small red onion, cut into 16 wedges

16 cherry tomatoes

¾ teaspoon salt, or to taste

¾ teaspoon black pepper, or to taste

1 tablespoon extra-virgin olive oil

1 teaspoon balsamic vinegar

1 garlic clove, finely chopped

¼ cup lightly packed fresh basil leaves, torn

1 Preheat grill to medium-high or place ridged grill pan over medium-high heat.

2 Alternate pieces of sausage, bell pepper, and onion and tomatoes on each of 8 skewers. (If using wooden skewers, soak in water at least 20 minutes to prevent charring.)

3 Lightly coat skewers with nonstick spray; sprinkle skewers all over with ½ teaspoon salt and ½ teaspoon black pepper. Grill skewers, turning occasionally, until sausage is browned and vegetables are tender, 12–15 minutes. Transfer to platter.

4 In small cup, combine oil, vinegar, garlic, remaining ¼ teaspoon salt, and remaining ¼ teaspoon black pepper; brush dressing evenly over skewers and sprinkle with basil.

Per serving (2 skewers): 178 Cal, 10 g Total Fat, 2 g Sat Fat, 998 mg Sod, 9 g Total Carb, 4 g Sugar, 2 g Fib, 15 g Prot.

Mini Turkey Meatball Gratins
POLPETTINE DI TACCHINO AL FORNO

serves 6

Every once in a while, I spend some time on a Sunday making meatballs. We eat a few that day and I freeze the rest. Then when I need them for a recipe—like these pretty mini gratins—I don't need to make them from scratch. The fully assembled gratins can also be made ahead: Just cover them with foil or plastic wrap and refrigerate for up to 4 days. When you're ready to serve, remove the wrap, cover loosely with wax paper, and reheat in a microwave on Medium-High until hot, about 3 minutes. This kind of planning helps me get dinner on the table in a snap.

1 (8-ounce) package cremini mushrooms

1 pound ground skinless turkey

¼ cup seasoned whole wheat bread crumbs

2 large eggs, lightly beaten

1 teaspoon dried oregano

¼ teaspoon salt

¼ teaspoon black pepper

1 (16-ounce) log prepared fat-free polenta, cut into 12 slices

1 (15-ounce) can crushed tomatoes

¾ cup (about 3 ounces) shredded part-skim mozzarella

2 tablespoons grated Parmesan

1 Heat oven to 400°F. Line rimmed baking sheet with foil and spray with nonstick spray.

2 Pulse mushrooms in food processor until very finely chopped. Place in large bowl and add turkey, bread crumbs, eggs, oregano, salt, and pepper. Mix well and form into 24 meatballs, using about 2 tablespoons turkey mixture for each. Place on baking sheet. Bake until meatballs are browned and cooked through, about 30 minutes.

3 Meanwhile, heat ridged grill pan over medium-high heat. Spray polenta with nonstick spray and grill until browned, about 4 minutes per side.

4 Spray 6 (8-ounce) ramekins or baking dishes with nonstick spray. Place 2 slices of polenta, 4 meatballs, and about ¼ cup tomatoes in each. Sprinkle each with 2 tablespoons mozzarella and 1 teaspoon Parmesan. Place ramekins on baking sheet. Bake until cheese melts and filling is heated through, about 10 minutes.

Per serving (1 gratin): 276 Cal, 11 g Total Fat, 4 g Sat Fat, 678 mg Sod, 20 g Total Carb, 3 g Sugar, 2 g Fib, 24 g Prot.

Roast Turkey
Breast with Sage

Roast Turkey Breast with Sage
PETTO DI TACCHINO ARROSTO ALLA SALVIA

serves 10 • gluten free

I've been lucky enough to enjoy delicious meals all over Italy, and the one thing I've noticed most Italian cooks do—besides make food in a wood-burning oven and use local, seasonal ingredients—is never, ever hurry a meal. Making food and enjoying it will take as long as it needs to. I know the idea of taking it slow can send some people running for the hills. Life is stressful and we're constantly juggling resources, trying to save time and energy. What gives me pause, though, is that food is where we often make a compromise, so I'm constantly trying to find effortless ways to get dinner on the table and make the time to savor it. This roast turkey will take a bit of time to cook, but most of it is hands-off. The fresh sage lends a lemony, if slightly bitter, taste, and the orange juice infuses sweetness.

1 (5-pound) bone-in turkey breast

1 tablespoon unsalted butter, softened

1 tablespoon olive oil

3 garlic cloves, minced

3 tablespoons chopped fresh sage

½ teaspoon finely grated lemon zest

¾ teaspoon kosher salt

⅛ teaspoon coarsely ground black pepper

1 cup chicken broth

¾ cup orange juice

¼ cup water

1 tablespoon cornstarch

2 teaspoons lemon juice

1 Position rack in middle of oven; preheat oven to 400°F.

2 Pat turkey dry. Combine butter, oil, garlic, 2 tablespoons sage, the lemon zest, salt, and pepper in small bowl. Loosen skin on breast and rub 2 tablespoons of mixture under skin. Rub remaining mixture over turkey. Place on rack in roasting pan. Roast until browned and instant-read thermometer inserted in thickest part of breast but not touching bone registers 165°F, about 1¼ hours. Transfer turkey to cutting board and let rest 15 minutes.

3 Pour juices from roasting pan into glass measuring cup; allow to sit until fat rises to top.

4 Meanwhile, combine broth and orange juice in small saucepan. Bring to boil, reduce heat, and simmer until reduced to ⅔ cup, about 8 minutes. Spoon off fat from pan juices and add remaining liquid to saucepan. Combine water and cornstarch in small bowl; stir into orange juice mixture. Bring to boil; boil until thickened, about 1 minute. Stir in lemon juice and remaining 1 tablespoon sage. Slice breast into 20 slices. Remove skin before eating. Serve with sauce.

Wine pairing:

Celebratory, medium-bodied red, like Barbera d'Alba or Barbera d'Asti.

Per serving (2 slices turkey without skin and 2 tablespoons sauce): 227 Cal, 6 g Fat, 2 g Sat Fat, 591 mg Sod, 5 g Total Carb, 3 g Sugar, 0 g Fib, 39 g Prot.

Chapter 7

Beef, Veal, and Lamb (manzo, vitello e agnello)

Classic Steak Florentine
BISTECCA ALLA FIORENTINA

serves 4 • gluten free • under 20 minutes

Like risotto Milanese, pesto Genovese, Caprese salad, and *ragù alla Bolognese*, steak Florentine is a recipe that's connected to a specific place and culture. Eating it for the first time allowed me to experience the simple, natural, yet refined cuisine of Tuscany.

Although grilling is now considered the "modern" healthy way to cook meat, it is a very traditional Tuscan method. I find it appealing because although I don't cook steak often, I want to get it absolutely right when I do: How do I achieve different degrees of doneness? What is a healthy balance of lean meat to fat? Which seasonings and herbs enhance the meat as it cooks? How long do I let the meat rest? It's a little intimidating. Fortunately, generations of Tuscans have answered all my questions.

1 teaspoon dried basil

1 teaspoon dried oregano

½ teaspoon fennel seeds, crushed

¾ teaspoon salt

½ teaspoon cracked black pepper

2 (1-pound) lean T-bone steaks, ¾-inch thick, trimmed

Lemon wedges

2 teaspoons extra-virgin olive oil

1 Combine basil, oregano, fennel seeds, salt, and pepper in small bowl. Rub mixture over both sides of each steak.

2 Preheat grill to medium-high or place large ridged grill pan over medium-high heat. Grill steaks, turning once, until instant-read thermometer inserted into side of each steak (not touching bone) registers 145°F for medium, 8–10 minutes.

3 Transfer steaks to cutting board and let rest 5 minutes. Squeeze lemon over steaks and slice. Drizzle with oil and serve.

Wine pairing:

Rich, Tuscan classic, like Barolo or Barbera.

10 SmartPoints value™

Per serving (½ steak): 344 Cal, 24 g Total Fat, 10 g Sat Fat, 493 mg Sod, 2 g Total Carb, 0 g Sugar, 1 g Fib, 29 g Prot.

To crush the fennel seeds, wrap them in plastic wrap and place them on a cutting board. Rap them several times with a meat mallet or the bottom of a heavy skillet.

Classic Steak
Florentine

**Stracotto with
Lemon Gremolata**

Stracotto with Lemon Gremolata

STRACOTTO CON GREMOLATA

serves 6

Stracotto is Italy's version of pot roast, and the name literally means "overcooked." It's the perfect name for meat that's slow braised and disappears into a tomatoey–mushroomy red-wine sauce. The sharpness of the lemon gremolata acts as a foil to the richness of the meat. I make this in the deepest days of winter.

Use a deep, heavy casserole or enameled cast-iron pot with a wide surface area. Nonstick pots won't work because they prevent caramelized meat juices from forming at the bottom of the pot.

1 (2-pound) lean beef chuck roast, trimmed

1½ teaspoons salt

½ teaspoon black pepper

2 tablespoons all-purpose flour

1 tablespoon olive oil

3 red onions, thinly sliced

2 large garlic cloves, minced

1 (8-ounce) package sliced white mushrooms

1 (14½-ounce) can crushed tomatoes

1 cup dry red wine

½ cup chopped fresh parsley leaves

Grated zest of 1 lemon

1 Sprinkle beef with salt and pepper; coat evenly with flour, pressing lightly so it adheres.

2 Heat oil in Dutch oven or large saucepan over medium heat. Add beef and cook until browned on all sides, about 10 minutes; transfer to plate. Add onions to pan and cook, stirring, until softened, about 5 minutes. Add half of garlic and cook, stirring, until fragrant, about 30 seconds.

3 Add mushrooms, tomatoes, and wine to pan; bring to boil, scraping up browned bits from bottom of pan. Reduce heat and simmer until mushrooms are softened, about 5 minutes. Return beef and any accumulated juices to pan; reduce heat and simmer, covered, stirring occasionally and turning beef every 30 minutes, until beef is fork-tender, about 2 hours. Transfer beef to cutting board and keep warm.

4 Bring vegetable mixture to boil over medium-high heat; boil, stirring frequently, until liquid is thickened, about 12 minutes.

5 Meanwhile, to make gremolata, stir together parsley, lemon zest, and remaining garlic in small bowl. Cut beef on diagonal into 12 slices. Serve sprinkled with gremolata and accompanied by vegetables with sauce.

Per serving (2 slices beef, generous ⅔ cup vegetables with sauce, and 1½ tablespoons gremolata): 323 Cal, 12 g Total Fat, 4 g Sat Fat, 810 mg Sod, 14 g Total Carb, 5 g Sugar, 3 g Fib, 35 g Prot.

Beef Braised in Red Wine

BRASATO AL VINO ROSSO

serves 8 • gluten free

One of the reasons I cook is because I get satisfaction from working with my hands. I feel industrious and connected to my physical world, which is increasingly rare given our cubicle lives and hours spent on electronic devices. The pleasure is even greater when I cook with someone by my side—like I did with my Zia Santa. Even in the heat of the summer, my aunt wore widow's black with a wool cardigan, but boy, oh boy, could she cook.

This fabulous braise gives me plenty of ingredients to tinker with, though it's not difficult to make. This dish is traditionally prepared with Barolo, one of Italy's finest red wines but a pricey one. Feel free to substitute another full-bodied red wine, like Valpolicella or Primitivo.

1 (2½-pound) bottom round roast

½ teaspoon kosher salt

¼ teaspoon black pepper

2 ounces (about ¼ cup) diced pancetta

2 carrots, diced

1 large onion, chopped

1 small fennel bulb, chopped

2 large garlic cloves, finely chopped

1½ teaspoons chopped fresh rosemary leaves

2 teaspoons chopped fresh thyme leaves

2 tablespoons tomato paste

1½ cups dry red wine

1 (14½-ounce) can crushed tomatoes

1 cup beef broth

1 Preheat oven to 325°F.

2 Spray Dutch oven or large saucepan with nonstick spray and set over medium-high heat. Sprinkle beef with salt and pepper. Add beef to Dutch oven and cook until browned on all sides, about 10 minutes. Transfer to plate.

3 Add pancetta to Dutch oven, reduce heat, and cook, stirring frequently, until browned and crisp, about 3 minutes. Add carrots, onion, and fennel; cook, stirring occasionally, until softened, about 6 minutes. Add garlic, rosemary, and 1 teaspoon thyme; cook, stirring constantly, until fragrant, about 30 seconds. Add tomato paste and cook, stirring, about 1 minute. Add wine, scraping up browned bits from bottom of pan. Stir in tomatoes and broth; bring to boil. Add beef and any accumulated juices. Cover and bake until beef is fork-tender, about 3 hours, turning beef halfway through cooking time.

4 Transfer beef to cutting board and tent loosely with foil. Skim off and discard fat from cooking liquid; stir in remaining 1 teaspoon thyme. Cook over medium-high heat until sauce is thickened, about 15 minutes. Cut beef across grain into 16 slices and serve with sauce.

Wine pairing:

Barolo, Valpolicella, or Primitivo (for cooking and drinking).

Per serving (2 slices beef and generous ½ cup sauce): 378 Cal, 19 g Total Fat, 7 g Sat Fat, 462 mg Sod, 10 g Total Carb, 4 g Sugar, 2 g Fib, 32 g Prot.

Beef Spiedini
SPIEDINI DI MANZO

serves 4

Spiedini are Italy's version of skewers or kebabs. Chicken, beef, fish, or vegetables are skewered on either metal sticks or sprigs of rosemary. Here, we make ours with beef that's seasoned, breaded, and rolled, then skewered and broiled. You can grill them if you like, over medium heat until browned, for about 6 minutes. Essentially it's food on a stick. Who doesn't love that?

¼ cup Italian-seasoned panko (bread crumbs)

3 tablespoons grated pecorino Romano cheese

2 tablespoons chopped fresh parsley leaves

1 garlic clove, finely chopped

1 pound thin-cut lean top round steak (8 slices), trimmed

½ teaspoon salt

¼ teaspoon black pepper

5 tablespoons plus 1 teaspoon shredded part-skim mozzarella

1 small red onion, cut into thin wedges

16 bay leaves, preferably fresh

6 cups lightly packed baby arugula

½ lemon

1 Combine bread crumbs, pecorino, parsley, and garlic in small bowl.

2 Cut each piece of steak in half crosswise to make 16 slices. Pound beef slices between pieces of plastic wrap until ⅛ inch thick. Sprinkle with salt and pepper. Sprinkle bread crumb mixture evenly over beef slices and press lightly so it adheres. Sprinkle each slice with 1 teaspoon shredded mozzarella. Roll up each beef slice beginning with a short side.

3 Preheat broiler. Line rimmed baking sheet with foil and spray foil with nonstick spray.

4 To assemble, thread 1 beef roll on metal skewer, piercing skewer through the top and bottom of roll. Skewer a piece of onion, then a bay leaf, then another beef roll, onion piece, and bay leaf. Lay skewer on prepared pan. Repeat with remaining ingredients to make 8 skewers. Spray with nonstick spray.

5 Broil skewers 6 inches from heat, turning once, until beef is lightly charred in places and cooked through, about 8 minutes.

6 Arrange 1½ cups arugula on each of 4 plates; squeeze lemon juice evenly over arugula. Top each plate with 2 skewers; remove bay leaves before eating.

 Per serving (2 skewers and 1½ cups arugula): 272 Cal, 12 g Total Fat, 5 g Sat Fat, 545 mg Sod, 9 g Total Carb, 2 g Sugar, 1 g Fib, 30 g Prot.

Tuscan Beef Stew with Polenta
SPEZZATINO ALLA TOSCANA CON POLENTA

serves 4 • gluten free

This is a fragrant beef stew made with onions, carrots, and celery. Cannellini beans add body, and the tomato paste adds depth and sweetness. Serve it over wet and creamy polenta, perfect to soak up the juices.

STEW

½ pound lean beef chuck or other lean stew meat, cut into 1-inch chunks

1 teaspoon olive oil

1 large carrot, sliced

1 large celery stalk, diced

1 small onion, diced

4 garlic cloves, finely chopped

1 tablespoon tomato paste

2 tablespoons balsamic vinegar

3 cups reduced-sodium beef broth

1 cup chopped drained canned whole tomatoes

2 fresh rosemary sprigs

1 bay leaf

¼ teaspoon salt, or to taste

½ teaspoon black pepper

1 (19-ounce) can cannellini (white kidney) beans, rinsed and drained

1 tablespoon finely chopped fresh parsley leaves (optional)

POLENTA

1½ cups chicken broth

1½ cups water

1 large garlic clove, minced

1 teaspoon minced fresh rosemary

¼ teaspoon kosher salt

¾ cup instant polenta

1 To make stew, spray large saucepan or Dutch oven with nonstick spray and place over medium-high heat. Add beef and cook, stirring occasionally, until browned, 5–6 minutes. Remove from saucepan and set aside.

2 Add oil, carrot, celery, and onion to pan. Cook, stirring frequently, until vegetables soften, about 5 minutes. Add garlic and cook until fragrant, about 1 minute. Add tomato paste and cook, stirring, 1 minute. Add vinegar and cook 30 seconds.

3 Add broth and tomatoes to pot. Scrape bottom of pan with spoon to release any browned bits. Stir in rosemary sprigs, bay leaf, salt, pepper, and reserved beef. Bring to boil. Reduce heat, cover, and simmer 40 minutes. Remove lid and stir in beans; simmer uncovered until meat is very tender and stew is thickened, about 30 minutes more. Remove from heat, discard rosemary sprigs and bay leaf, and sprinkle with parsley, if using. Let sit, covered, while you make polenta.

4 To make polenta, combine broth, water, garlic, rosemary, and salt in medium saucepan and bring to boil. Slowly whisk in polenta. Lower heat to medium-low and continue to stir 3 minutes. Serve with stew.

Per serving (generous 1 cup stew and ½ cup polenta): 364 Cal, 5 Total Fat, 2 g Sat Fat, 1,572 mg Sod, 52 g Total Carb, 6 g Sugar, 9 g Fib, 27 g Prot.

Tuscan Beef Stew
with Polenta

**Spaghetti Squash
with Meatballs**

Spaghetti Squash with Meatballs

ZUCCA SPAGHETTI CON POLPETTE

serves 4 • gluten free

A playful riff on spaghetti and meatballs: In this case spaghetti squash stands in for noodles, and meatballs are enhanced with zucchini and mushrooms for a lighter, fluffier texture. We like the low SmartPoints value, too.

1 small (2-pound) spaghetti squash, halved

1 pound ground lean beef (7% fat or less)

1 cup shredded zucchini

1 cup finely chopped cremini mushrooms

2 scallions, finely chopped

1 garlic clove, minced

1 tablespoon chopped fresh parsley

½ teaspoon salt

½ teaspoon olive oil

1 onion, chopped

⅛ teaspoon red pepper flakes

3 cups basil-and-garlic tomato sauce

¼ cup fresh basil leaves, thinly sliced

1 Preheat oven to 375°F. Use spoon to scoop out and discard seeds from middle of each squash half. Place squash cut side down in roasting pan. Pour ½ cup water into pan. Bake until squash is tender when pressed, 30–35 minutes. Let cool slightly.

2 Meanwhile, mix together beef, zucchini, mushrooms, scallions, garlic, parsley, and salt in large bowl until combined. With damp hands, shape mixture into 12 meatballs.

3 Heat oil in large nonstick skillet with lid over medium heat. Add 6 meatballs and cook, turning occasionally, until browned on all sides, about 8 minutes. With slotted spoon, transfer meatballs to plate. Repeat with remaining 6 meatballs.

4 Add onion to skillet and cook, covered, stirring occasionally, until tender, about 5 minutes. Add pepper flakes and cook, stirring, until fragrant, about 30 seconds. Stir in tomato sauce and meatballs; bring to boil. Reduce heat; cover and simmer until meatballs are cooked through, about 20 minutes, turning meatballs once halfway through cooking time.

5 With fork, scrape out squash pulp and divide evenly among 4 bowls. Top evenly with meatballs and sauce and sprinkle with basil.

Per serving (3 meatballs, ¾ cup sauce, and ¾ cup squash): 345 Cal, 12 g Total Fat, 4 g Sat Fat, 1,304 mg Sod, 32 g Total Carb, 8 g Sugar, 4 g Fib, 29 g Prot.

Italian Beef-and-Pork Meat Loaf

POLPETTONE DI MANZO E MAIALE

serves 8

Here's our Italian take on meat loaf. This version is flecked with portobello mushrooms, carrots, scallions, and parsley, and seasoned with fennel and lemon zest. If you want to make the recipe ahead and freeze it, bake it without the tomato sauce topping, let it cool completely, then wrap it in heavy-duty foil and freeze up to 3 months. Thaw it in the refrigerator overnight, brush with tomato sauce, and reheat in a 350°F oven until hot, about 30 minutes.

1 portobello mushroom, cut into chunks

5 scallions, coarsely chopped

½ cup lightly packed fresh parsley sprigs

1 carrot, coarsely chopped

4 garlic cloves, crushed

1½ teaspoons grated lemon zest

1 teaspoon anise or fennel seeds

1 pound ground lean beef (7% fat or less)

½ pound ground lean pork

½ cup Italian-seasoned bread crumbs

1 large egg

½ teaspoon salt

½ teaspoon black pepper

⅓ cup tomato sauce

1 Preheat oven to 375°F. Line baking sheet with foil and set aside.

2 Pulse mushroom, scallions, parsley, carrot, garlic, lemon zest, and anise seeds in food processor to make fine-textured paste, scraping down sides of bowl once or twice. Transfer mixture to large bowl.

3 Crumble beef and pork into same bowl; add bread crumbs, egg, salt, and pepper; mix until combined. Transfer meat mixture to prepared baking sheet and form into 10 x 4 x 2-inch loaf. Brush tomato sauce over loaf.

4 Bake until meat loaf is cooked through and center of loaf registers 160°F on instant-read thermometer, 50–60 minutes. Let stand 10 minutes before cutting into 16 slices.

Wine pairing:

Simple red, like Chianti or Sangiovese.

Per serving (2 slices): 201 Cal, 10 g Total Fat, 3 g Sat Fat, 368 mg Sod, 9 g Total Carb, 1 g Sugar, 1 g Fib, 20 g Prot.

Veal Scallopine Milanese
COTOLETTE DI VITELLO ALLA MILANESE

serves 4

Before there were chicken cutlets in the DiMasi household, there was veal scallopine Milanese. My mom's butcher would slice the scallopine and she'd cook them once or twice a week. This recipe is similar to Chicken Milanese, and like the chicken version it makes for a quick weeknight dinner: Because the meat is sliced very thin, the cooking time is brief. Just before digging in, I drizzle the cutlets with a generous squeeze of lemon.

3 tablespoons instant flour (such as Wondra) or all-purpose flour

1 teaspoon salt

1 large egg

2 tablespoons water

⅔ cup Italian-seasoned bread crumbs

8 (2-ounce) lean veal scallopine, trimmed, ⅛ to ¼ inch thick

3 teaspoons olive oil

2 red onions, halved and thinly sliced

1 (5-ounce) container baby arugula

¼ teaspoon black pepper

Lemon wedges for serving

1 Place 3 sheets wax paper on work surface. Combine flour and ½ teaspoon salt on first sheet of paper. Beat egg with water in small bowl. Place bread crumbs on second sheet of paper. Working one piece at a time, first coat veal in flour, then dip in egg, then coat in crumbs. Place on remaining wax paper sheet.

2 Heat 1½ teaspoons oil in large skillet over medium heat. Cook veal in two batches until golden brown, 2–3 minutes per side, adding remaining 1½ teaspoon oil for second batch. Remove from skillet and drain on paper towels. Keep warm.

3 Add onions to skillet, raise heat to medium-high, and cook, tossing frequently, until softened, about 4 minutes. Transfer to large bowl. Add arugula, remaining ½ teaspoon salt, and the pepper and toss.

4 Divide salad among 4 plates and top each with 2 scallopine. Serve with lemon wedges to squeeze over top.

Wine pairing:

Fresh rosé (*rosato*) or light red, like Dolcetto.

Per serving (2 pieces veal and 1½ cups salad): 307 Cal, 10 g Total Fat, 2 g Sat Fat, 947 mg Sod, 25 g Total Carb, 4 g Sugar, 3 g Fib, 30 g Prot.

Veal Involtini with Asparagus

INVOLTINI DI VITELLO E ASPARAGI

serves 4

Involtini means something that is stuffed and rolled. In this recipe, veal cutlets are wrapped around silky prosciutto, tangy provolone, and crisp asparagus. The entire bundle is coated in breading then pan-fried. I usually make these when I'm entertaining over the weekend or for a holiday, when good friends are gathered in the kitchen for an informal dinner.

8 asparagus spears

¼ cup lightly packed chopped fresh parsley leaves

1 garlic clove, minced

8 (2-ounce) veal cutlets, pounded ¼ inch thick

¼ teaspoon kosher salt

¼ teaspoon black pepper

4 (½-ounce) slices prosciutto, trimmed and cut in half crosswise

4 (¾-ounce) slices reduced-fat provolone cheese, halved

¼ cup plain dried bread crumbs

2 teaspoons olive oil

4 lemon wedges

1 Trim asparagus spears so each is about 5 inches long. Bring small saucepan filled two-thirds with salted water to a boil. Add spears; boil until spears are crisp-tender, about 3 minutes. Drain and rinse under cold water. Drain again and pat spears dry.

2 Combine parsley and garlic in cup. Sprinkle both sides of cutlets with salt and pepper. Top each slice with 1 piece prosciutto, 1 piece provolone, ½ tablespoon parsley mixture, and 1 asparagus spear. Roll up each cutlet and secure seam with toothpick. Spread bread crumbs on sheet of wax paper; coat rolls with bread crumbs.

3 Heat oil in large nonstick skillet over medium heat. Add rolls and cook, turning occasionally, until browned and cooked through, 8–10 minutes. Remove toothpicks and serve rolls with lemon wedges.

Wine pairing:

Medium-dry Pinot Grigio or rosé (*rosato*).

Per serving (2 rolls): 324 Cal, 15 g Total Fat, 6 g Sat Fat, 896 mg Sod, 10 g Total Carb, 2 g Sugar, 2 g Fib, 38 g Prot.

Veal Involtini
with Asparagus

Veal with Tuna Sauce
VITELLO TONNATO

serves 6 • gluten free

This classic, elegant dish hails from Italy's Piedmont region, where it's a summer favorite. Poached veal is chilled, then covered in a creamy tuna sauce made with anchovies, capers, and lemon. Make sure to refrigerate the finished dish long enough for the meat to macerate in the sauce and for the flavors to blend. Bring it to room temperature just before serving.

1 (2 ¼-pound) boneless veal shoulder, trimmed, rolled, and tied by your butcher

10 flat anchovy fillets, drained

2 garlic cloves, thinly sliced

3 cups water

1 (14 ½-ounce) can chicken broth

1 cup dry white wine

1 onion, quartered

2 carrots, sliced

1 celery stalk, sliced

1 bay leaf

1 (5-ounce) can tuna in olive oil, drained

⅓ cup reduced-fat mayonnaise

1 tablespoon lemon juice

⅛ teaspoon black pepper

2 tablespoons drained capers

3 tablespoons thinly sliced fresh parsley leaves

1 With sharp knife, make slits all over veal. Coarsely chop 6 anchovies; insert chopped anchovies and garlic into slits.

2 Transfer veal to 4-quart Dutch oven or large saucepan. Add water, broth, wine, onion, carrots, celery, and bay leaf and bring just to boil. Skim off and discard foam. Reduce heat; cover and simmer until veal is tender, about 1½ hours.

3 Remove pan from heat and let veal cool in broth 1 hour. Transfer veal to plate and refrigerate until cooled completely, about 2 hours. Strain broth through fine sieve and discard solids. Transfer ⅓ cup broth to blender (save remaining broth for another use). Add tuna, remaining 4 anchovies, the mayonnaise, lemon juice, pepper, and 1 tablespoon capers to blender; puree until smooth, adding more broth if sauce is too thick.

4 Cut veal into 18 slices. Arrange overlapping slices on platter large enough to hold veal in one layer. Pour sauce over veal; cover and refrigerate at least 1 hour or up to 24 hours. Serve chilled or at room temperature, sprinkled with parsley and remaining 1 tablespoon capers.

Per serving (3 slices veal and about 2½ tablespoons sauce): 360 Cal, 13 g Total Fat, 3 g Sat Fat, 894 mg Sod, 7 g Total Carb, 3 g Sugar, 1 g Fib, 45 g Prot.

Leg of Lamb with Rosemary

COSCIOTTO DI AGNELLO CON ROSMARINO

serves 8 • gluten free

This recipe might sound a bit complicated, maybe even intimidating, but I urge you to try it. Ask your butcher for a well-trimmed leg of lamb, bring it home, and lay it flat on a cutting board. Rub it with a mixture of shallots, garlic, fresh rosemary, lemon, and some salt and pepper; then roll and tie it with kitchen string. Let it sit in the refrigerator for at least 8 hours. Put it in a hot oven and roast—no need to poke, prod, stir, or turn it over. When it's done you'll get mouth watering, incredibly juicy meat with a crisp, golden crust. I like to serve it with an herbaceous sauce.

LAMB

1 (2½-pound) lean boneless leg of lamb, trimmed

2 shallots, finely chopped

3 garlic cloves, finely chopped

2 tablespoons chopped fresh rosemary

1 teaspoon grated lemon zest

2 tablespoons lemon juice

½ teaspoon kosher salt

¼ teaspoon coarsely ground black pepper

HERB SAUCE

2 garlic cloves, coarsely chopped

¾ cup lightly packed fresh mint leaves

¼ cup lightly packed fresh parsley leaves

2 tablespoons extra-virgin olive oil

1 tablespoon red-wine vinegar

¼ teaspoon kosher salt

⅛ teaspoon red pepper flakes, or to taste

2 tablespoons water

1 To make lamb, place leg flat on cutting board. Combine shallots, garlic, rosemary, lemon zest and juice, salt, and pepper in small bowl. Spread mixture on lamb. Roll lamb up and tie at 2- to 3-inch intervals with kitchen string. Cover and refrigerate 8–24 hours.

2 Remove lamb from refrigerator and allow to come to room temperature before roasting.

3 Preheat oven to 400°F. Place lamb on rack in roasting pan. Roast 20 minutes. Reduce temperature to 350°F and roast until instant-read thermometer inserted in thickest part of lamb registers 145°F for medium, about 35 minutes longer. Remove from oven; tent with foil and let rest 15 minutes.

4 Meanwhile, to make herb sauce, combine all ingredients in food processor and pulse until very finely chopped.

5 Cut lamb into 16 slices and serve with herb sauce.

Wine pairing:

Primitivo, or splurge on a Brunello or Amarone.

Per serving (2 slices lamb and 2 tablespoons sauce): 213 Cal, 8 g Total Fat, 2 g Sat Fat, 295 mg Sod, 3 g Total Carb, 1 g Sugar, 1 g Fib, 31 g Prot.

Roman-Style
Lamb Chops

Roman-Style Lamb Chops
ABBACCHIO ALLA ROMANA

serves 4 • gluten free

This method of preparing lamb chops is typical of Rome and Southern Italy and is sometimes called *scottadito*, or "finger-burning," because the chops are so irresistible that diners might snatch them hot off the grill and eat them straight from the bone. Have extra napkins on hand because diners may be too impatient to bother with knife and fork!

Since I'm already grilling, I like to serve these chops with spring onions—after a quick charring, they pair perfectly with the grilled lamb.

2 tablespoons chopped fresh rosemary leaves

4 garlic cloves, finely chopped

1 teaspoon grated lemon zest

½ teaspoon salt

¼ teaspoon red pepper flakes

2 tablespoons lemon juice

1 tablespoon olive oil

8 (3-ounce) lean lamb rib chops, trimmed

4 lemon wedges

1 Combine rosemary, garlic, lemon zest, salt, and pepper flakes on cutting board. Chop with a heavy knife until mixture resembles a paste. Scrape into small bowl and stir in lemon juice and olive oil.

2 Rub mixture all over lamb chops to coat well. Place on plate and cover with plastic wrap. Marinate in refrigerator at least 2 hours or up to 8 hours.

3 Preheat grill to medium-high or place ridged grill pan over medium-high heat.

4 Grill lamb chops, turning once, until browned and instant-read thermometer inserted in side of each chop registers 145°F for medium, 3–4 minutes per side. Serve with lemon wedges.

Per serving (2 chops): 204 Cal, 10 g Total Fat, 3 g Sat Fat, 368 mg Sod, 4 g Total Carb, 1 g Sugar, 1 g Fib, 24 g Prot.

The ancient and the old

Italy was not unified until 1861, and a long history of independent states and territories has resulted in a land that sometimes seems less like a country and more like a clutch of regions. Like its food, Italy's architecture is a feast for the eyes.

1. Standing in Gerace, a medieval town that sits above a vertical rock.

2. A café gets ready to open.

3. Nuns at the entrance to Gerace, with the Ionian Sea in the distance. The town can be reached only through four gates (originally there were 12).

Grand cities

When you picture Italy, it's often the main cities and their iconic images that come to mind: the gondolas and town squares of Venice, the opera house and design houses in Milan, the art and domes of Florence, or the ancient ruins and churches in Rome.

Though these cities are grand, they're accessible. Italy invites you to interact, pause, and reflect. Walking through the streets, you realize that you are in a country that has inherited one of the greatest ancient civilizations in the world, and yet is completely modern, especially when it comes to fashion, design, architecture, sports cars, and yes, food.

1. A canal in Venice.

2. Gold dome in Amalfi.

3. The view from St. Peter's Basilica in Vatican City, the world's largest Catholic church.

Pork (maiale)

Pork Braciole with Prosciutto
ROTOLO DI MAIALE CON PROSCIUTTO

serves 6 • *gluten free*

From chops and loin to prosciutto and pancetta, pork is ubiquitous in Italy. My dad would cook pig's feet, cheeks, and ears in the winter and pack them in jars that he'd keep cool in our attic or garage. We'd also cure soppressata, capocollo, and *salamini* (little salami) by hanging them from the rafters.

One of my favorite ways to eat pork is *braciole* (stuffed meat rolls). A rich mixture of Swiss chard, sun-dried tomatoes, capers, and pine nuts with sliced prosciutto is rolled in pork loin, then roasted for 45 minutes. It's a perfect meal for hungry friends or date night.

2 teaspoons olive oil

1 onion, diced

2 garlic cloves, finely chopped

⅛ teaspoon red pepper flakes

½ bunch (6 ounces) Swiss chard, tough stems removed, leaves chopped

½ teaspoon kosher salt

½ teaspoon cracked black pepper

¼ cup sun-dried tomatoes (not packed in oil), thinly sliced

1 tablespoon drained capers

1 tablespoon toasted pine nuts

1 teaspoon chopped fresh rosemary

1 (2-pound) piece lean center-cut boneless pork loin, trimmed

1 ounce thinly sliced prosciutto

1 Preheat oven to 400°F.

2 Heat oil in large skillet over medium heat. Add onion and cook, stirring occasionally, until translucent, about 5 minutes. Stir in garlic and pepper flakes and cook 1 minute. Add Swiss chard, ¼ teaspoon salt, and ¼ teaspoon pepper; cover and cook until chard is tender, about 3 minutes. Stir in sun-dried tomatoes, capers, pine nuts, and rosemary. Cool.

3 Slice pork loin horizontally (lengthwise), cutting to within ½ inch of side. Open pork loin like a book and pound gently with bottom of small heavy skillet until loin is even in thickness (about ½ inch thick).

4 Spread chard mixture evenly over pork, leaving ½-inch border around edges. Top evenly with prosciutto slices. Roll up loin securely; tie at 2-inch intervals with kitchen string. Sprinkle with remaining ¼ teaspoon salt and remaining ¼ teaspoon pepper.

5 Place pork in small roasting pan lined with foil. Roast until instant-read thermometer inserted into center of pork registers 145°F, about 45 minutes. Transfer to platter, tent with foil, and let rest 10 minutes. Cut into 12 slices.

Wine pairing:
Light red, like Dolcetto.

Per serving (2 slices): 271 Cal, 11 g Total Fat, 4 g Sat Fat, 495 mg Sod, 5 g Total Carb, 2 g Sugar, 1 g Fib, 36 g Prot.

Pork Braciole
with Prosciutto

Porchetta-Style Pork Loin
LONZA DI MAIALE IN PORCHETTA

serves 8 • gluten free

Porchetta is classic street food in Italy. This juicy, tender pork roast is also a popular dish served during the holidays, or thinly sliced and layered into rolls for a picnic. You'll find many variations, but most of them use fennel, garlic, rosemary, and sage to season the pork. Onions are scattered in the pan and cooked with the porchetta. We use cipollini onions as they are a favorite Italian variety with a rich, earthy flavor. You can substitute pearl or baby onions, or use halved shallots.

6 garlic cloves, finely chopped

1½ tablespoons chopped fresh rosemary leaves

1½ tablespoons chopped fresh sage leaves

2 teaspoons fennel seeds, coarsely chopped

3 teaspoons olive oil

1 teaspoon kosher salt

1 (2-pound) piece lean boneless center-cut pork loin, trimmed

½ teaspoon black pepper

6 thin slices (about 3 ounces) pancetta

1 pound cipollini onions or other very small onions, peeled

1 cup chicken broth

⅔ cup dry white wine

1 Combine garlic, rosemary, sage, fennel, 1 teaspoon oil, and ½ teaspoon salt in mini–food processor and pulse to chunky paste, or chop on cutting board with heavy knife.

2 Butterfly pork by placing on work surface with short end facing you. Starting at top of loin, use sharp knife to score down length of loin toward you, creating a 1-inch flap. Continue slicing down loin, opening pork like a book but not cutting all the way through, until you have rectangular slab about 1 inch thick.

3 Sprinkle both sides of pork with pepper and remaining ½ teaspoon salt. Spread herb paste over cut surface. Roll pork up tightly. Overlap pancetta on top and tie at 2-inch intervals with kitchen string. Place pork in roasting pan; scatter onions around pork and drizzle with remaining 2 teaspoons oil. (Can be refrigerated up to 1 day.)

4 Preheat oven to 450°F. Pour ⅓ cup broth and ⅓ cup wine into pan. Roast 10 minutes; reduce temperature to 400°F and roast until instant-read thermometer inserted into center registers 145°F, about 30 minutes. Leave oven on. Transfer pork and onions to cutting board; tent with foil.

5 Pour pan drippings into cup and spoon off fat. Add remaining ⅔ cup broth, remaining ⅓ cup wine, and skimmed drippings back into roasting pan, scraping bottom of pan with wooden spoon. Return pan to oven and allow liquid to reduce by half, about 12 minutes. Stir accumulated juices from cutting board into sauce. Remove twine from roast. Cut into 16 slices. Serve with onions and pan sauce.

6 SmartPoints value™

Per serving (2 slices pork, about 3 onions, and 1 tablespoon sauce): 282 Cal, 14 g Total Fat, 4 g Sat Fat, 460 mg Sod, 7 g Total Carb, 3 g Sugar, 1 g Fib, 28 g Prot.

Herb-Roasted Pork Primavera

ARROSTO DI MAIALE AGLI AROMI

serves 6 • *gluten free*

There's no better way to settle differences and defuse arguments than by sharing a good meal. My mom has been saying this for years: Food is what keeps families and friends together. I urge you to consider this succulent, herb-crusted roast for your next family gathering.

2 teaspoons chopped fresh
rosemary leaves

2 teaspoons chopped fresh
thyme leaves

1 garlic clove, minced

½ teaspoon black pepper

¾ teaspoon salt

1 (1½-pound) piece lean
boneless center-cut
pork loin, trimmed

2 teaspoons olive oil

1 pound small red
potatoes, halved

1 (9-ounce) package frozen
artichoke hearts, thawed
and patted dry

1 cup baby-cut carrots

1 Preheat oven to 450°F. Spray large shallow roasting pan with nonstick spray.

2 Stir together rosemary, thyme, garlic, pepper, and ¼ teaspoon salt in cup. Rub mixture all over pork. Heat 1 teaspoon oil in large skillet over medium-high heat. Add pork and cook until browned on all sides, about 5 minutes.

3 Transfer pork to prepared roasting pan. Toss together potatoes, artichoke hearts, carrots, remaining 1 teaspoon oil, and remaining ½ teaspoon salt in large bowl. Scatter vegetables around pork. Roast, stirring vegetables once or twice, until instant-read thermometer inserted into center of pork registers 145°F and vegetables are tender, 35–40 minutes. Transfer pork to cutting board and let stand 5 minutes. Cut pork into 12 slices and serve with vegetables.

Wine pairing:

Medium-bodied white, like Gavi or Pinot Bianco.

5 SmartPoints value™

Per serving (2 slices pork and 1 cup vegetables): 252 Cal, 7 g Total Fat, 2 g Sat Fat, 410 mg Sod, 18 g Total Carb, 2 g Sugar, 5 g Fib, 27 g Prot.

If you like, you can use a sliced fennel bulb in place of the artichoke hearts and add 2 teaspoons of finely chopped fennel fronds to the herb mixture.

Pork with Tuscan Beans

MAIALE CON FAGIOLI ALLA TOSCANA

serves 4 • gluten free • under 20 minutes

Italians adore beans, and white cannellini with olive oil, garlic, and herbs are classic in Tuscany. I feed my family lots of beans, usually with greens. (Escarole is my favorite.) Here we serve the beans and greens with pork that's grilled over medium-hot flames, and finished with a splash of lemon. Very juicy.

4 teaspoons olive oil

1 onion, sliced

3 garlic cloves, sliced

1 large head escarole, cut into 2-inch slices

½ cup chicken broth

2 teaspoons finely chopped fresh sage or 1 teaspoon dried sage

1 teaspoon salt

1 (15-ounce) can cannellini (white kidney) beans, drained and rinsed

1 teaspoon chopped fresh thyme leaves or ¼ teaspoon dried thyme

¼ teaspoon black pepper

1 (1-pound) lean pork tenderloin, trimmed and cut into 12 slices

Lemon wedges for serving

1 Heat 2 teaspoons oil in large skillet over medium-high heat. Add onion and cook, stirring frequently, until onion softens, about 3 minutes. Stir in garlic and cook 1 minute. Add escarole, broth, half of sage, and ½ teaspoon salt; cover and cook, stirring occasionally, until escarole is tender, about 7 minutes. Stir in beans and cook until heated through, about 2 minutes.

2 Meanwhile, in small bowl, combine thyme, pepper, remaining sage, and remaining ½ teaspoon salt. Sprinkle mixture over pork slices and drizzle with remaining 2 teaspoons oil. Heat ridged grill pan over medium-high heat. Add pork and grill until just browned and barely pink in center, about 2 minutes per side. Divide pork and escarole mixture among 4 plates. Serve with lemon wedges.

Per serving (3 pork medallions and 1¼ cups escarole and beans): 279 Cal, 7 g Total Fat, 2 g Sat Fat, 1,121 mg Sod, 21 g Total Carb, 1 g Sugar, 7 g Fib, 32 g Prot.

Pork Chops Marsala
BRACIOLE DI MAIALE AL MARSALA

serves 4

This recipe is spot-on. The earthy depth of mushrooms is balanced by the sweetness of the dry
Marsala wine, and fresh chopped parsley just makes the dish taste brighter, as parsley does.
We use cremini mushrooms here. They're darker and firmer than white button mushrooms.
Creminis are sometimes called "baby bellas" since they're actually young portobello mushrooms.
But just about any variety of mushroom would work in this dish, so feel free to improvise.

**4 (¼-pound) lean boneless
pork loin chops, trimmed**

¾ teaspoon salt

**¼ teaspoon plus ⅛ teaspoon
black pepper**

1½ tablespoons flour

1½ teaspoons olive oil

**¾ pound cremini
mushrooms, sliced**

1 large shallot, chopped

**2 garlic cloves, finely
chopped**

⅔ cup dry Marsala

½ cup chicken broth

**1½ teaspoons chopped fresh
thyme leaves**

1 tablespoon unsalted butter

**2 tablespoons chopped
fresh parsley leaves**

1 Sprinkle pork with ½ teaspoon salt and ¼ teaspoon pepper. Coat chops with 1 tablespoon flour.

2 Heat 1 teaspoon oil in large nonstick skillet over medium heat. Add pork and cook until browned and instant-read thermometer inserted into side of each chop registers 145°F, 3–4 minutes per side. Transfer to plate; keep warm.

3 Heat remaining ½ teaspoon oil in same skillet over medium heat. Add mushrooms and cook, stirring, until lightly browned and liquid evaporates, 5–7 minutes. Add shallot and garlic; cook, stirring frequently, until shallot is softened, about 3 minutes.

4 Stir in Marsala and cook over medium-high heat, scraping bottom of skillet with wooden spoon to loosen browned bits, 1 minute. Whisk broth and remaining ½ tablespoon flour in cup and stir into skillet. Stir in thyme and bring to boil. Reduce heat and simmer, stirring occasionally, until slightly thickened, about 2 minutes.

5 Stir remaining ¼ teaspoon salt and remaining ⅛ teaspoon pepper into skillet. Remove from heat and swirl in butter. Spoon mushrooms and sauce evenly over chops. Sprinkle with parsley.

Per serving (1 pork chop and ½ cup mushrooms and sauce): 293 Cal, 12 g Total Fat, 4 g Sat Fat, 836 mg Sod, 12 g Total Carb, 5 g Sugar, 2 g Fib, 27 g Prot.

Pork Chops with
Fava Puree

Pork Chops with Fava Puree

BRACIOLE DI MAIALE CON PUREA DI FAVE

serves 4 ● gluten free

Many Italians think that if you don't eat with passion you can't be trusted. That's how important food is to them. Cook these pork chops over medium to fierce heat, then serve with an earthy side of mashed favas.

PUREE

3 cups frozen fava beans, thawed, skins slipped off

1 cup chicken broth

1 garlic clove, minced

1 rosemary sprig

1½ teaspoons extra-virgin olive oil

½ teaspoon finely grated lemon zest

1½ teaspoons lemon juice

¼ teaspoon salt, or to taste

⅛ teaspoon black pepper

PORK CHOPS

1 tablespoon chopped fresh rosemary leaves

1 garlic clove, chopped

1 teaspoon fennel seeds

½ teaspoon kosher salt

¼ teaspoon black pepper

4 (5-ounce) lean bone-in center-cut pork loin chops, trimmed

1 teaspoon olive oil

1 lemon, cut into wedges

1 To make puree, combine fava beans, broth, garlic, and rosemary in medium saucepan and bring to boil over medium-high heat. Reduce heat, cover, and simmer, stirring occasionally, until fava beans are tender, about 6 minutes. Remove from heat; discard rosemary sprig. Mash beans with fork and stir in oil, lemon zest and juice, salt, and pepper. Cover and keep warm.

2 To make pork chops, put rosemary, garlic, fennel seeds, salt, and pepper on cutting board. Chop mixture with heavy knife until it forms a paste. Sprinkle evenly over pork chops, pressing into pork to adhere.

3 Heat oil in large skillet over medium-high heat. Add pork and cook, turning once, until lightly browned and instant-read thermometer inserted into side of each chop registers 145°F, about 3 minutes per side.

4 To serve, reheat fava bean puree if necessary and divide among 4 plates. Top with pork chops and drizzle with any juices left in skillet. Serve with lemon wedges.

Per serving (1 pork chop and ½ cup puree): 249 Cal, 9 g Total Fat, 2 g Sat Fat, 640 mg Sod, 20 g Total Carb, 9 g Sugar, 8 g Fib, 26 g Prot.

Hearty Pork Ragù with Porcini

RAGÙ DI MAIALE CON PORCINI

serves 6 • gluten free

Whenever I make this recipe I get fist-pumps across the table. The porcini mushrooms have a rich, meaty texture that stands up well in the pork sauce, and the flavor is divine. The best part: The meat is so tender you can eat it with a spoon. I ladle the *ragù* over creamy polenta and save any leftover sauce for pappardelle the following day.

1 ounce dried porcini mushrooms

1 (1-pound) lean pork tenderloin, trimmed

1 teaspoon salt

2 teaspoons olive oil

1 large carrot, chopped

1 large onion, chopped

3 large garlic cloves, finely chopped

2 tablespoons tomato paste

½ cup red wine

1 (28-ounce) can whole tomatoes, tomatoes chopped, juice reserved

½ teaspoons dried oregano

1½ teaspoon dried thyme

¼ teaspoon red pepper flakes, or to taste

1 Place mushrooms in 2-cup glass measuring cup and pour in boiling water to cover. Let soak until softened, about 20 minutes. Lift mushrooms out of water; reserve liquid. Chop mushrooms.

2 Meanwhile, cut pork crosswise into 4 pieces. Sprinkle with ½ teaspoon salt.

3 Heat oil in Dutch oven or large saucepan over medium heat. Add pork and brown on all sides, about 6 minutes. Stir in carrot, onion, garlic, and mushrooms; cook, stirring, until vegetables soften, about 4 minutes. Stir in tomato paste. Add wine and scrape bottom of pan with wooden spoon to loosen any browned bits.

4 Pour in 1 cup of reserved mushroom soaking liquid, pouring carefully so that any grit in bottom of cup is left behind. (Save any additional soaking liquid.) Stir in tomatoes and juice, oregano, thyme, pepper flakes, and remaining ½ teaspoon salt. Bring to boil, reduce heat, cover, and simmer until pork is fork-tender, turning 3 or 4 times, 1½–2 hours. Remove pan from heat.

5 Using 2 forks, shred pork into bite-size pieces; stir into sauce. If sauce is too thick, thin with ½ cup or more mushroom water. Reheat ragù before serving.

Wine pairing:

Rich red, such as Brunello or Chianti Classico.

Per serving (1 cup ragù): 172 Cal, 3 g Total Fat, 1 g Sat Fat, 667 mg Sod, 13 g Total Carb, 6 g Sugar, 3 g Fib, 19 g Prot.

Pork Piccata with Spinach
MAIALE PICCATA CON SPINACI

serves 4

My mom and dad grew up poor. Meat was a treat that they could afford only a few times a year, usually on holidays. But when they talked about the food they were lucky enough to have, it sounded just as good and healthy as anything wealthier folks would eat. Even the poorest citizens seemed to eat like royalty.

I still think of meat more as a side dish than a main, even though these days I eat it more often than my parents did. This recipe could easily be called Spinach with Pork Piccata, though maybe I wouldn't include it in a chapter on pork.

3 tablespoons all-purpose flour

1 teaspoon salt

½ teaspoon black pepper, or to taste

1 pound lean pork tenderloin, trimmed and cut into 16 thin slices

2½ teaspoons olive oil

¾ cup chicken broth

¼ cup lemon juice

2 teaspoons cornstarch

2 teaspoons salted butter

1 tablespoon drained capers

2 garlic cloves, finely chopped

12 ounces baby spinach

1 Combine flour, ½ teaspoon salt, and ¼ teaspoon pepper on plate; dredge pork in flour, coating both sides and shaking off excess.

2 Heat 2 teaspoons oil in large skillet over medium-high heat. Add pork (in 2 batches if necessary) and cook just until cooked through and golden, about 1½ minutes per side; set aside on platter and cover.

3 In cup, whisk broth, lemon juice, cornstarch, ¼ teaspoon salt, and ⅛ teaspoon pepper together until blended. Pour into same skillet and stir with wooden spoon to scrape up browned bits from bottom of skillet. Simmer until slightly thickened, about 1 minute. Remove skillet from heat; stir in butter until melted. Stir in capers and spoon mixture over pork; cover to keep warm.

4 Heat remaining ½ teaspoon oil in same skillet over medium-high heat. Add garlic and cook, stirring, until fragrant, about 30 seconds. Add spinach to skillet in batches, tossing mixture and adding more spinach as it cooks down; add remaining ¼ teaspoon salt and remaining ⅛ teaspoon pepper. Cook, tossing, until wilted and tender, about 2 minutes more. Serve spinach with pork.

Wine pairing:

Full-bodied white, like Pinot Bianco or Soave Classico.

Per serving (4 slices pork, about 3 tablespoons sauce, and ½ cup spinach): 227 Cal, 8 g Total Fat, 3 g Sat Fat, 930 mg Sod, 11 g Total Carb, 1 g Sugar, 2 g Fib, 28 g Prot.

Sausage and Peppers on a Roll
PANINO DI SALSICCIA E PEPERONI

serves 4

We ever-so-slightly updated this Italian-American sandwich: sausage with sweet peppers and onion. We add broccoli rabe to up the veg.

1 teaspoon olive oil

2 (3½-ounce) links Italian sausage, split lengthwise

1 (8-ounce) bunch broccoli rabe, tough stems trimmed, stalks chopped

1 small red bell pepper, sliced

1 small onion, halved and sliced

⅛ teaspoon salt

⅛ teaspoon black pepper

4 (2-ounce) whole wheat hoagie rolls or ciabatta, halved lengthwise

8 teaspoons low-fat pesto

1 Heat oil in medium nonstick skillet over medium heat. Place sausages cut sides down in skillet and cook, turning once, until browned and no longer pink, about 4 minutes per side. Transfer to plate, leaving any drippings in skillet.

2 Meanwhile, bring large saucepan filled two-thirds with salted water to boil. Add broccoli rabe and cook until tender, about 5 minutes. Drain and cool under cold water. Drain again and set aside.

3 Return same skillet to medium heat. Add bell pepper, onion, salt, and black pepper. Cook, stirring occasionally, until onion begins to brown, about 8 minutes. Stir in broccoli rabe and heat through.

4 Pull out soft centers from tops of rolls (discard or save for bread crumbs). Spread inside of each roll with 2 teaspoons pesto. Place ½ sausage in bottom of each roll. Top evenly with vegetable mixture and cover with tops.

Per serving (1 sandwich with ½ sausage and ½ cup vegetables): 358 Cal, 22 g Total Fat, 7 g Sat Fat, 737 mg Sod, 27 g Total Carb, 6 g Sugar, 6 g Fib, 13 g Prot.

Sausage and
Peppers on a Roll

Sausage, Lentil, and Kale Stew

STUFATO DI SALSICCE, LENTICCHIE E CAVOLO RICCIO

serves 6 • gluten free

Once the clock strikes midnight on New Year's Day, Italians far and wide eat lentils and sausage. The coin-shaped lentils symbolize wealth, and pork sausage represents health and the bounty of the land. If they're the first things you eat, tradition says, you'll enjoy prosperity in the year to come. Sounds good to me, which is why I serve this dish on New Year's Day. Italians also believe in throwing old pots and pans, toys, clothes, and even furniture out the window for the new year. This is their way of letting go of the past to make room for the future.

2 (4-ounce) links Italian sausage, casings removed

2 carrots, chopped

1 onion, chopped

2 garlic cloves, minced

6 cups chicken broth

1¾ cups brown lentils, picked over and rinsed

½ teaspoon kosher salt

¼ teaspoon black pepper

1 teaspoon chopped fresh thyme leaves

5 ounces (about 8 lightly packed cups) chopped kale leaves, tough ribs removed

2 tablespoons lemon juice

1 Cook sausage in large saucepan over medium heat, breaking up chunks with side of wooden spoon, until browned, 5–7 minutes. Add carrots and onion; cook until vegetables soften, about 5 minutes. Stir in garlic.

2 Stir in broth, lentils, salt, and pepper; bring mixture to boil. Skim off any foam that forms on surface. Add thyme, reduce heat, and simmer, covered, until lentils are tender, about 30 minutes.

3 Stir in kale and continue to simmer until kale wilts, about 5 minutes. Stir in lemon juice.

Wine pairing:

Rich, medium-bodied Sangiovese.

5 SmartPoints value

Per serving (1½ cups): 395 Cal, 14 g Total Fat, 5 g Sat Fat, 1,207 mg Sod, 43 g Total Carb, 4 g Sugar, 8 g Fib, 25 g Prot.

Use your choice of either spicy or mild (sweet) Italian sausage.

Pork-and-Ricotta Meatballs
POLPETTE DI MAIALE E RICOTTA

serves 4

When I was young, sometimes I'd catch my favorite aunt or cousin throwing some secret ingredient into their tomato sauce when no one was looking. When I'd ask them what was in the sauce, they'd just shrug, hand me a bowl of something delicious and say, "Mangia." I'm still asking for some of those recipes, but I did manage to get a few.

1 pound ground lean pork

½ cup part-skim ricotta

1 small red onion, grated

1 (1-ounce) slice firm white sandwich bread, grated into crumbs

1 large egg, lightly beaten

3 tablespoons chopped fresh parsley leaves

½ tablespoon chopped fresh oregano leaves

2 garlic cloves, minced

½ teaspoon kosher salt

¼ teaspoon ground fennel seeds

⅛ teaspoon red pepper flakes

1 teaspoon olive oil

2 cups fat-free marinara sauce

1 Combine pork, ricotta, onion, bread crumbs, egg, 2 tablespoons parsley, the oregano, garlic, salt, fennel seeds, and pepper flakes in large bowl. Shape into 12 meatballs.

2 Heat oil in large nonstick skillet over medium heat. Add meatballs and cook, turning occasionally, until browned on all sides, about 10 minutes. Add marinara and bring to boil. Reduce heat and simmer, covered, until cooked through, about 20 minutes, turning meatballs once halfway through cooking time. Serve meatballs and sauce sprinkled with remaining 1 tablespoon parsley.

7 SmartPoints value™

Per serving (3 meatballs and ⅓ cup sauce): 290 Cal, 9 g Total Fat, 4 g Sat Fat, 662 mg Sod, 18 g Total Carb, 6 g Sugar, 2 g Fib, 32 g Prot.

These saucy meatballs are fabulous served over spaghetti: ½ cup cooked spaghetti per serving will increase the SmartPoints value by 3.

Chapter 9

Seafood (pesce e frutti di mare)

Pan-Grilled Calabrian Swordfish

PESCE SPADA ALLA CALABRESE

serves 4 • gluten free

In Italy, I learned to tie knots, bait hooks, and handle knives. We'd snag fish in nets and cast lines off the side of red, white, and green skiffs. Hours later we'd take our catch home and grill them whole. On days when the fish weren't biting, we'd go to the *pescheria* (fish market) and buy tuna, red mullet, or swordfish, but we wouldn't bring it home to cook. Instead my uncle would take us to visit a friend my brother and I called *Signor Pesce* (Mr. Fish—the Signor short for Signore), because he'd grill the fish for us. When the fish was done, Signor Pesce would give each of us a piece to eat, my uncle would pay him, and we'd bring the rest of the fish home for dinner.

1 fennel bulb

4 (6-ounce) skinless swordfish steaks, about ¾ inch thick

Zest and juice of 1 small lemon

¾ teaspoon kosher salt

4 teaspoons olive oil

2 garlic cloves, thinly sliced

1 large leek, halved, rinsed, and thinly sliced

1 fresh hot cherry pepper or red jalapeño pepper, chopped (remove seeds for milder dish)

½ cup chicken broth

2 tablespoons drained capers

1 cup grape tomatoes, quartered

2 tablespoons chopped fresh parsley leaves

Lemon wedges (optional)

1 Trim green stalks from fennel; chop 2 tablespoons fennel fronds and reserve. Cut fennel bulb into quarters and remove and discard tough core from each quarter. Thinly slice quarters.

2 Cut any deep-red spots out of swordfish steaks. Press reserved fennel fronds and lemon zest onto steaks and season with ½ teaspoon salt; set aside.

3 Heat 3 teaspoons oil in large nonstick skillet over medium-low heat. Add garlic and cook, stirring occasionally, until lightly golden, about 4 minutes. Remove garlic with slotted spoon to paper towel and reserve.

4 Add fennel bulb, leek, and hot pepper to skillet. Raise heat to medium; cook, stirring frequently, until fennel softens, about 8 minutes. Add broth, lemon juice, capers, and remaining ¼ teaspoon salt. Cook, tossing mixture once or twice, until juices thicken, about 3 minutes. Remove from heat; stir in tomatoes, parsley, and reserved garlic.

5 Meanwhile, spray ridged grill pan with nonstick spray and place over medium-high heat. Drizzle remaining 1 teaspoon oil over swordfish. Grill until just opaque in center, about 3 minutes per side. Spoon fennel mixture onto plates and top with swordfish. Serve with lemon wedges, if desired.

Per serving (1 swordfish steak and ¾ cup vegetables): 337 Cal, 16 g Total Fat, 3 g Sat Fat, 733 mg Sod, 12 g Total Carb, 3 g Sugar, 3 g Fib, 36 g Prot.

Pan-Grilled
Calabrian
Swordfish

Sicilian-Style Grilled Tuna Steaks
TONNO GRIGLIATO ALLA SICILIANA

serves 4 • gluten free • under 20 minutes

Tuna fishing has played a central role in Sicily's history, and the coast was once dotted with lively *tonnare* where the fish were brought in and processed. Today local stocks are depleted, but tuna both fresh and canned remains a beloved part of the island's cuisine.

2 teaspoons olive oil

2 tablespoons finely chopped red onion

1 garlic clove, finely chopped

2 large ripe tomatoes, seeded and diced

8 pitted Gaeta or Kalamata olives, sliced

1 tablespoon drained capers

2 teaspoons finely chopped fresh oregano leaves

½ teaspoon kosher salt

4 (5-ounce) tuna steaks

¼ teaspoon black pepper

1 Heat oil in small skillet over medium heat. Add onion and cook until onion softens, about 2 minutes. Stir in garlic and cook 1 minute. Stir in tomatoes, olives, capers, oregano, and ¼ teaspoon salt. Cook until mixture is heated through, about 3 minutes. Cover and set aside.

2 Preheat grill to medium-high or place ridged grill pan over high heat. Sprinkle tuna with pepper and remaining ¼ teaspoon salt. Grill until steaks are browned and just pink in the center, about 3 minutes per side. Top with warm sauce.

Wine pairing:

Assertive white, like Sicilian Etna Bianco, or Sicilian rosé (*rosato*).

Per serving (1 tuna steak and about ⅓ cup sauce): 202 Cal, 5 g Total Fat, 1 g Sat Fat, 404 mg Sod, 5 g Total Carb, 3 g Sugar, 2 g Fib, 34 g Prot.

This recipe calls for classic Sicilian ingredients: tuna, which turns succulent when grilled; bright tomatoes; tangy capers; and olives for a sweet-salty note.

Baked Salmon Puttanesca

SALMONE ALLA PUTTANESCA

serves 4 • gluten free

Sometimes people ask if I ever get tired of cooking. The truth is I don't cook every day because I don't have the energy, but no, I never get tired of cooking. It's not just because I'm passionate about cooking (though everything about food excites me). Passion ebbs and flows. It's great, but it takes you only so far. To me, it's about desire, the unwavering need to create and share what I create with family and friends. This recipe is a family favorite and comes together in a flash. I buy only wild salmon from Alaska, fresh or frozen.

1 tablespoon olive oil

1 shallot, finely chopped

2 garlic cloves, minced

½ teaspoon red pepper flakes

1 tablespoon anchovy paste (or 3 fillets, mashed with a fork)

1 (28-ounce) can whole tomatoes, drained and chopped

1 tablespoon tomato paste

10 pitted Gaeta or Kalamata olives, coarsely chopped

2 tablespoons drained capers

4 (¼-pound) skinless salmon fillets

1 Preheat oven to 350°F. Heat oil in large ovenproof skillet over medium heat. Add shallot, garlic, and pepper flakes; cook, stirring occasionally, until vegetables soften, 2–3 minutes.

2 Add anchovy paste and cook, stirring, until it melts into pan, about 1 minute. Add tomatoes and tomato paste; reduce heat to medium-low and simmer until sauce thickens, about 5 minutes. Stir in olives and capers; remove from heat.

3 Nestle salmon fillets into sauce; spoon some sauce over salmon. Cover skillet; bake until fish is just opaque in center, 10–12 minutes.

Wine pairing:

Dry rosé (*rosato*) or medium-bodied Soave.

Per serving (1 fillet and ½ cup sauce): 258 Cal, 13 g Total Fat, 2 g Sat Fat, 700 mg Sod, 11 g Total Carb, 6 g Sugar, 3 g Fib, 25 g Prot.

Don't care for anchovies? If you like, leave them out and double the amount of olives for no change in SmartPoints.

Roast Cod
with Tomato

Roast Cod with Tomato

MERLUZZO AL FORNO CON POMODORI

serves 4 • gluten free

Cod is a fish with many names in Italian: It's called *merluzzo* when it's fresh or frozen, *stoccafisso* when it's dried, and *baccala* when dried then cured with salt. Preserving techniques were developed so that sailors, mainly from the Veneto region, could bring fish on long journeys. Salt cod is a popular dish traditionally served on Christmas Eve and as an alternative to meat during Lenten fasting.

2 teaspoons olive oil

1 red onion, finely chopped

3 garlic cloves, minced

1 cup drained, diced whole tomatoes

10 pitted oil-cured black olives, chopped

¼ cup dry red wine

3 tablespoons drained capers

¼ teaspoon red pepper flakes

1 anchovy fillet, minced (optional)

4 (5-ounce) cod fillets

¼ cup thinly sliced fresh basil leaves

1 Preheat oven to 425°F.

2 Heat oil in large ovenproof skillet over medium-high heat. Add onion; cook, stirring, until onion is softened, about 4 minutes. Stir in garlic and cook 1 minute. Add tomatoes, olives, wine, capers, pepper flakes, and anchovy, if using; bring to boil. Reduce heat and simmer until flavors blend, about 3 minutes.

3 Remove skillet from heat. Add cod, turning to coat with sauce. Transfer skillet to oven. Roast until fillets are just opaque in center, 8–10 minutes. Sprinkle with basil just before serving.

Per serving (1 cod fillet and about ⅓ cup sauce): 203 Cal, 6 g Total Fat, 1 g Sat Fat, 543 mg Sod, 8 g Total Carb, 3 g Sugar, 1 g Fib, 26 g Prot.

Venetian Sweet-Savory Flounder
PESCE IN SAOR

serves 4 • gluten free

In Venice, this traditional marinated fish is often made with fresh sardines and anchovies. The basic technique is simple: First dredge the fish in flour, fry until crisp and golden, layer it in a baking dish or casserole. Then sauté the onion with wine and vinegar and pour the sauce over the fish, adding raisins and pine nuts. Here, we use the same technique, except we swap in flounder and bake the fish instead of frying it. The melding of sweet-and-sour flavors is mouthwateringly delicious.

4 teaspoons olive oil

2 large Vidalia onions, halved and thinly sliced

¾ teaspoon salt

¾ cup chicken broth

⅓ cup golden raisins

¼ cup red-wine vinegar

½ teaspoon black pepper

4 (5-ounce) flounder fillets

1 tablespoon chopped fresh chives

1 Heat 2 teaspoons oil in large nonstick skillet over medium-low heat. Add onions and ½ teaspoon salt. Slowly cook onions, covered, stirring frequently, until lightly caramelized, 20–25 minutes.

2 Preheat oven to 425°F. Spray 9 x 13-inch baking dish with nonstick spray.

3 When onions are caramelized, raise heat to medium and add broth and raisins; simmer until broth is reduced by half, about 3 minutes. Add vinegar and ¼ teaspoon pepper; cook, stirring, 1 minute.

4 Spoon onion mixture into prepared baking dish. Top with flounder, folding under thin tail ends. Season fillets with remaining ¼ teaspoon salt and remaining ¼ teaspoon pepper and drizzle with remaining 2 teaspoons oil. Bake until fish flakes easily when tested with fork, 8–10 minutes.

5 Transfer fillets to plates. Spoon onion mixture and juices over fillets and sprinkle with chives. Serve warm, at room temperature, or chilled.

Per serving: (1 flounder fillet and ½ cup onion mixture): 243 Cal, 7 g Total Fat, 1 g Sat Fat, 695 mg Sod, 17 g Total Carb, 10 g Sugar, 2 g Fib, 29 g Prot.

Sea Bass with Artichoke Sauté

BRANZINO CON CARCIOFI SALTATI IN PADELLA

serves 4 • gluten free

This recipe reminds me of my brother because he's an avid fisherman and he likes to cook, especially fish. You can't find a better fish than a line-caught sea bass, he says. His love of fish is what makes it taste so good when he cooks it. He's also a tinkerer, always trying new flavors or pairing unusual ingredients. His creativity really kicks in on the Feast of the Seven Fishes, when many Italian families eat seven different types of fish on Christmas Eve over the course of several hours. Sea bass is always on the menu, as are calamari, salt cod, shrimp, salmon, scallops, and sardines in oil. The trick is to start with spanking-fresh fish and prepare it simply.

4 teaspoons olive oil

1 red onion, chopped

2 garlic cloves, minced

1 (9-ounce) package frozen artichoke hearts, thawed

1 red bell pepper, chopped

1 tablespoon lemon juice

3 tablespoons thinly sliced fresh basil leaves

½ teaspoon salt

¼ teaspoon black pepper

4 (6-ounce) sea bass fillets

1 Spray broiler rack with nonstick spray; preheat broiler.

2 Heat 2 teaspoons oil in large skillet over medium-high heat. Add onion and cook, stirring occasionally, until onion softens, 2–3 minutes. Add garlic and cook 1 minute. Stir in artichoke hearts and bell pepper and cook until onion begins to brown, 4–5 minutes longer. Add lemon juice. Remove skillet from heat and stir in basil, ¼ teaspoon salt, and ⅛ teaspoon black pepper. Cover and keep warm.

3 Drizzle sea bass with remaining 2 teaspoons oil and sprinkle with remaining ¼ teaspoon salt and remaining ⅛ teaspoon black pepper. Transfer fish to broiler pan and broil 5 inches from heat until fish is just opaque in center, 7–8 minutes. Serve topped with artichoke mixture. Remove skin before eating.

Wine pairing:

Crisp, dry Pinot Grigio.

Per serving (1 sea bass fillet and ½ cup vegetables): 240 Cal, 8 g Total Fat, 1 g Sat Fat, 437 mg Sod, 8 g Total Carb, 3 g Sugar, 4 g Fib, 33 g Prot.

I recommend becoming friends with your fishmonger. He or she will let you know what fish is freshest, and can even clean or fillet it for you.

Glorious Fish

Fish is abundant in Italy: Four different seas flank the peninsula (the Adriatic, Ionian, Ligurian, and Tyrrhenian seas) and the country has two major islands, Sicily and Sardinia in the Mediterranean, not to mention many lakes and rivers. No wonder seafood is such a popular part of the country's cuisine. Picture fishermen in skiffs catching fish with lines and nets, and little seaside restaurants filled with diners intent on enjoying the bounty of the Mediterranean.

We packed this chapter with some of the most classic preparations, but don't stand on ceremony: One of the great things about seafood is that you barely need a recipe. Italians like their fish simple—lemon, herbs, and olive oil will do. Most preparations aim for a crisp, caramelized outside and tender, succulent flesh inside. When a fish comes off the grill all charred skin and steaming flesh, your senses come alive.

Fish, like most food in Italy, is regional. In fact, most restaurants that line the coasts don't have set menus; what gets caught that day goes on the table. We recommend you explore the local offerings in your own area. For variety, consider going beyond salmon and cod and cooking smaller, sustainable species like anchovies and sardines and explore shellfish like mussels, clams, and scallops.

Here are some simple techniques for cooking seafood, a zero SmartPoints food*. We've included sauce pairings from our Building Block Recipes section in case you want to change things up a bit.

Fish Fillets

1 Choose a nonstick skillet large enough to hold the fillets in a single layer with enough space to turn them easily; if necessary, use two separate skillets or cook in two batches. Run your fingers along fillets to feel for pinbones; if you find any, pull them out with clean needle-nose pliers or tweezers. Season fillets with salt and pepper.

2 Heat 2 teaspoons olive oil in the skillet over medium heat. When the oil is hot, place the fillets in the skillet, skin side down if they have skin. Cook until browned on the bottom, typically 3 to 4 minutes. Using a wide spatula, carefully turn the fillets and cook the other side until white-fleshed fish (like tilapia or halibut) flakes easily or until salmon or tuna are opaque with just a hint of pink or red at the center, 3 to 4 minutes longer (the exact timing will depend on the thickness of the fillets).

NOTE that although seafood itself is a 0 SmartPoints food, cooking it in olive oil, as recommended here, will add 1 SmartPoints per teaspoon of olive oil used; remember to calculate the per-serving SmartPoints accordingly. Sauce suggestions will also add SmartPoints. See individual recipes for complete information.

Best Sauces

- Salsa Verde (page xxxiii) is especially good with delicate white-fleshed fish.

- For hearty fish like salmon or tuna, Light Aïoli (page xxxiii) topped with your favorite chopped herb is superb.

- Artichoke Pesto (page xxxiii) thinned with a little lemon juice is a winner on just about any fish.

Whole Fish

1 Have your fish seller clean and scale your fish. Cut a few slits into the side of the fish, cutting almost to the bone, to help it cook more evenly. Brush the fish all over with olive oil. Season with salt and pepper, inside and out. Stuff a few herb sprigs or citrus wedges in the cavity if you like.

2 Heat an outdoor grill for medium-heat cooking or heat a grill pan over medium-high heat. Place the fish on the grill or in the pan; let sit undisturbed until the skin begins to brown and you see the flesh toward the bottom of the fish begins to turn opaque. Using a wide, long spatula (or two spatulas for very large fish), flip fish and cook the other side until cooked all the way through. Cooking times for whole fish are usually 10 to 12 minutes per inch of thickness; the fish is done when the flesh flakes and is opaque at the center when you check it with the tip of a paring knife.

3 Transfer the whole fish to platter or cutting board. Let rest for a few minutes, then use a long, wide knife to cut behind the head just to the bone. Slide the knife parallel to the bone to remove the flesh in one or more even, bone-free pieces. Flip the fish over and repeat with the flesh on the other side.

Best Sauces

- Italian Vinaigrette (page xxxv) makes a great quick marinade for whole fish, or you can drizzle fish with it after cooking.

- Light Aïoli (page xxxiii) is fantastic spooned over cooked whole fish, with or without a sprinkle of chopped capers.

- Salsa Verde (page xxxiii) is excellent over whole fish; add a few pinches of red pepper flakes to the sauce for the best match for rich fish like bluefish, sardines, and mackerel.

Shrimp and Scallops

1 Peel and devein shrimp (see page xxix). For scallops, remove any white tags on their edges (this is a bit of tough muscle) and rinse well. Pat shellfish dry with paper towels. Shrimp and scallops release a lot of liquid when cooked, so use a skillet large enough to allow evaporation; 1 pound of shellfish should be cooked in a skillet at least 12 inches in diameter.

2 Heat 2 teaspoons olive oil over high heat until it almost shimmers. Add shellfish and sprinkle with salt and pepper (a few cloves sliced garlic is also excellent!). Let sit until shrimp begin to turn pink on bottom or scallops begin to brown. Turn shrimp or scallops over, sprinkle again with salt and pepper, and continue cooking until just opaque in the center; total cooking time should be 4 to 6 minutes, depending on size.

Best Sauces

- Italian Béchamel (page xxxiv) makes a rich topping for shellfish; a sprinkle of chopped parsley or chives makes a colorful garnish.

- Shellfish with Quick-Cook Tomato Sauce or Classic Tomato Sauce (both on page xxxii) is superb, with or without pasta.

- Toss shellfish with pasta and Basil Pesto (page xxxii) for a light, flavorful meal.

Grilled Branzino with Fennel

BRANZINO ALLA GRIGLIA CON FINOCCHIO

serves 8 • gluten free

Grilling is one of the easiest ways to prepare fish. To keep it from falling apart on the grill,
I season the fish well and brush it with olive oil or let it marinate for 15 to 20 minutes before
cooking. I also brush the grill with a little oil. Branzino's delicate texture means it cooks
quickly when filleted, so watch it carefully to avoid overcooking it.

6 medium red bell peppers

1 large garlic clove, minced

3 celery stalks, thinly sliced

4 tablespoons
extra-virgin olive oil

3 tablespoons lemon juice

1¾ teaspoons salt

8 (¼-pound) skin-on
branzino (sea bass) fillets
or red snapper fillets

¼ teaspoon black pepper

1 cup coarsely chopped
fresh basil leaves

½ small fennel bulb,
very thinly sliced

1 Preheat grill to medium-high.

2 Place whole bell peppers on grill; cook, turning occasionally
with tongs, until blackened all over, about 15 minutes.
Immediately transfer peppers to large bowl, cover tightly
with plastic wrap, and let steam until cool enough to handle,
10–15 minutes. Hold peppers one at a time under running
water; rub off charred skin with your fingers. Pat peppers dry
and scrape out seeds. Coarsely chop peppers.

3 In bowl, combine chopped peppers, garlic, celery,
3 tablespoons oil, the lemon juice, and ¾ teaspoon salt;
let sit, stirring occasionally. Coat fish with remaining
1 tablespoon oil and sprinkle with the black pepper and
remaining 1 teaspoon salt.

4 Spray 2 large pieces of foil with nonstick spray; place
4 fillets on each piece of foil, skin side up, and poke a few
holes in foil using skewer. Slide foil onto hot grill; cook fillets
until golden brown on bottom, 3–4 minutes. Flip fillets; cook,
skin side down, until opaque and browned, 2–3 minutes.
Arrange fish on platter. Stir basil into pepper relish and spoon
over fish. Sprinkle with fennel. Remove skin before eating.

Wine pairing:

Crisp, minerally Vermentino or Verdicchio.

Per serving (1 fillet without skin and ⅓ cup relish and fennel): 212 Cal,
10 g Total Fat, 2 g Sat Fat, 618 mg Sod, 6 g Total Carb, 2 g Sugar, 2 g Fib,
25 g Prot.

*If your market only
sells branzino whole,
ask the fishmonger to
fillet the fish for you.*

**Grilled Branzino
with Fennel**

Halibut Braised with Orzo

Halibut Braised with Orzo
HALIBUT BRASATO CON ORZO

serves 4

Plenty of people don't like fish. If you're one of these people I hope this recipe changes your mind.

2 teaspoons olive oil

1 onion, chopped

2 garlic cloves, finely chopped

2 celery stalks, chopped, leaves reserved

1 teaspoon fennel seeds, lightly crushed

1 (14½-ounce) can crushed tomatoes

1¾ cups water

1 cup (about 6 ounces) orzo

12 pitted Gaeta or Kalamata olives, halved

1 tablespoon drained capers

½ teaspoon salt

¼ teaspoon black pepper

4 (5-ounce) skinless halibut fillets

1 Heat oil in 10-inch nonstick skillet over medium-high heat. Add onion and cook, stirring frequently, until softened, about 3 minutes. Add garlic, celery, and fennel seeds and cook, stirring, until fragrant, about 2 minutes.

2 Stir in tomatoes, water, orzo, olives, capers, ¼ teaspoon salt, and ⅛ teaspoon pepper; bring to boil, stirring occasionally. Reduce heat and simmer, covered, 5 minutes.

3 Sprinkle halibut with remaining ¼ teaspoon salt and remaining ⅛ teaspoon pepper. Add halibut to skillet, spooning some tomato mixture over fish. Cover and simmer until fish is just opaque in center and orzo is tender, 10–12 minutes. Chop a few reserved celery leaves for garnish.

Per serving (1 halibut fillet and 1 cup orzo mixture): 355 Cal, 6 g Total Fat, 1 g Sat Fat, 689 mg Sod, 41 g Total Carb, 5 g Sugar, 4 g Fib, 33 g Prot.

Roast Monkfish and Potatoes
RANA PESCATRICE E PATATE AL FORNO

serves 4 • gluten free

Salmoriglio is a simple yet packed-with-flavor marinade used in many Sicilian and Calabrian dishes. It's made by whisking together lemon, minced garlic, olive oil, oregano, parsley, salt, and pepper. My mom marinates chicken, lamb, fish, and even vegetables with this lush and versatile sauce. Here we serve it with monkfish that's baked on a layer of baby potatoes and sweet peppers. The vegetables soak up all the juices from the fish, and not a drop of flavor is wasted.

½ pound baby yellow potatoes, sliced ½ inch thick

½ pound mixed mini–sweet peppers, split, seeded, and sliced ½ inch thick

1 teaspoon salt

4 (6-ounce) monkfish fillets

½ cup chicken broth

2 tablespoons lemon juice

1 teaspoon cornstarch

⅛ teaspoon red pepper flakes, or to taste

1 tablespoon extra-virgin olive oil

1 large garlic clove, minced

2 tablespoons chopped fresh parsley leaves

2 teaspoons chopped fresh thyme leaves

1 Preheat oven to 425°F. Coat baking sheet with nonstick spray.

2 Arrange potatoes and peppers on baking sheet in even layer; lightly coat with nonstick spray and sprinkle with ½ teaspoon salt. Roast 10 minutes; turn potatoes and peppers with spatula and continue to bake until vegetables are almost tender, about 5 minutes.

3 If monkfish has grayish, translucent membrane covering it, ask your fish seller to remove it, or slip a thin knife under membrane and cut it carefully away from flesh. Spray monkfish with nonstick spray and season with ¼ teaspoon salt. Place on top of vegetable mixture. Roast until fish is firm to the touch and just opaque in center, about 15 minutes.

4 While fish roasts, whisk broth, lemon juice, cornstarch, pepper flakes, and remaining ¼ teaspoon salt in small saucepan until cornstarch dissolves. Cook over medium heat, stirring, until mixture boils. Continue to cook, stirring, about 1 minute longer. Whisk in oil and garlic; cook 1 minute longer. Stir in parsley and thyme.

5 Transfer fish and vegetables to 4 plates. Pour accumulated juices from baking sheet into sauce and stir. Spoon 2 tablespoons sauce over each serving.

Per serving (1 piece monkfish, ½ cup vegetables, and 2 tablespoons sauce): 228 Cal, 6 g Total Fat, 1 g Sat Fat, 717 mg Sod, 14 g Total Carb, 3 g Sugar, 3 g Fib, 27 g Prot.

Shrimp Fra Diavolo with Farro
GAMBERI PICCANTI CON FARRO

serves 4

At the beginning of a meal, when people first sit down to eat, there's silence. No one talks because they're too busy eating (it's a sign that the food is good, says my mother). By the time the second course arrives, and hunger is appeased, people start talking, telling jokes, debating which sports team is the best, discussing politics. Just like lively conversations, this recipe serves up heat and substance. Pan-searing shrimp brings out their sweetness and deepens the overall flavor. I buy shrimp with shells on because they're firmer, but those already shelled work, too.

¾ *cup farro*

3 *cups water*

¾ *teaspoon salt, or to taste*

2 *teaspoons olive oil*

1¼ *pounds large shrimp, peeled and deveined*

1 *small onion, thinly sliced*

4 *garlic cloves, sliced*

⅓ *cup dry white wine*

2 *tablespoons tomato paste*

1 *(14½-ounce) can crushed tomatoes*

1 *teaspoon dried oregano*

½ *teaspoon red pepper flakes, or to taste*

¼ *cup sliced fresh basil leaves*

1 Place farro, water, and ¼ teaspoon salt in medium saucepan. Cover and bring to boil; reduce heat and simmer, covered, until farro is tender, about 30 minutes. Drain.

2 Meanwhile, heat oil in large skillet over medium-high heat. Sprinkle shrimp with ¼ teaspoon salt and cook, turning once, until shrimp are just cooked through, 3–4 minutes. Transfer shrimp to plate.

3 Return skillet to medium-high heat and add onion; cook, stirring frequently, until softened, about 3 minutes. Add garlic and cook 1 minute. Add wine and simmer until most liquid has evaporated. Stir in tomato paste and cook 1 minute; add crushed tomatoes, oregano, pepper flakes, and remaining ¼ teaspoon salt. Adjust heat and simmer, uncovered, 5 minutes.

4 Return shrimp to skillet and heat through. Stir in basil. Spoon farro onto 4 plates and top with shrimp and sauce.

Wine pairing:

Pinot Bianco, if you prefer white; Sangiovese, if you favor red.

Per serving (1 cup shrimp and sauce and generous ½ cup farro): 302 Cal, 4 g Total Fat, 0 g Sat Fat, 824 mg Sod, 32 g Total Carb, 7 g Sugar, 6 g Fib, 35 g Prot.

Mariner's Tart with Sardines
SARDE FRESCHE IN TORTIERA

serves 6

"Blue-scale fish" are popular all over Italy; they include sardines, mackerel, and anchovies. I like them because their flesh is fatty, so I don't have to use much oil or butter. This pretty tart takes a bit of work but its flavors are spectacular. Sardines are layered with potatoes and tomatoes and sprinkled with oregano, then baked. The aroma and flavors instantly transport me to a cliff on the Amalfi Coast, which is where, incidentally, I ate it for the first time. Sit back, enjoy, and let the magic find you.

2 tablespoons plain dried bread crumbs

1 teaspoon dried oregano, crushed

¾ teaspoon kosher salt

¼ teaspoon black pepper

1¼ pounds large fresh sardines or anchovies (about 8 sardines or 30 anchovies)

1 pound plum tomatoes, sliced

½ pound Yukon Gold potatoes, peeled and thinly sliced

4 teaspoons olive oil

1 tablespoon chopped fresh parsley leaves

Lemon wedges

1 Preheat oven to 425°F. Spray 1½-quart round baking dish or 9-inch pie plate with nonstick spray. Put bread crumbs in dish and tilt dish to coat bottom and sides.

2 Combine oregano, salt, and pepper in cup. Rinse sardines under cold water and cut off heads. Slit each fish down the belly and pull out and discard guts. Hook a finger behind spine toward the head of each fish and lift out bones; cut off tails. Arrange sardines in concentric circles in bottom of prepared baking dish, overlapping them slightly. Sprinkle half of oregano mixture evenly over fish; spray with nonstick spray.

3 Set aside 4 tomato slices. Arrange remaining tomatoes around edge of dish in concentric circle, overlapping slices slightly. Arrange potatoes in concentric circle alongside tomatoes, overlapping slices slightly. Arrange reserved tomatoes in center. Sprinkle top with remaining oregano mixture; drizzle evenly with oil. Cover top with foil.

4 Bake 45 minutes. Uncover and bake until potatoes are tender, about 15 minutes longer. Let stand 10 minutes before serving. Sprinkle with parsley, cut into 6 wedges, and serve with lemon wedges.

Per serving (1 wedge): 200 Cal, 8 g Total Fat, 2 g Sat Fat, 366 mg Sod, 11 g Total Carb, 3 g Sugar, 2 g Fib, 21 g Prot.

**Mariner's Tart
with Sardines**

Roast Shrimp Scampi

Roast Shrimp Scampi

GAMBERI ALL'AGLIO

serves 4 • gluten free

I love the sound of shrimp sizzling in the oven. You don't need a lot of extraneous ingredients for this delicious dish—just some herb butter, lemon, garlic, olive oil, wine, and shallots for flavoring.

1½ teaspoons olive oil

3 garlic cloves, finely chopped

1 small shallot, finely chopped

4 tablespoons dry white wine

1 tablespoon lemon juice

2 teaspoons finely chopped fresh parsley leaves

1 teaspoon finely chopped fresh tarragon leaves

1 teaspoon finely chopped fresh thyme leaves

½ teaspoon salt

¼ teaspoon black pepper

2 tablespoons unsalted butter, at room temperature

20 jumbo shrimp (about 1¾ pounds), peeled and deveined, tail shells left on

Lemon wedges

1 Warm medium skillet over medium-low heat; add oil and heat until hot. Add garlic and cook, stirring constantly, about 1 minute. Add shallot and cook, stirring, 2 minutes. Add 2 tablespoons wine and ½ tablespoon lemon juice; stir, scraping bottom of pan occasionally with wooden spoon, until most liquid evaporates, about 3 more minutes. Allow to cool.

2 In small bowl, combine shallot-wine mixture, parsley, tarragon, thyme, salt, and pepper. Mash in butter; refrigerate until butter hardens. (Can be made up to 1 day ahead.)

3 Preheat oven to 475°F.

4 In medium ovenproof casserole dish or skillet, arrange shrimp in ring, tails up and touching one another for support; place bits of chilled herbed butter around shrimp. Pour remaining 2 tablespoons wine and remaining ½ tablespoon lemon juice in bottom of dish.

5 Roast in oven until shrimp turns pink and butter starts to sizzle, 8–10 minutes. Serve shrimp with pan sauce and lemon wedges.

Per serving (5 jumbo shrimp and 2 teaspoons sauce): 254 Cal, 8 g Total Fat, 4 g Sat Fat, 530 mg Sod, 2 g Total Carb, 1 g Sugar, 0 g Fib, 40 g Prot.

Prosciutto-Wrapped Scallops
CAPESANTE AVVOLTE NEL PROSCIUTTO

serves 4 • gluten free • under 20 minutes

Scallops are meaty, yet meltingly tender. In this recipe, we wrap them in prosciutto to bring earthiness and complexity to them, then serve them with a vinegary fennel and parsley salad to balance the flavors.

1 fennel bulb, thinly sliced

¼ cup diced red onion

¼ cup lightly packed fresh parsley leaves

1 tablespoon red-wine vinegar

3 teaspoons extra-virgin olive oil

¼ teaspoon salt

12 large sea scallops (about 1 pound), rinsed and patted dry

2 ounces thinly sliced prosciutto, cut into 12 (1-inch-wide) strips

1 Toss together fennel, onion, parsley, vinegar, 1 teaspoon oil, and ⅛ teaspoon salt in medium bowl.

2 Sprinkle scallops with remaining ⅛ teaspoon salt. Wrap 1 strip prosciutto around each scallop.

3 Heat remaining 2 teaspoons oil in large skillet over medium-high heat. Add scallops and cook until prosciutto is browned and scallops are just opaque in center, 2–3 minutes per side. Serve scallops with fennel salad.

Wine pairing:

Medium-bodied Soave or Pinot Bianco.

Per serving (3 scallops and ½ cup salad): 185 Cal, 8 g Total Fat, 2 g Sat Fat, 1,094 mg Sod, 9 g Total Carb, 1 g Sugar, 2 g Fib, 20 g Prot.

The cracks in the tops of sea scallops can harbor grit, so be sure to rinse them well. Pat them dry thoroughly so they'll take a good sear.

Clams in Wine and Tomato

VONGOLE AL VINO E POMODORO

serves 4 • gluten free • under 20 minutes

Tomatoes, garlic, and white wine are a classic combination for flavoring fish and seafood in Southern Italian cooking. This recipe takes less than 20 minutes to make and its garlicky goodness leaves me feeling satisfied and happy. I eat it with gratitude.

4 teaspoons olive oil

6 garlic cloves, minced

1 cup dry white wine

1 (14½-ounce) can crushed tomatoes, with juice

½ teaspoon dried oregano

⅛ teaspoon salt

⅛ teaspoon red pepper flakes

4 dozen littleneck clams, scrubbed

¼ cup lightly packed fresh basil leaves, chopped

¼ cup lightly packed fresh parsley leaves, chopped

1 Heat 1½ teaspoons olive oil in Dutch oven or large saucepan over medium-low heat. Add garlic and cook, stirring, until just barely golden, about 2 minutes.

2 Add wine and raise heat to medium-high; bring to boil and boil 1 minute. Stir in tomatoes, oregano, salt, and pepper flakes. Bring to boil, reduce heat, and simmer 5 minutes for flavors to blend.

3 Increase heat to high. Stir in clams; cover and cook, stirring occasionally, until clams open, about 7 minutes. Discard any clams that do not open.

4 Divide clams among 4 bowls using slotted spoon. Stir remaining 2½ teaspoons olive oil, the basil, and parsley into pan, then pour sauce over clams.

Wine pairing:

A medium-dry white, like Gavi, or a dry rosé (*rosato*).

3 SmartPoints value

Per serving (12 clams and ¾ cup sauce): 210 Cal, 5 g Total Fat, 1 g Sat Fat, 872 mg Sod, 11 g Total Carb, 3 g Sugar, 1 g Fib, 17 g Prot.

Want to serve the clams over pasta? Cook 5 ounces of linguine or spaghetti according to the package directions and add another can of diced tomatoes to the clams. The per-serving SmartPoints value will increase by 4.

Mussels with Garlicky Bruschetta
COZZE CON BRUSCHETTA ALL'AGLIO

serves 4

Mussels are a favorite ingredient in Neapolitan cuisine and these brothy, briny, garlicky mussels are magical. They're also fun to eat, which is why my youngest son gobbles them up and mops up the broth with the bruschetta.

3 garlic cloves

1 (6-ounce) baguette, cut into 12 slices

4 teaspoons olive oil

1 onion, finely chopped

⅛ teaspoon red pepper flakes

½ cup dry white wine

2 tablespoons drained capers

¼ teaspoon kosher salt

3 pounds mussels, scrubbed and debearded

½ cup lightly packed fresh parsley leaves, chopped

1 Preheat oven to 400°F.

2 Cut 1 garlic clove in half. Place slices of bread on baking sheet and spray with nonstick spray. Bake until golden and crisp, about 8 minutes. With cut garlic clove halves, lightly rub tops of bruschetta; discard garlic.

3 Finely chop remaining 2 garlic cloves. Heat oil in large Dutch oven over medium-high heat. Add chopped garlic, onion, and pepper flakes; cook, stirring frequently, until onion softens, about 2 minutes. Add wine, capers, and salt; bring to boil. Boil 1 minute.

4 Add mussels; reduce heat and cook, covered, until they open, about 10 minutes. Discard any mussels that do not open. Stir in parsley. Divide mussels and sauce among 4 bowls and serve with bruschetta.

Wine pairing:
A medium-dry white, like Gavi or Soave.

6 SmartPoints value

Per serving (about 18 mussels, scant ⅔ cup sauce, and 3 bruschetta): 286 Cal, 8 g Total Fat, 1 g Sat Fat, 730 mg Sod, 33 g Total Carb, 3 g Sugar, 3 g Fib, 15 g Prot.

Sometimes mussels have long hair-like strands, known as beards, protruding from their shells. It's usual (but not mandatory) to remove them before cooking by scraping the beards off with the edge of a paring knife.

**Mussels with
Garlicky
Bruschetta**

Lazing in
emerald-green
waters.

Only in Italy

...do people celebrate going on holiday
with a holiday (unofficially). Ferragosto
takes place on August 15, and kicks off
a one- or two-week-long summer vacation
for most Italians. Ferragosto traditionally
marked the end of the harvest season,
but today it's all about going to the beach,
eating, and gathering with family and
friends to enjoy summer.

**Mussels with
Garlicky
Bruschetta**

Grilled Squid
with Salsa Cruda

Grilled Squid with Salsa Cruda

CALAMARI GRIGLIATI CON SUGO DI POMODORO CRUDO

serves 4 • gluten free

This is one of the easiest summer meals you can make. Squid (a.k.a. calamari) is flavorful and tender when cooked properly, but toughens quickly when overcooked. To keep it juicy during grilling, use very high heat and skewer the pieces so that they lay even and flat on the grill; in just a few minutes the squid will be moist and nicely chewy rather than rubbery.

1½ pounds cleaned squid tubes and tentacles

1 tablespoon olive oil

2 small garlic cloves, minced

¼ teaspoon paprika

⅛ teaspoon cracked black pepper

Zest and juice of ½ lemon

½ teaspoon kosher salt

2 large tomatoes, seeded and diced

2 tablespoons finely chopped red onion

3 tablespoons chopped fresh basil leaves

1 Cut each squid tube in half lengthwise. Lightly score flesh in crosshatch pattern, being sure not to cut all the way through. Thread squid pieces evenly on 8 small skewers. (If using wooden skewers, soak in water at least 20 minutes to prevent charring.) If squid has tentacles separated, skewer them separately from tubes. Place skewers in glass 9 x 13-inch baking dish.

2 Combine oil, half of minced garlic, the paprika, pepper, lemon juice, and ¼ teaspoon salt in small bowl; brush evenly over squid, turning to coat. Cover and chill 30 minutes.

3 Meanwhile, stir together tomatoes, onion, basil, lemon zest, remaining garlic, and remaining ¼ teaspoon salt. Set aside.

4 Preheat grill to high. Grill skewers, turning once, until squid is just opaque, about 4 minutes (do not overcook). Serve immediately with salsa.

 Per serving (2 skewers and ½ cup salsa): 210 Cal, 6 g Total Fat, 1 g Sat Fat, 319 mg Sod, 10 g Total Carb, 3 g Sugar, 1 g Fib, 28 g Prot.

If you buy squid with the tentacles separated, skewer them separately from the tubes since they tend to cook a bit faster.

Lazing in
emerald-green
waters.

Only in Italy

...do people celebrate going on holiday
with a holiday (unofficially). Ferragosto
takes place on August 15, and kicks off
a one- or two-week-long summer vacation
for most Italians. Ferragosto traditionally
marked the end of the harvest season,
but today it's all about going to the beach,
eating, and gathering with family and
friends to enjoy summer.

When it comes to summer leisure, Italian women do it in style: fabulous sunglasses, two-piece suits, and big, floppy hats. Men wear swim trunks.

Chapter 10

Vegetables and Side Dishes (verdure e contorni)

Broccoli Rabe with Cannellini

CIME DI RAPA CON FAGIOLI CANNELLINI

serves 6 • gluten free • vegetarian • under 20 minutes

Vegetables lie at the center of Italian cooking. From the tender green peas of spring to the fiery orange squash of autumn, vegetables are abundant year-round and Italians can't get enough of them. The markets reflect the region and season, and for Italians, cooking starts there. An entire meal is built around what's available. We kick off this chapter with one of the most versatile vegetables: broccoli rabe. I like mine sautéed with lots of garlic and *peperoncino*, or as a side to sausage. Here we pair it with cannellini beans and just a bit of lemon (we don't want to discolor the greens). Peperoncino are a specialty of the Basilicata region and come in a variety of sizes and shapes. My dad would bring a few long, tapered peppers to the table, cut a few slices from the end, and add them to whatever he was eating.

1 (1-pound) bunch broccoli rabe, bottoms of thick stems trimmed and discarded

1½ tablespoons olive oil

3 large garlic cloves, thinly sliced

1 (15½-ounce) can cannellini (white kidney) beans, rinsed and drained

2 tablespoons lemon juice

¼ teaspoon salt

⅛ teaspoon red pepper flakes

1 Bring large pot filled two-thirds with salted water to boil over high heat. Coarsely chop broccoli rabe and add to pot. Cook until just tender, 3–4 minutes; drain in colander and set aside.

2 Meanwhile, combine oil and garlic in middle of large nonstick skillet and set over low heat. Cook, stirring, until garlic is very tender but not colored, about 8 minutes, keeping garlic in center of pan to avoid browning.

3 Add broccoli rabe, beans, lemon juice, salt, and pepper flakes to skillet. Increase heat to medium and cook, stirring, until very hot, about 4 minutes.

Per serving (1 cup): 106 Cal, 4 g Total Fat, 1 g Sat Fat, 372 mg Sod, 13 g Total Carb, 0 g Sugar, 4 g Fib, 6 g Prot.

Cooking sliced garlic slowly without browning tames its pungency and turns it sweet and pleasantly aromatic.

**Broccoli Rabe
with Cannellini**

Braised Artichokes with Favas

CARCIOFI BRASATI CON FAVE

serves 4 ⚬ gluten free ⚬ vegetarian

Some days, the time I spend cooking is the only time I get to myself. Chopping, dicing, sniffing, roasting, and baking soothes me, gets me out of my head, and lets the clutter that fills my mind melt away, allowing me to focus. This recipe has the added bonus of using two of my favorite ingredients: artichokes and fava beans. *Fava* is taken from the Latin *faba* meaning "bean." Romans adore artichokes as well as favas, and this recipe is a riff on *carciofi alla Romana.*

1 large lemon, cut in half

4 globe artichokes

2 teaspoons plus 1 tablespoon extra-virgin olive oil

1 shallot, chopped

6 large garlic cloves, minced

1 cup dry white wine

1 cup vegetable or chicken broth

¾ teaspoon salt

2 cups frozen fava beans, thawed and skins slipped off

Freshly ground black pepper to taste

¼ cup chopped fresh mint or parsley leaves

Lemon wedges

1 Squeeze lemon halves into large bowl of cold water; drop in lemon halves.

2 Working with one artichoke at a time, snap off and discard dark-green outer leaves. Trim end of stem; with sharp knife, peel tough skin from remaining stem section. Slice off and discard 1 inch from top of artichoke. Cut artichoke in half through stem. With small spoon, scrape out and discard fuzzy choke at center. Drop artichoke halves into lemon water to prevent browning. Repeat with remaining artichokes.

3 Heat 2 teaspoons oil in large, deep, nonstick skillet over medium heat. Add shallot and garlic and cook, stirring, until fragrant, about 30 seconds. Stir in wine, broth, and ½ teaspoon salt; raise heat to high and bring to boil. Add artichoke halves, cut sides down. Cover skillet, reduce heat, and simmer, turning artichokes occasionally and adding water as needed, until almost tender, 25–30 minutes.

4 Scatter fava beans around artichokes. Cover and cook until fava beans and artichokes are tender, about 5 minutes.

5 Transfer artichokes and fava beans to platter with slotted spoon. Sprinkle with remaining ¼ teaspoon salt, the pepper, remaining 1 tablespoon oil, and mint. Serve with lemon wedges.

Per serving (2 artichoke halves and ½ cup fava beans): 244 Cal, 7 g Total Fat, 1 g Sat Fat, 766 mg Sod, 33 g Total Carb, 8 g Sugar, 13 g Fib, 11 g Prot.

Swiss Chard with Almonds
BIETOLE CON MANDORLE

serves 4 • gluten free • vegetarian

I find most recipes have a story behind them, whether they're passed down generation to generation or shared by a neighbor. They're born of a place and time and carry special meaning for people. This one is inspired by *la maestra* (the teacher) who lived next door to the house where my mom grew up. By the time I met the teacher she was an elderly woman, but every day after our midday meal I'd go to her house and she'd teach me needlepoint. She was a seamstress by trade, and unlike most of the neighborhood, she didn't sleep during the siesta. We'd sew for a little, then I'd help her chop vegetables for her dinner. I remember a picture of the Virgin Mary on the wall and a rosary hanging from its frame. And the oil and garlic sizzling in the pan, ready for my chopped vegetables to be dropped in.

2 tablespoons slivered almonds

1½ teaspoons olive oil

1 large shallot, chopped

2 pounds Swiss chard, ends trimmed, cut into ¾-inch-wide pieces

2 tablespoons golden raisins, chopped

2 tablespoons water

½ teaspoon salt, or to taste

¼ teaspoon red pepper flakes, or to taste

1 tablespoon red-wine vinegar

1 Set large pot over medium heat. When hot, add almonds and cook, stirring often, until toasted and golden, about 3 minutes. Remove from pot, chop, and set aside.

2 Heat oil in same pot over medium heat. Add shallot; cook, stirring often, until golden, about 4 minutes. Add Swiss chard to pot and increase heat to high; cook, tossing, until chard wilts, about 3 minutes. Add raisins, water, salt, and pepper flakes; cover and cook, stirring occasionally, until chard is tender, 5–7 minutes.

3 Remove from heat and stir in vinegar. Transfer to serving bowl and sprinkle with toasted almonds.

Per serving (about ¾ cup Swiss chard and 1½ teaspoons almonds): 101 Cal, 4 g Total Fat, 0 g Sat Fat, 772 mg Sod, 15 g Total Carb, 6 g Sugar, 5 g Fib, 5 g Prot.

Choose chard that has crisp leaves and firm stalks. The combination of raisins, vinegar, nuts, and red pepper flakes is a classic Southern Italian way to flavor braising greens, and you can use it with other sturdy greens like escarole and kale.

In Season

The first rule of Italian cuisine is to cook what's in season and buy locally grown or locally raised ingredients. Nothing defines seasonality more than fresh fruits and vegetables. This approach is so ingrained in the Italian way of eating that there's a word for it: *scorpacciata*, meaning "to consume a large amount of what's in season before it disappears." Scorpacciata celebrates the changing bounty of the seasons and urges us to enjoy it while we can.

The following list includes ingredients you'd typically find grown in Italy, and some that you would not. The key is to use a seasonal approach to your cooking. If possible, buy more of what's at its peak than you'll need and freeze or preserve the extra, just like the Italians do. They know that ripeness in fruit and vegetables can hardly be improved upon, so they do a little extra work up front to ensure they can enjoy its flavor year-round.

Spring: *A season of renewal—sunshine, light, greenness*

Vegetables

- Arugula
- Asparagus
- Baby artichokes
- Carrots
- Chicory
- Dandelion greens
- Fava beans
- Leeks
- Peas
- New potatoes
- Radishes
- Rhubarb
- Scallions
- Spinach
- Sprouts
- Wild garlic
- Young lettuces

Fruit

- Lemons
- Mangoes
- Passionfruit
- Strawberries

Herbs

- Mint
- Dill
- Chives
- Parsley
- Thyme

Summer: *Time for open air, ripe and juicy, smoke and char*

Vegetables

- Beets
- Bell peppers
- Corn
- Cucumbers
- Eggplant
- Fava beans
- Globe artichokes
- Green beans
- Lettuces
- Radicchio
- Radishes
- Summer squash
- Swiss chard
- Tomatoes
- Zucchini

Fruit

- Apricots
- Blackberries
- Blueberries
- Cherries
- Figs
- Grapes
- Mangoes
- Melons
- Nectarines
- Peaches
- Plums
- Raspberries
- Strawberries
- Watermelon

Herbs

- Oregano
- Basil
- Thyme
- Sage
- Rosemary

Fall: A chance to enjoy cooler weather, the harvest, and vivid colors

Vegetables

- Arugula
- Beets
- Belgian endive
- Broccoli
- Brussels sprouts
- Cabbage
- Carrots
- Cauliflower
- Celery root
- Escarole
- Fennel
- Kale
- Late tomatoes
- Leeks
- Mushrooms
- Onions
- Parsnips
- Potatoes
- Pumpkin
- Sunchokes
- Swiss chard

Fruit

- Apples
- Grapes
- Late figs
- Pears
- Pomegranates

Herbs

- Rosemary
- Sage
- Thyme

Winter: Moments to reflect and revel in comforting dishes and glowing fruit

Vegetables

- Beets
- Broccoli
- Butternut squash
- Cabbage
- Carrots
- Cauliflower
- Celery root
- Chicory greens
- Fennel
- Kale
- Leeks
- Onions
- Parsnips
- Potatoes
- Rutabagas
- Turnips
- Winter squash

Fruit

- Blood oranges
- Clementines and mandarins
- Cranberries
- Grapefruit
- Oranges
- Pomegranates

Herbs

- Rosemary
- Thyme

**Cauliflower
Pizzaiola**

Cauliflower Pizzaiola

CAVOLFIORE ALLA PIZZAIOLA

serves 4 • gluten free • vegetarian

Pizzaiola, or "in a pizza style," means something cooked in a sauce of tomato, olive oil, garlic, white wine, basil, and oregano (a *pizzaiolo* is someone who makes pizza in a pizzeria, particularly in Naples). We do without the wine, but the rest is all here. Cauliflower is one of those ingredients that can take on the bold flavors of other ingredients it's paired with, yet retain its own character. Make this recipe and see for yourself.

1 large cauliflower

3 teaspoons olive oil

1 teaspoon dried oregano

½ teaspoon salt

¼ teaspoon black pepper

½ red bell pepper, cut into ¼-inch-thick slices

½ green bell pepper, cut into ¼-inch-thick slices

1 small onion, cut into ¼-inch-thick slices

1 garlic clove, finely chopped

1 cup drained canned whole tomatoes, diced

1¼ cups (about 5 ounces) shredded part-skim mozzarella

1 Heat oven to 400°F. Spray rimmed baking sheet with nonstick spray.

2 Trim green leaves off cauliflower, leaving cauliflower whole. Cut into 4 thick slices and place on prepared baking sheet. Brush slices with 2 teaspoons oil and sprinkle with ½ teaspoon oregano and the salt and black pepper. Bake until tender, about 30 minutes.

3 Meanwhile, heat remaining 1 teaspoon oil in large skillet over medium-high heat. Add bell peppers and onion; cook, stirring occasionally, until crisp-tender, about 5 minutes. Stir in garlic. Stir in tomatoes and remaining ½ teaspoon oregano. Simmer 5 minutes.

4 Spoon pepper and onion mixture over cauliflower and scatter mozzarella over top. Bake until cheese melts, about 3 minutes.

Wine pairing:

Young Dolcetta or Sangiovese.

Per serving (1 slice cauliflower): 229 Cal, 10 g Total Fat, 4 g Sat Fat, 801 mg Sod, 25 g Total Carb, 13 g Sugar, 8 g Fib, 15 g Prot.

Penne pasta is an ideal accompaniment to this dish. A ½-cup serving per person of cooked whole wheat penne will increase the SmartPoints value by 2.

Asparagus with Fontina

ASPARAGI CON FONTINA

serves 6 • gluten free • vegetarian

The crucial component in this dish is the asparagus, so look for firm, vibrant green or violet-tinged spears. The Piedmontese like to serve asparagus with a little cheese sauce. I highly recommend you do, too. You won't regret it.

1½ pounds medium-thick asparagus, trimmed

½ teaspoon salt

3 tablespoons dry white wine

1¼ teaspoons cornstarch

5 tablespoons fat-free half-and-half

½ teaspoon Dijon mustard

½ cup (about 2 ounces) shredded fontina cheese

Pinch freshly grated nutmeg

Freshly ground black pepper

1 Preheat oven to 450°F. Spray baking sheet with nonstick spray.

2 Arrange asparagus in single layer on baking sheet. Spray asparagus with nonstick spray and sprinkle with ¼ teaspoon salt; roll asparagus from side to side on baking sheet to coat. Roast, shaking baking sheet halfway through cooking, until asparagus is lightly browned and tender, about 10 minutes. Transfer asparagus to warm platter.

3 Meanwhile, to make fontina sauce, whisk wine, cornstarch, and remaining ¼ teaspoon salt in small saucepan until blended. Stir in half-and-half and mustard. Bring to simmer over medium heat; reduce heat to low and simmer, stirring, until thickened, about 1 minute.

4 Remove from heat; stir in cheese and nutmeg, stirring until cheese is melted and sauce is thickened and smooth (if sauce is grainy, pour through fine-mesh sieve and scrape sauce through holes with rubber spatula). Pour sauce over asparagus and sprinkle with pepper.

Per serving (about 5 asparagus spears and 1½ tablespoons sauce): 75 Cal, 3 g Total Fat, 2 g Sat Fat, 293 mg Sod, 6 g Total Carb, 3 g Sugar, 2 g Fib, 5 g Prot.

A thrifty way to trim asparagus is to slice off the woody ends with a knife at the point where the stems turn from white to pale green, then peel about 2 inches of stem with a vegetable peeler.

Summer Squash Gratin
ZUCCHINE VERDI E GIALLE GRATINATE

serves 4 • vegetarian

Vegetables are a pillar of Apulian cuisine. The region is known for broccoli, tomatoes, bell peppers, zucchini, potatoes, eggplant, cauliflower, fennel, spinach—you name it. We love vegetables, too, and this cheery summer dish is full and robust.

2 zucchini, cut on the diagonal into ½-inch-thick slices

2 yellow squash, cut on the diagonal into ½-inch-thick slices

3 teaspoons olive oil

½ teaspoon kosher salt

¼ teaspoon black pepper

1 garlic clove, minced

3 tablespoons panko (Japanese bread crumbs)

¼ cup (about 1 ounce) grated Parmesan

¼ cup loosely packed fresh basil leaves, thinly sliced

1 teaspoon grated lemon zest

1 Preheat oven to 375°F. Spray grill rack with nonstick spray; preheat grill to medium.

2 Toss together zucchini, yellow squash, 2 teaspoons oil, the salt, and pepper in large bowl. Place zucchini and yellow squash on grill rack; grill until browned and tender, about 3 minutes per side. Set aside.

3 Meanwhile, heat remaining 1 teaspoon oil in nonstick skillet over medium-low heat. Add garlic and cook until fragrant, about 10 seconds. Add panko and cook, stirring occasionally, until golden, about 5 minutes. Set aside.

4 Spray shallow 1½- or 2-quart baking dish with nonstick spray. Toss vegetables with Parmesan, basil, and lemon zest in large bowl. Arrange vegetables in concentric circles or other pattern in baking dish, overlapping slices. Top evenly with panko and bake until heated through, about 13 minutes.

Per serving (⅔ cup): 112 Cal, 6 g Total Fat, 2 g Sat Fat, 397 mg Sod, 11 g Total Carb, 6 g Sugar, 2 g Fib, 5 g Prot.

Grilling the zucchini and yellow squash before baking them keeps this gratin firm and delicious, not watery. You can also roast the squash on a parchment-lined baking sheet in a 400°F oven until lightly browned, 10 to 12 minutes.

Balsamic-Roasted Vegetables

VERDURE AL FORNO CON ACETO BALSAMICO

serves 8 • gluten free • vegetarian

This roasted dish will bring sweet and tangy and soft and creamy to the table. We use a baking sheet instead of a roasting pan to avoid steaming the veggies, which are cut to the same size to ensure they cook evenly. Basil goes on last, topping a heaping plate of vegetables.

3 tablespoons balsamic vinegar

2 tablespoons olive oil

4 garlic cloves, finely chopped

1 tablespoon chopped fresh oregano leaves

1 teaspoon chopped fresh rosemary leaves

½ teaspoon salt

¼ teaspoon black pepper

2 zucchini, cut into 1-inch chunks

2 eggplants, cut into 1-inch chunks

2 cups grape tomatoes

2 tablespoons chopped fresh basil leaves

1 Preheat oven to 425°F. Coat 2 rimmed baking sheets with nonstick spray; set aside.

2 In large bowl, whisk together vinegar, oil, garlic, oregano, rosemary, salt, and pepper. Add zucchini and eggplant; toss well. Divide mixture between baking sheets; roast 10 minutes.

3 Divide tomatoes between baking sheets. Stir and continue to roast until vegetables are tender, 10–15 minutes longer. Spoon vegetables into serving bowl; stir in basil. Serve hot or at room temperature.

Per serving (1 cup): 82 Cal, 4 g Total Fat, 1 g Sat Fat, 156 mg Sod, 12 g Total Carb, 6 g Sugar, 4 g Fib, 2 g Prot.

These veggies can be served over pasta or grains, with eggs at breakfast, or added to sandwiches or salads.

Balsamic-Roasted
Vegetables

Zucchini with Mint
and Almonds

Zucchini with Mint and Almonds

ZUCCHINE ALLA MENTA CON MANDORLE

serves 8 • gluten free • vegetarian

One day, on a trip from Roccella, Calabria, to Sicily, we all got hungry. Having already devoured the *panini* we had packed, we looked for a roadside *osteria*. No luck. After driving for a while we saw an older man with a basket of eggplants sitting next to a shack by the side of the road. We stopped to ask if he knew of a place to grab a bite. The closest spot would take us out of our way but he said he could help us. He led us behind his house where, to our surprise, we saw a field with rows and rows of vegetables. He snipped some escarole and gathered some tomatoes, at which point his daughter, son, and wife joined in to help. Within 25 minutes we all sat, hosts included, at a table with plates of mixed green salad, shaved artichokes with lemon and oil, sliced tomatoes, and grilled zucchini that tasted like sunshine, pillowy bocconcini ("little mouthfuls" of fresh mozzarella), *mortadella* (cured pork), olives, and bread. Problem solved. Like the zucchini we ate that day, this dish works as a side or as part of an antipasto platter. Grill the zucchini until it is crisp and golden. Mint makes it refreshing.

2 tablespoons sliced almonds

4 (8-ounce) zucchini, sliced into ½-inch-thick rounds

1 tablespoon olive oil

½ teaspoon coarse sea salt

⅛ teaspoon black pepper

½ cup lightly packed fresh mint leaves, chopped

1 Heat small skillet over medium heat; add almonds and cook, tossing frequently, until golden brown, 3–4 minutes. Transfer to small plate to cool.

2 Preheat grill to medium-high or place large skillet over medium-high heat.

3 Combine zucchini, oil, salt, and pepper in large bowl and toss to coat; place in large grill wok and place wok on grill grate, or place in skillet. Cook, tossing occasionally, until softened and browned in spots, about 15 minutes in grill wok or 10–15 minutes in skillet.

4 Toss zucchini with mint and sprinkle with almonds just before serving.

Per serving (⅔ cup): 41 Cal, 3 g Total Fat, 0 g Sat Fat, 126 mg Sod, 4 g Total Carb, 3 g Sugar, 1 g Fib, 2 g Prot.

I use medium or large zucchini for this recipe because even though they're more watery than smaller ones, they work well when the heat of grilling removes some of their moisture. I save the smallest zucchini for eating raw or adding to pasta where a full-bodied flavor is essential.

Tri-Color Vegetable Ribbons
NASTRI DI VERDURE TRICOLORI

serves 4 • gluten free • vegetarian • under 20 minutes

This dish is a riot of color on a plate. More important, it connects me directly with the world around me. One reason I love to cook is that it bonds me to what's growing in nearby fields and gardens. It gives me the opportunity to engage with the rhythms of nature and the seasons. I make this dish—gorgeous, vibrant carrots, summer squash, and zucchini with bright herbs and lemons—knowing that nature provides all I need for survival.

2 small zucchini

2 small yellow squash

4 carrots, peeled

1 teaspoon olive oil

1 red onion, halved and thinly sliced

1 garlic clove, minced

½ teaspoon kosher salt

⅛ teaspoon black pepper

¼ cup (about 1 ounce) shredded pecorino Romano cheese

1½ teaspoons chopped fresh thyme

¾ teaspoon grated lemon zest

1 Pull vegetable peeler down length of each zucchini and yellow squash to make "ribbons" (stop when you reach seedy center). Use same technique to make long carrot ribbons.

2 Heat oil in large deep skillet over medium-high heat. Add onion and cook, stirring, until softened, about 5 minutes. Add zucchini, yellow squash, carrots, garlic, salt, and pepper; cook, tossing often, until vegetables are tender, about 3 minutes longer. Spoon onto platter; sprinkle with pecorino, thyme, and lemon zest.

Per serving (about 1 cup vegetables and 1 tablespoon cheese): 88 Cal, 3 g Total Fat, 1 g Sat Fat, 391 mg Sod, 13 g Total Carb, 8 g Sugar, 3 g Fib, 3 g Prot.

Use these tasty vegetable ribbons in place of noodles the next time you make your favorite pasta sauce.

**Tri-Color
Vegetable
Ribbons**

Charred Cherry Tomato Skewers
SPIEDINI DI POMODORINI ABBRUSTOLITI

serves 6 • gluten free • vegetarian • under 20 minutes

Enjoy these superb grilled tomatoes bubbly and hot. They're so sensual and sweet you might need to eat them behind closed doors.

24 red cherry tomatoes

24 yellow cherry tomatoes

1 tablespoon extra-virgin olive oil

1 teaspoon kosher salt, or to taste

½ teaspoon balsamic vinegar

1 tablespoon sliced fresh basil leaves

1 Toss red and yellow tomatoes, oil, and salt together in medium bowl. Thread 8 tomatoes on each of 6 large metal skewers, alternating red and yellow. (If using wooden skewers, soak in water at least 20 minutes to prevent charring.)

2 Preheat grill to high. Grill skewers, turning several times for even cooking, until tomatoes start to blister, 6–7 minutes. Place skewers on platter, drizzle with vinegar, and sprinkle with basil.

Per serving (1 skewer): 45 Cal, 3 g Total Fat, 0 g Sat Fat, 328 mg Sod, 5 g Total Carb, 4 g Sugar, 2 g Fib, 1 g Prot.

Leftovers are great tossed into pasta and sprinkled with cheese, added to salads, or used in frittatas or sandwiches.

Tomatoes with Farro

POMODORI CON FARRO

serves 6 • vegetarian

The sole purpose of this salad is to showcase two ingredients: tomatoes and farro. That's it.
The rest of the ingredients are meant only to enhance.

¾ *cup farro*

½ *teaspoon plus*
⅛ *teaspoon salt*

3 *cups water*

2 *tomatoes, diced*

½ *cup coarsely chopped*
fresh parsley leaves

3 *tablespoons diced*
red onion

1 *tablespoon*
balsamic vinegar

1 *tablespoon*
extra-virgin olive oil

1 Combine farro, ½ teaspoon salt, and water in medium saucepan; bring to boil over high heat. Reduce heat to low and simmer, covered, until farro is tender, 20–30 minutes for pearled or semi-pearled farro, 45–60 minutes for whole farro. (Check your package carefully and adjust cooking time if necessary.) Drain farro and allow to cool slightly.

2 Meanwhile, in medium bowl, combine tomatoes, parsley, onion, vinegar, oil, and remaining ⅛ teaspoon salt.

3 Add farro to tomato mixture and toss to coat; cover and chill at least 30 minutes for flavors to blend.

Per serving (about ¾ cup): 107 Cal, 3 g Total Fat, 0 g Sat Fat, 253 mg Sod, 18 g Total Carb, 3 g Sugar, 3 g Fib, 4 g Prot.

You don't need it, but crumbled feta cheese or ricotta salata is a savory addition to this dish. A tablespoon of either sprinkled over each serving will increase the SmartPoints value by 1.

Roasted
Parmesan
Potatoes

Roasted Parmesan Potatoes

PATATE AL FORNO CON PARMIGIANO

serves 6 • gluten free • vegetarian

These are a wonderful side for roast chicken, but also delicious on their own. If I don't have fingerling potatoes I use baby potatoes and smash them so they have a flat surface for the Parmesan, rosemary, and garlic mixture to adhere to (depending on the size of the potatoes, I may parboil them before roasting). You want a nice balance of crunchy exterior to soft middle. Be sure to scatter the potatoes loosely in the pan so they cook evenly.

1½ pounds mixed fingerling potatoes, halved lengthwise

½ teaspoon salt

3 tablespoons grated Parmesan

1 tablespoon chopped fresh rosemary leaves

2 garlic cloves, minced

½ teaspoon black pepper

2 teaspoons olive oil

1 tablespoon snipped fresh chives

1 Soak potatoes in bowl of cold water for 15 minutes. Preheat oven to 425°F. Spray large baking sheet with nonstick spray.

2 Drain potatoes, but do not blot dry; arrange, cut side down, on baking sheet. Lightly spray potatoes with nonstick spray and sprinkle with salt. Roast 20 minutes.

3 Stir together Parmesan, rosemary, garlic, and pepper in small bowl using fork. Remove potatoes from oven and turn cut side up; sprinkle with Parmesan mixture. Drizzle with oil. Continue roasting until potatoes are golden and flesh is tender when pierced with knife, about 8 minutes.

4 Sprinkle with chives. Transfer potatoes with large spatula, Parmesan side up, to platter.

Per serving (¾ cup): 84 Cal, 2 g Total Fat, 1 g Sat Fat, 251 mg Sod, 14 g Total Carb, 1 g Sugar, 1 g Fib, 2 g Prot.

Adding herbs and garlic toward the end of the roasting time keeps them from scorching, resulting in vivid flavor and great aroma.

The simple life

1. Italians are known for their ability to find joy in life, even in difficult times. They've endured erupting volcanoes and earthquakes, continual conquest and oppression, disease and mass emigration, and yet they've survived. The source of their strength is family and their ability to take pleasure in the everyday—eating, drinking, laughing, singing, dancing, and sleeping. Italians bring magic to everything they do—where most people see rough weeds and rubble, they set up a table for lunch and watch horses graze in the background.

2. In some towns, clotheslines still stretch across buildings.

Desserts (dolci)

Ricotta Tart

CROSTATA DI RICOTTA

serves 12 · vegetarian

My cousin Pepe's wife, Lina, grew up in Stignano, a small village at the top of a mountain in Calabria. Her family made everything from scratch; the first time I ate an egg that had just been laid, saw that walnuts grow on trees, and made ricotta was when I visited their farm. To make the ricotta, we'd stand in front of the stove and cook milk and whey from the farm's sheep in a large pot, adding rennet and then lemon and vinegar until the mixture curdled. With plastic baskets, we'd scoop up the curds; once the baskets were filled, we'd set them in a tray so the curds could drain and dry. The whole process was beautiful, and I think about that experience when I make this stunning ricotta tart.

1 refrigerated pie crust (from 15-ounce package of 2), softened according to package directions

1½ cups part-skim ricotta

3 ounces light cream cheese (Neufchâtel), at room temperature

2 large egg whites

¼ cup confectioners' sugar

1 tablespoon honey

½ teaspoon grated orange zest or lemon zest

Pinch salt

1 Preheat oven to 400°F.

2 Ease crust into 9-inch tart pan with removable bottom, pressing dough evenly onto bottom and up sides of pan. Fold overhang of dough inward and press against side of pan to reinforce edge. Line tart shell with foil and fill with pie weights or dried beans. Bake until dough looks set around edges, about 15 minutes; remove foil and weights. Return tart shell to oven and continue to bake just until dough is golden, about 10 minutes longer. Cool crust in pan on rack.

3 Meanwhile, reduce oven temperature to 350°F. Puree ricotta and cream cheese in food processor. Add egg whites, confectioners' sugar, honey, zest, and salt; pulse until blended.

4 Pour filling into cooled crust and spread evenly. Bake until filling is puffed and golden, about 40 minutes. Cool in pan on rack. Remove tart ring and cut tart into 12 slices.

Wine pairing:

Sparkling, floral Lambrusco or Moscato d'Asti.

Per serving (1 slice): 161 Cal, 9 g Total Fat, 4 g Sat Fat, 161 mg Sod, 15 g Total Carb, 5 g Sugar, 0 g Fib, 6 g Prot.

If you like, top this tart with berries, sliced plums, diced mango, or other seasonal fruit.

Ricotta Tart

Zabaglione-and-Berry Parfaits
ZABAGLIONE CON FRUTTI DI BOSCO

serves 6 • gluten free • vegetarian • under 20 minutes

This is my husband's favorite dessert—and who can blame him? It's warm, rich, creamy, frothy, boozy, and fragrant. Some people think it tastes like eggnog; I find it much lighter. It's essentially egg yolks whipped with sweet wine and a bit of sugar. Marsala is the most common wine used, but I've also made zabaglione with Vin Santo and Moscato d'Asti. And although we use berries here, let the season dictate the fruit: Plums, figs, oranges, and pears are all quite delicious.

3 large egg yolks

3 tablespoons sugar

¼ cup dry Marsala

Pinch salt

1 pound strawberries, hulled and quartered

1 pint blueberries

1 Bring 1 inch water to boil in large saucepan. Meanwhile, place egg yolks and sugar in large heatproof bowl. With hand-held mixer on high speed, beat until mixture is thick and sugar is completely dissolved, about 1 minute. On low speed, gradually beat in Marsala and salt.

2 Set bowl over saucepan; reduce heat to maintain simmer. On medium-high speed, beat until mixture holds soft peaks when beaters are lifted and temperature reaches 150°F on instant-read thermometer, about 5 minutes. Remove bowl from saucepan; continue to beat until cooled slightly, about 1 minute longer.

3 Divide strawberries and blueberries among 6 parfait or sundae glasses; top each evenly with zabaglione. Serve at once.

Per serving (about ⅔ cup berries and ½ cup zabaglione): 114 Cal, 3 g Total Fat, 1 g Sat Fat, 114 mg Sod, 20 g Total Carb, 15 g Sugar, 3 g Fib, 2 g Prot.

To make this dessert ahead, beat the zabaglione in step 2 until completely cool, about 5 minutes. Cover and refrigerate up to 1 hour and serve chilled. Save leftover egg whites to make an omelette, or use them in the Hazelnut Meringue Kisses, page 263.

Plums Poached in Vin Santo

PRUGNE COTTE NEL VIN SANTO

serves 6 • gluten free • vegetarian

A bowl of poached fruit is a thing of beauty. Making it is a simple and straightforward process: Choose a fruit, pick a poaching liquid, then add sugar and flavorings like spices, herbs, or citrus zest. We poach our plums until they're tender (not mushy) in sweet wine with cinnamon and orange zest, then chill them. When you're ready to serve, add a dollop of mascarpone, a rich cream cheese traditionally made in Lombardy. You can also enjoy this dish for breakfast, though I'd use yogurt instead of mascarpone.

2 cups Vin Santo or other sweet white wine

2 (4-inch) strips orange peel removed with vegetable peeler

1 cinnamon stick

1 tablespoon sugar

1½ pounds plums (about 9 small), pitted and quartered

¼ cup mascarpone

1 Put Vin Santo, orange peel, cinnamon stick, and sugar in large skillet and bring to boil over medium-high heat. Cover, lower heat, and simmer 10 minutes.

2 Add plums and return to boil. Cover and simmer over low heat, stirring occasionally, until plums are very soft, about 12 minutes.

3 Lift plums out of poaching liquid with slotted spoon and place in bowl. Boil poaching liquid until syrupy and reduced to ¼ cup, about 5 minutes. Spoon over fruit; cover and refrigerate until chilled. (Can be made several days ahead.)

4 Spoon plums into 6 dessert bowls or wine glasses. Top each serving with 2 teaspoons mascarpone.

Per serving (½ cup plums, about 1 tablespoon poaching liquid, and 2 teaspoons mascarpone): 167 Cal, 5 g Total Fat, 3 g Sat Fat, 7 mg Sod, 18 g Total Carb, 14 g Sugar, 2 g Fib, 1 g Prot.

Nectarines with Ricotta and Nuts

Nectarines with Ricotta and Nuts

PESCHE NOCI CON RICOTTA E PINOLI

serves 4 • gluten free • vegetarian • under 20 minutes

This dish sings of summer. Split ripe nectarines in two, roast, top with a sweet syrup, then roast again (baking the fruit concentrates its flavors). Finish with a scoop of fresh ricotta and a sprinkle of pine nuts. Other baked fruit variations I enjoy year-round: figs + almonds + balsamic + mascarpone; and pears + cinnamon + grappa + crème fraîche.

4 nectarines, halved and pitted

1 tablespoon balsamic vinegar

2 teaspoons honey

Pinch salt

¾ cup part-skim ricotta

2 tablespoons toasted pine nuts

1 teaspoon grated lemon zest

1 Preheat oven to 425°F. Line medium baking sheet with parchment paper.

2 Place nectarines, cut side up, on baking sheet. Roast until heated through and caramelized on top, about 10 minutes.

3 Stir together vinegar, honey, and salt in small bowl. Brush nectarines with mixture and continue roasting until lightly browned, about 15 minutes longer. Top with ricotta, then sprinkle with pine nuts and zest.

Wine pairing:

Prosecco or Vin Santo.

Per serving (2 filled nectarine halves and ½ tablespoon pine nuts): 164 Cal, 6 g Total Fat, 3 g Sat Fat, 120 mg Sod, 22 g Total Carb, 15 g Sugar, 3 g Fib, 7 g Prot.

For a more caramelized flavor, you can broil the nectarines: Spray a broiler pan with non-stick spray, place the fruit directly on the pan, and broil 6 inches from the heat for 2 minutes; brush with the balsamic mixture and continue broiling until caramelized, 3 to 4 minutes longer.

Panna Cotta with Berries

PANNA COTTA CON FRUTTI DI BOSCO

serves 8 • gluten free

This is my husband's other favorite dessert (second only to zabaglione). *Panna cotta* means "cooked cream" in Italian, and it's basically dairy thickened with gelatin. Our version replaces cream with a mixture of milk and Greek yogurt, making it wonderfully tangy. Serve with seasonal fruit.

3 tablespoons plus 1 cup low-fat (1%) milk

1½ teaspoons unflavored gelatin

6 tablespoons sugar

1¼ cups plain low-fat Greek yogurt

1 teaspoon vanilla extract

1 tablespoon grated lemon zest

4 cups mixed berries

1 tablespoon Framboise or Grand Marnier liqueur

1 Spray 8 (4-ounce) ramekins or 8 standard cups of a muffin tin with nonstick spray; wipe out excess.

2 Pour 3 tablespoons milk into small bowl and sprinkle gelatin over top; let stand 10 minutes.

3 Meanwhile, heat remaining 1 cup milk and 5 tablespoons sugar in small saucepan over medium heat. Add gelatin mixture and stir until sugar and gelatin are completely dissolved (do not boil). Remove from heat and let cool slightly. Whisk in yogurt and vanilla until smooth; stir in ½ tablespoon zest. Divide mixture equally among prepared ramekins, cover with plastic wrap, and chill until firm, at least 6 hours or overnight.

4 About 30 minutes before serving, combine berries with remaining 1 tablespoon sugar and the liqueur in medium bowl; stir occasionally with rubber spatula until juicy, at least 10 minutes.

5 Unmold each panna cotta onto small plate; serve each with ½ cup berries and sprinkle of remaining zest.

Wine pairing:

Lightly sparkling Moscato d'Asti.

Per serving (1 panna cotta and ½ cup berries): 134 Cal, 1 g Total Fat, 1 g Sat Fat, 37 mg Sod, 24 g Total Carb, 18 g Sugar, 3 g Fib, 7 g Prot.

You can prepare the puddings up to 2 days ahead.

Panna Cotta
with Berries

Fruit Salad with Limoncello

MACEDONIA CON LIMONCELLO

serves 6 • gluten free • vegetarian • under 20 minutes • no cook

Nothing is sweeter than fresh fruit, and Italians know it. That's why they mostly eat fruit for dessert. Cake and pastries are reserved for breakfast, and gelato is enjoyed in the afternoon at the neighborhood café or during the evening *passegiata* (a leisurely stroll in the streets).

Our fruit salad is made with colorful strawberries, peaches, blueberries, and melon, but you can use any fruit that's in season. We mix honey, lemon, and limoncello, then toss in the juicy fruit. Limoncello is a sweet, aromatic liqueur made from lemons, produced mainly in the citrus-growing areas of Southern Italy. It's widely available, but since it's fairly easy to make at home many Italians and Italian-Americans make their own. I highly recommend you try it. (Full disclosure: My family in Italy manufactured limoncello.) This salad is best eaten in the sun.

2 tablespoons honey

3 tablespoons Italian lemon-flavored liqueur (such as limoncello)

1 teaspoon grated lemon zest

1 tablespoon lemon juice

3 cups cubed honeydew melon

2 peaches, peeled, pitted, and sliced

2 cups strawberries, hulled and quartered

1 cup blueberries

3 tablespoons thinly sliced fresh basil or mint leaves

Stir honey, liqueur, and lemon zest and juice together in large bowl. Add melon, peaches, strawberries, and blueberries; toss to combine. Serve at once or cover and refrigerate up to 4 hours and serve chilled. Stir in basil just before serving.

Per serving (generous 1 cup): 132 Cal, 1 g Total Fat, 0 g Sat Fat, 18 mg Sod, 30 g Total Carb, 26 g Sugar, 3 g Fib, 2 g Prot.

Vanilla and Orange Biscotti

BISCOTTI ALLA VANIGLIA E ARANCIA

serves 20 • vegetarian

Generosity came easily to my parents. They had a willingness to offer what they could. When friends visited, my dad would bring out some of his homemade wine, and my mom would whip up a multi-course meal followed by a bowl of fruit and her cookies—sweet little bites made from nuts, chocolate, honey, or wine. My parents sent everyone home with a bottle of wine, a tray of lasagna, or a plate of cookies.

My mom still bakes her favorite, biscotti—a crunchy cookie that we'd dip in Vin Santo, an amber-colored dessert wine from Tuscany. According to my parents, tradition says that if you fight with your significant other the two of you should eat biscotti with Vin Santo so you won't go to sleep angry.

1 cup all-purpose flour

*½ cup plus
1 tablespoon sugar*

1 pinch salt

½ teaspoon baking powder

*3 tablespoons cold
unsalted butter, diced*

1 large egg

*1½ teaspoons
vanilla extract*

*Grated zest of
2 large oranges*

*1 tablespoon orange-
flavored liqueur*

*⅓ cup toasted
unsalted pistachios,
coarsely chopped*

1 Preheat oven to 350°F. Line large baking sheet with parchment paper.

2 Place flour, ½ cup sugar, salt, and baking powder in bowl of food processor; pulse to combine. Add butter and pulse until no pieces are larger than peas.

3 In small bowl, whisk together egg, vanilla, orange zest, liqueur, and pistachios; add to food processor and pulse just to blend. (Mixture should be moist but crumbly.) Turn dough out onto work surface. Gather dough together and knead gently once or twice until just smooth; form into ball. Cut dough in half; roll each section into a 1-inch-thick rope (dust hands with flour if dough is sticky).

4 Place ropes a few inches apart on prepared baking sheet and flatten tops slightly with hands; sprinkle lightly with remaining 1 tablespoon sugar. Bake until golden, about 30 minutes; remove baking sheet from oven and let cool 5 minutes (logs can break when slicing if too hot).

5 When logs are cool enough to remove from baking sheet, transfer to flat surface. Cut logs on angle into ½-inch-thick slices, using quick, clean strokes with sharp chef's knife. (Don't use a serrated knife and avoid sawing motion or biscotti may break.)

6 Place biscotti, cut side up, on baking sheet; bake until lightly browned, about 10 minutes. Cool on rack. Store biscotti in cookie jar or basket covered with tea towel for up to 1 week.

3 SmartPoints value™

Per serving (1 biscotto): 87 Cal, 3 g Total Fat, 1 g Sat Fat, 31 mg Sod, 14 g Total Carb, 8 g Sugar, 1 g Fib, 2 g Prot.

Espresso with
Ice Cream,
page 265

Hazelnut
Meringue
Kisses

Vanilla and
Orange
Biscotti,
page 261

Hazelnut Meringue Kisses

BACI DI MERINGA ALLA NOCCIOLA

serves 24 • gluten free • vegetarian

Hazelnuts are grown in many regions of Italy, but most famously in Piedmont. They're often paired with chocolate, but we opted for cocoa powder to keep these cookies delicious yet low in fat and SmartPoints.

Enjoy these pretty, petite cookies with an espresso; add a shot of Frangelico or grappa to your coffee to make *caffè corretto* ("corrected coffee").

½ cup hazelnuts

4 large egg whites, at room temperature

¼ teaspoon cream of tartar

⅛ teaspoon salt

1 cup sugar

1 tablespoon unsweetened cocoa powder

1 teaspoon vanilla extract

1 Preheat oven to 400°F. Line 2 large baking sheets with parchment paper.

2 Heat medium skillet over medium heat. Add hazelnuts and cook, shaking pan occasionally, until lightly browned, about 5 minutes. Transfer to plate and let cool. Scrape into food processor and process until finely ground, about 1 minute. Set aside.

3 Combine egg whites, cream of tartar, and salt in medium bowl and beat with electric mixer on medium-high speed until mixture holds soft peaks, about 2 minutes. Slowly beat in sugar; continue beating until meringue is glossy and holds stiff peaks. Add cocoa and vanilla and beat 1 minute longer. Gently fold in hazelnuts with rubber spatula.

4 Transfer egg white mixture to pastry bag without tip or large zip-close plastic bag with one corner snipped off. Pipe about 96 kiss-shaped mounds (each about 1 rounded tablespoon) onto baking sheets. Place in oven and reduce temperature to 250°F. Bake until meringues are dried and crisped, about 1 hour. Remove from oven and cool completely on baking sheets. Store in cool, dry place in airtight container for up to 3 weeks.

Per serving (4 meringues): 54 Cal, 2 g Total Fat, 0 g Sat Fat, 21 mg Sod, 9 g Total Carb, 9 g Sugar, 0 g Fib, 1 g Prot.

Frozen Peach Bellinis

BELLINI GHIACCIATI

serves 8 • gluten free • vegetarian • under 20 minutes • no cook

Make these zippy, refreshing cocktails for friends. They'll thank you for it.

1 tablespoon lemon juice

1 tablespoon superfine sugar

16 ounces unsweetened frozen peaches

2½ cups Prosecco or other sparkling wine

⅓ cup peach schnapps

1 small fresh peach, sliced into 8 thin pieces (optional)

1 In small bowl, combine lemon juice and sugar; stir until sugar dissolves.

2 In large blender, combine frozen peaches, Prosecco, schnapps, and lemon mixture. Let bubbles from Prosecco settle before processing; blend on high until smooth. Pour into 8 glasses and garnish each with fresh peach slice, if using.

Per serving (generous ½ cup): 126 Cal, 0 g Total Fat, 0 g Sat Fat, 7 mg Sod, 14 g Total Carb, 12 g Sugar, 1 g Fib, 1 g Prot.

Prepare this recipe in two batches if you have a small blender, or halve the recipe for four servings total. If peaches are out of season, you can garnish each glass with a thin round of lemon; cut a small slit in each round so it will slide easily over the rim of the glass.

Espresso with Ice Cream
AFFOGATO AL CAFFÈ

serves 2 • vegetarian • under 20 minutes • no cook

Meals in Italy usually end with a strong espresso. That is, unless you want a scoop of ice cream "drowned" (*affogato* in Italian) in hot espresso. Just thinking about the contrast of hot and cold, bitter and sweet makes me happy. Affogato is an Italian classic that couldn't be quicker and easier to make; it will even leave you time to contemplate the question: What would life be like if one did only what was easy?

⅔ *cup vanilla bean reduced-fat ice cream*

⅓ *cup hot brewed espresso*

2 small biscotti

Scoop ice cream into 2 small dessert dishes. Pour espresso over ice cream, dividing evenly. Serve at once with biscotti.

Per serving (1 dish): 162 Cal, 5 g Total Fat, 2 g Sat Fat, 74 mg Sod, 25 g Total Carb, 18 g Sugar, 1 g Fib, 4 g Prot.

Though I'm a big fan of keeping it really simple, the one thing I always like to add to affogato is a sprinkling of crushed biscotti or amaretti cookies for texture.

In her hands, a basket of peaches becomes a peach *crostata* (tart). Just like that.

Recipes by SmartPoints value

4 SmartPoints

5 SmartPoints

6 SmartPoints

Contadini are Italian peasants who usually own a little plot of land, a single-family house, and maybe a mule with a saddle for getting around town. Many live in the mountains or by the sea and grow and fish for food, selling it at the market in wooden crates. They don't describe their food as local or organic or artisanal or clean or sustainable or this thing or that thing. They just grow it or catch it, then eat it themselves and offer it to others.

Index